# THE GLORY AND THE POWER

# THE GLORY AND THE POWER

## The Fundamentalist Challenge
## to the Modern World

Martin E. Marty and R. Scott Appleby

Beacon Press
Boston

Beacon Press
25 Beacon Street
Boston, Massachusetts  02108-2892


Beacon Press books
are published under the auspices of
the Unitarian Universalist Association of Congregations.

99  98  97  96  95  94  93  92    8  7  6  5  4  3  2  1


Text design by Micah Marty
All photographs © 1992 by Micah Marty except as noted

Library of Congress Cataloging-in-Publication Data

Marty, Martin E., 1928–
        The glory and the power : the fundamentalist challenge to the
    modern world / Martin E. Marty and R. Scott Appleby.
            p.    cm.
        "Companion to . . . a series of film and radio documentaries that
    aired on PBS and NPR in June 1992"—Acknowledgments.
        Includes bibliographical references and index.
        ISBN 0–8070–1216–5. — ISBN 0–8070–1217–3 (pbk.)
        1. Fundamentalism—Comparative studies. I. Appleby, R. Scott.
    1956– . II. Glory and the power (radio program)  III. Glory and
    the power (Television program)  IV. Title.
    BL238.M37  1992
    291'.09'04—dc20                                      92-32840
                                                              CIP

# CONTENTS

# ACKNOWLEDGMENTS

This book is intended as a companion to "The Glory and the Power: Fundamentalisms Observed," a series of film and radio documentaries that aired on the Public Broadcast System (PBS) and National Public Radio (NPR) in 1992. The series was produced by the William Benton Broadcast Project of the University of Chicago, in association with the British Broadcasting Corporation (BBC) and WETA-TV in Washington, D.C. We thank John Callaway, who succeeded the late Lewis Freedman as director of the William Benton Broadcast Project and made funds available to support the production of this book.

The authors served as consultants to the series producers and as the editors of *Fundamentalisms Observed* (University of Chicago Press, 1991), an encyclopedic volume that provides fourteen detailed case studies of fundamentalist-like movements around the world. *Fundamentalisms Observed* was one important reference source for the film and radio series, and we have drawn on it here as well. Our thanks to the University of Chicago Press and to editor Alan Thomas, who is supervising the publication of five additional such volumes over the next three years.

*The Glory and the Power* also draws upon quotes from the interviews with Christian, Jewish, and Muslim fundamentalists presented in the PBS/NPR series. We gratefully acknowledge the film directors, who had a keen ear for revealing and incisive comment: Bill Jersey, on Christian fundamentalism (*Fighting Back*), Jane Treays, on Jewish fundamentalism (*This Is Our Land*), and Steve York, on Islamic fundamentalism (*Remaking the World*). Claudia Daly, the producer of the radio broadcasts, was also a valuable colleague and enthusiastic supporter of this book.

As directors of the Fundamentalism Project of the American Academy of Arts and Sciences, we thank the Academy's Executive Officer, Joel Orlen, and President, Leo Beranek, for their continuing support and guidance.

We are also grateful to our colleague Barbara Lockwood, to copy editor Chris Kochansky, and to Patricia Mitchell and Angela Appleby, who assisted in preparing the manuscript and the index. Jeffrey Kaplan reviewed the chapters on Judaism and Islam and suggested corrections. Micah Marty played a central role as photographer and graphic artist. Lori Foley of Beacon Press ably supervised production of the book. Editor Lauren Bryant was unfailingly patient and encouraging. She also helped conceptualize the book and offered many useful criticisms of the manuscript.

# THE GLORY AND THE POWER

# INTRODUCTION

"Every nation is better off in a culture that is dominated by, that is led by, that is undergirded by, the principles and the laws of the Word of God."[1]

Thus says Randall Terry, leader of the Christian anti-abortion movement Operation Rescue. The Word of God to which Terry refers is the Christian Bible, including the New Testament of faith in Jesus the Christ, sent to save humanity from sin and death. The God to whom Terry refers is one who will, any day now, clear his threshing floor, separating the wheat from the chaff, the righteous from the fallen. The righteous, in this vision of supernatural justice, are believers who have heeded the laws of King Jesus; most blessed are those who have risked their freedom and even their lives in the battle against the agents of immorality and atheism who rule, and are ruled, by human laws. Referring to the courts and congresses of the United States, Terry claims that "our forefathers' biblical principles were involved in bringing these power bases to existence. We abandoned them for the past two generations." Now, he argues, "those very power bases are turning on us and literally seek to crush the life out of the Christian family. So what we're boiling down to is a war, a civil war in this country that is a war of allegiances: whose God and whose laws are going to prevail in the culture?"

The passion of the Jewish activist Daniela Weiss for her God and Holy Book rivals that of Terry for his. A prominent spokesperson for the radical Jewish settler movement Gush Emunim (Bloc of the Faithful), Weiss envisions a day when the land promised by God to the Chosen People—"the Whole Land of

Israel"—is restored to them finally and definitively, never again to be taken away. People are trying to take that land away even now—not only Arabs who claim that Palestine is theirs, but Israelis who disgrace their Jewish heritage, the Gush believes, by their willingness to compromise with *chukos ha goyim* (the ways of the Gentiles). The efforts of the enemies of the Gush are doomed to failure, though, for today is "Messiah-time." The God of the Jews, who sent the prophets and gave the law of the Torah to his chosen people, is sending a messiah to fulfill the final promises. "If I don't use history, what do I do?" Weiss asks. "Do I live here because the view is nice? There are nicer views in Norway! I live here because this is my home—in the deep and large sense of a land being a home for a nation. This is why I am here." "Here" is the West Bank territory occupied by Israel after the 1967 Six-Day War and claimed by the indigenous Arab population.

Adil Hussein is fighting his own holy war, but on different terms from those of Randall Terry or Daniela Weiss. Hussein, a prominent leader of the Muslim Brotherhood of Egypt, is fighting for Allah, the one who created all things in heaven and earth and to whom all creatures must submit. The word *Islam* means "submission," and each devout Muslim fights an internal battle against his passions and selfish will, bending them in obedience to the law of Allah revealed to the Prophet Muhammad and contained in the Holy Qur'an. Adil Hussein fights this internal *jihad,* or holy struggle, but he also carries on an external jihad to help bring others into submission to Islamic law. Unlike the armed radicals who hide in Cairo's alleyways and Asyut's shadows, Hussein and the Muslim Brothers do not seek to overthrow the Egyptian government. Rather, they seek to overwhelm the government by the petitions and politics of aggrieved Muslims who are demanding that the state be governed in conformity not with Western expectations but with the rule of Islamic law. "Islam is the one home-grown marvel of the Arab world," Hussein comments. "It offers the only comprehensive system of human relations capable of meeting the unique needs of Muslims everywhere." Hussein is an organizer, politician, and publicist. Some say that he uses Islam to forward his own political ambitions, but the movement he represents has left no doubt in the mind of the devout Muslim populace that the Muslim Brotherhood intends to bring Egypt gradually into line with Allah's ordinances—

not only those governing the dress of women and the conduct of marital relations, but also those governing trade, conscription, banking, relations with non-Muslims, and a host of similar matters associated with the governance of a modern state.

What do Randall Terry, Daniela Weiss, and Adil Hussein have in common beyond the fact that each is a dynamic leader whose religious activism spills over into domestic or international politics? The answers to this question lie in an understanding of *fundamentalism*, a pattern of belief and behavior that has emerged in all the major world religions over the past twenty-five years and is gaining prominence and influence in the 1990s. This book, based in part on the film series "The Glory and the Power" and in part on the work of over one hundred scholars involved in the Fundamentalism Project of the American Academy of Arts and Sciences, is intended to enhance understanding of this worldwide phenomenon by discussing its major attributes and illustrating its manifestations in three settings—the United States, Israel, and Egypt. The motto of the Fundamentalism Project, taken from a line of the seventeenth-century philosopher Baruch Spinoza, also informs the present inquiry: we come not to laugh, not to cry, but to understand. Our purpose is not to bash or praise fundamentalists but to present the results of research about their endeavors as fairly and accurately as possible.

Fundamentalists do not often get fair treatment from nonfundamentalists or, for that matter, from fundamentalists of different religious traditions. To many scholars and much of the public, fundamentalists seem to be spectres haunting the civil world, paragons of unreason, reminders of unenlightened human pasts.[2] The word *fundamentalism*, patented in Baptist battles in the United States in 1920, is now applied and will be applied, whether members of a given group like it or not, to a certain kind of intentionally disruptive movement that can erupt in any conservative religion, in any traditional culture.

Fundamentalism is an exported term; certain Muslims, Jews, and Hindus, among others, will reject analysis that seems to be based on the case of American Protestantism. For that matter, some Protestant fundamentalists, though they invented the term and wore it proudly, now grow restive about being classed and compared with radical Muslims, Jews, or Hindus. Fundamentalisms cannot be compared, insist some believers who feel they are in all respects unique; one should not even suggest that other faiths have truths that deserve to be called fundamental to human destiny. Yet to make sense of anything, people will and must compare. In this book we hope to compare fundamentalists to non-fundamentalists, and to fundamentalists of different traditions, in ways that will illuminate both the common human experiences of fundamentalists across traditions and the distinctive and incomparable aspects of each group.

The best case against the word *fundamentalism* comes from those who say it represents a Western linguistic encroachment. Asked to offer alternatives, scholars come up with adjectives like "neo-traditionalist," "extremist," "radical-reformist," and "ultra-orthodox" to describe patterns of belief and behavior that the broadcasting networks, the wire services, and politicians simply describe as fundamentalism. For present purposes, we ask those who are offended by the term to think of it in its most general, comparative sense; we are looking at "fundamentalist-like" movements in three religious traditions. Fundamentalism, like liberalism and conservatism, republicanism and democracy, religious and secular, is never precisely definable. In employing the term, however, we will offer a general definition and then explore its many meanings and the various contexts in which it is used.

In using one term, we do not mean to imply that all fundamentalisms are alike in their orientation to the world or to the other-world. Fundamentalism takes a different form in the actions of militant Buddhists in Sri Lanka than it does in the actions of Operation Rescue protestors in Wichita, Kansas. In regard to specific religious beliefs, Muslim guerrilla fighters in Afghanistan have little or nothing in common with the religious Zionists who make up Gush Emunim and inhabit the newest West Bank settlements; Hindu nationalists who seek to define India in narrow religious terms disagree violently with their Muslim neighbors in Pakistan about almost everything. But all of these groups and individuals share certain common characteristics that together may be said to comprise a certain style of religiopolitical activism in today's world.

These shared characteristics also set each fundamentalist group apart from fellow believers within the same religious tradition. In every case, nonfundamentalists outnumber fundamentalists by a large margin; that is, Muslim fundamentalists are a minority within Islam, Christian fundamentalists a minority within Christianity, and so on. But these minority groups within each tradition, often led by charismatic figures who excel in attracting devoted followers, have made a powerful argument that is appealing to a number of people "on the fence," people who feel that traditional faith is slipping away. And they support this argument with the assertion that they are upholding and defending "the true faith." Nonfundamentalist Christians, Muslims, or Jews believe, of course, that *they* follow the basic teachings or fundamentals of their respective faiths, and they often resent the practice of fundamentalists who claim sole possession of "authentic" Islam or Christianity or Judaism. What sets fundamentalists apart from nonfundamentalists within each tradition, then, is not the attempt to live the religious faith with conviction. It is the characteristic ways that fundamentalists select, present, and understand the "fundamentals" that sets them apart from liberal or moderate or orthodox believers.

The first chapter of this book describes those basic shared characteristics. Chapters 2, 3, and 4 explore their manifestations in modern Christianity, Judaism, and Islam, respectively. Chapter 5 notes the emergence and increasing importance of movements in South Asia that resemble fundamentalisms elsewhere in certain aspects, but which do not have the "natural resources" of fundamentalism, including revealed doctrines, canonized texts, and a linear view of history. This in turns leads us to some conclusions about the religious and political construction of modernity around the world, in response to which fundamentalist-like movements have arisen, even in the most unlikely religious traditions.

The topic of global religious fundamentalisms is so vast that an author must make choices in an introductory work such as this. Because the focus of the present book is the material covered in the film and radio series "The Glory and the Power," we have organized our presentation around the transcripts of interviews presented in the series. For commentary upon the opinions and descriptions offered by the fundamentalists interviewed, we have depended upon the research of the many specialists who have written extensively about the intricacies of each movement and historical period discussed. In so doing we have attempted to be faithful to the scholarly consensus (such as it is) reflected in the secondary literature and in the primary works we consulted (many of them in translation). In the case of particularly controversial issues, we have presented the various sides of the debate.

While we have striven for accuracy and fairness in what follows, the present book can be no more than a starting point for a sophisticated understanding of this complex topic. In order to indicate the scope of the study of fundamentalisms currently being conducted by social scientists, historians, theologians, philosophers, literary critics, and journalists, we have included a list of recommended readings at the end of the book. Should the reader follow our advice and consult these for a more detailed and comprehensive presentation of each fundamentalist movement, he or she may well begin to construct new definitions of fundamentalism as a global phenomenon.

*CHAPTER ONE*

# THE FUNDAMENTALS
# OF FUNDAMENTALISM

Mr. Yoder is unhitching the horses while Mrs. Yoder and the black-clad children carry some full shopping bags into their farmhouse. They have just returned from what they call "the world" to their Amish *Gemeinde,* their spiritual enclave. Every seven days Frank Yoder grudgingly accedes to the law and the demands of safety—he mounts a phosphorescent red triangle on the back of the horse-drawn buggy as he takes the family to town. No Amish will have anything to do with automobiles. Such machines are unnecessary luxuries and they make it too easy for the Amish young to reach the world and its seductions. Of course, Anna Yoder also allows no television in their house. Another luxury, it would help the same beguiling world enthrall their young.

While Anna unpacks, the children hurry off to carry benches to a home where tomorrow the *Gemeinde* will worship. The Amish, scorning showy church buildings, use a different home for praising God each week. The Yoder family will also rest tomorrow. The dinner pies are already made; they will eat well. They will also read the Bible and talk a bit about the troubles of Frank's brother and his family. Brother Henry, it is said, adopted some worldly ways and sinned. The Amish leaders have commanded his wife to shun him. This means she cannot sleep with the man she loves, nor can their children eat with him.

The Yoders are adhering to the antique patterns and teachings that have been the fundamentals of the Amish way since at least 1697. They are ultra-traditional, but the Amish are not fundamentalists. They do not call themselves fundamentalists, nor do their friends or enemies or the scholars. As the Amish mind their own business, they hope that others will simply let them alone. They are not antagonistic and they do not proselytize.

For contrast, consider a second composite fictional family. Ray and Jenny Morris have just sped home from a large Southern Baptist church in Dallas in their new Lincoln Continental. They had poised it in the pole position in the parking lot of the church; on many Sundays the Morrises socialize at a coffee hour after church, but this week Ray has hurried away so he can be home in time for the kickoff at the Cowboys football game. Jenny would like to have lingered at church to chat with her adult Sunday school mates about a recent San Francisco business-and-pleasure trip with her husband.

The Morrises, too, have children. Merri Lee did stay after Sunday school. She was making the most of her status as a cousin of the newly crowned Miss Texas, who is also a Baptist. The Merri Lee generation was glorying in the testimony to Jesus that she had given on television the night before. And Steve will call, as he does most Sundays, to report on his week as a commodities trader in Chicago. This week he will tell his parents which church and country club his fiancee, a young corporate lawyer, has booked for next June's elaborate, alcohol-free wedding. All seems well in the world of the Morrises. They have prospered. They are thankful that they were not involved in the Savings and Loan scandals that took down some of their fellow church members. They are one of several couples from their church who are actively involved in organizing this season's major charity benefit at a posh downtown hotel.

The very modern Morrises, so at home in the Sunbelt world, are fundamentalists. They think of themselves as fundamentalist, and want to be called that. As upper-middle-class or lower-upper-class Southern Baptists, they are in the minority in a movement that has a large populist base, but they are soul mates of those who remain less well off. They are especially proud that their own pastor helped the fundamentalist faction win control of the conservative Southern

Baptist Convention. They have heard him preach that the other faction were "evangelical," or "new evangelical," which meant, among other things, that they made too many concessions to the modern world.

Traditionalisms and fundamentalisms are not unique to Protestant Christianity. They are present within Islam, and in Judaism as well.

Ehud and Shulamit Cohen have no buggy to hitch, no Lincoln to park. It is the Sabbath, so they have walked home from Kehillat Kodesh, the "holy community" that meets at their synagogue. College football is on television today, but Ehud must shun it; Shulamit will not open a refrigerator door. If either Cohen turns a switch and thus creates a light, he or she will have violated the Sabbath. The Cohens will rest, eat previously prepared kosher food, read, and talk.

At shul Ehud sat on the men's side and Shulamit on the women's in their Orthodox temple. The synagogue represents for them a world inside and apart from the larger world. Ehud is part of a minyan, a small gathering that meets each day to pray. One day this week he brought back word about a nephew who is going to marry a Conservative Jew. Shulamit was distressed. Conservatives, she knows, are now ordaining women, and a female rabbi will be at the wedding. Shulamit will not.

While the decor at the Cohen home is up-to-date, so far as Ehud and Shulamit are concerned their beliefs and behavior basically match what their great-grandparents aspired to preserve in the shtetls of Europe before World War I. They would never change anything important among those beliefs. The Cohens, however, are Orthodox and not fundamentalist. They do not call themselves fundamentalist, nor do those who admire, despise, or study them.

Take Moshe and Rachel Rosenblum as an alternative couple. They live well enough in their West Bank settlement in Israel. This does not mean they have all the comforts they knew when he first got his M.B.A. and she her Ph.D. at Ohio State, where they met. Of course they miss some of the comforts of suburban life back in Shaker Heights, but their twinges of homesickness quickly pass because they are now preoccupied with many causes and duties. They would like to raise children. They must fend off enemies, defend turf, and keep the Sabbath. They take their signals from Gush Emunim, "the Bloc of the Faithful," Israelis who recruited them after they converted to Orthodoxy and left behind the relaxed and compromising ways of their secular Jewish parents.

The Rosenblums do not oppose everything in the world around them. They enjoy parties and good food and television entertainment. Moshe's office in Hebron is spartan, but he uses the best computers the Israeli market has to offer. His machine gun is as technically up-to-date as anything the army uses. The couple plans to fly to Cleveland for forthcoming holy days and holidays.

The Rosenblums may not call themselves fundamentalists, and they do not want to be associated in the mind's eye with the Reverend Jerry Falwell or the Ayatollah Khomeini, but they understand what others mean when they use the word *fundamentalism* to describe the Gush Emunim movement. They part company with the ultra-Orthodox or *haredi* Jews (pl. *haredim,* "those who tremble [before God's word]"), anti-Zionists who might throw stones if you misbehave on the Sabbath in their enclave, Jerusalem's Mea Shearim, but will not lift a finger to fight for the State of Israel. No, the Rosenblums, willing to fight for the secular State of Israel, are of a distinctive fundamentalist cast, and they can understand why scholars and their enemies point that out.

The difference between the Yoders and the Cohens on one hand and the Morrises and the Rosenblums on the other is not between "nice" and "nasty" or between compromising and uncompromising. Like traditionalists and orthodox people, moderates and liberals, fundamentalists come in many personality styles and wear many guises. We have to look elsewhere than at their character as individuals to make sense of the people in movements which in recent decades have received front-page and prime-time coverage under the blanket term.

## Fundamentalists Fight Back against Modernity

What kinds of movements get called fundamentalist? First, religious fundamentalisms are movements that in a direct and self-conscious way fashion a response to modernity.

Most historians associate the first mature cultural expression of modernity with the Enlightenment, the eighteenth-century European intellectual movement that emerged in response to the rise of the bourgeoisie, or capitalist middle class, and in response to the influence of critical science. Forged by French *philosophes* like Voltaire and Diderot, the sensibilities associated with the Enlightenment also influenced American society through the efforts of political leaders and statesmen such as Thomas Paine, Benjamin Franklin, and Thomas Jefferson. These thinkers tended to reject centralized, hierarchical, and divinely sanctioned authority, as embodied in monarch and pope, and moved to outlaw intolerance, clerical privilege, and the union of church and state. They attacked traditional knowledge as being handed down routinely and uncritically from generation to generation, and they strove to replace folk wisdom and religious lore with a culture of critical reason and bureaucracy. Enchanted not by magic or religion but by the march of science, the Enlightenment *philosophes* and deists embraced the idea that intellectual and material progress are all but inevitable in the new modern secular era, that is, an era that honors human reason untangled from "priestcraft and superstition." Many of the assumptions of the Enlightenment, although refined by later developments, informed the policies of the colonizing powers of the West in the nineteenth and twentieth centuries, and persist to this day in the way Westerners think of themselves and relate to the non-Western world.

One assumption held by the Enlightenment thinkers and their successors was that there would be a gradual decline and eventual end of religion as a public force. According to the secular rationalist, knowledge comes from the faculty of human reason drawing conclusions on the basis of empirical evidence—that is, on the basis of observable phenomena in time and space—rather than from truths revealed to a select few by a God beyond time and space. The assumptions of secular rationality have conditioned the "liberal cultures" of legislators, social scientists, journalists and broadcasters, scholars—and even many religious leaders—around the world, in the Americas as well as in Asian, African, and Middle Eastern contexts. Ever since the Enlightenment, therefore, most members of the educated classes worldwide have tended to picture a future that would allow little room for religion. Whatever religions would survive, the generation of rationalists like Thomas Jefferson thought, would be reasonable. In order to coexist they would have to be tolerant and interactive.

Many post-Enlightenment academics and observers, according to the evidence of their writings, expected that the growth of criticism and the unfettered employment of human reason would lead to the end of religion altogether. While religion, in their view, had contended with and replaced mere superstition, mere magic, mere mythology, it still belonged to an earlier, waning stage of human development. Once upon a time, many reasoned, religion had been strong. It dominated cultures, sanctioned rulers and laws, provided boundaries, offered rewards and threatened punishments through official means, set forth the symbols of the society, and discouraged science and unaided human reason. By the turn of this century all that seemed changed; what had once been the loud march of the priests was becoming a long diminuendo.

Secular rationalists asked of religion: After what we have learned from the sciences, can one still believe? Do some people still hold to ancient scriptures? Do the laws of the Qur'an or the Torah still have the potential for a hold on a new generation? Can one still expect scientifically trained elites to worship an invisible, unseen force? Can one still expect devotion to God after constitutions are secularized, drawing lines of distinctions between religious and civil authority and making religion irrelevant to the process of statecraft? Can faith still motivate urban industrialized peoples as it did rural and peasant peoples? The word *still*, one scholar has said, represented a kind of canker in the fruit or cancer in the marrow.[1]

The smug assumption of the Enlightenment regarding religion's fate has been manifestly proven wrong by the twentieth-century dynamism of fundamentalisms. Religion did not "go away;" even by the beginning of the twentieth century, scholars writing in the spirit of the Enlightenment were aware that many, many people "still" believed. The *World Christian Encyclopedia* estimates that in 1900 there were 1.6 billion people on earth, 560 million of whom were Christian, 200 million Muslim, 200 million Hindu, 127 million Buddhist, and 106 million "tribal religionists." Despite these numbers, post-Enlightenment scholars anticipated a drastic decline of religious allegiance and practice by the year 2000. Yet recently the *World Christian Encyclopedia* projected religious numbers for the year 2000, and according to these estimates, there will be 2.1 billion Christians, down not even half a percentage point from the 34 percent of the human race called Christian a hundred years earlier. They envision 1.2 billion Muslims, six times as many as in 1900 in a world population that will have grown by less than four times. There may be 860 million Hindus, 360 million Buddhists, and "still" 100 million "tribal religionists," the only category to see decline. What would the enlightened scholars of the Euro-American West of the turn of the century and their counterparts elsewhere make of these projected statistics ?

Admittedly, these figures are rounded to a few tens of millions and the reported allegiances do not tell much about degrees of loyalty. But they do tell us something else: that peoples of the world have not "thrown off the shackles" of religion. Even in the colleges and universities of the United States, where the secular rational ethos is supposed to dominate, only 30 percent tell poll takers they have "no religion" or "no religious preference," a figure significantly higher than the 8 percent of the general public which says the same, but hardly a sign of wholesale rejection of faith.

The general assumption at the turn of the century was that whatever religion would survive modernity would tend to be "enlightened" and "modern." In other words, religion would become semi-secular, rational, tolerant, and individualistic. And, when adaptations progressed in this direction at various rates in many religious traditions, the conservatives, traditionalists, and orthodox began to see what they were up against. Moderate, liberal, and modernist believers were ever more interactive, ecumenical, responsive to and empathic with each other, but the liberal wave was not destined to set the direction or pace of progress without a serious challenge. Enduring and effective competition arose from some of the very people the post-Enlightenment secularists had relegated to the margins.

The biggest mistake American modernists made when Protestant fundamentalists opposed them early in the century, for example, was to see the movements as vestiges. Journalist H. L. Mencken and lawyer Clarence Darrow, and even some moderate evangelical Protestants, portrayed fundamentalists as Bible Belt rednecks, mountaineer mossbacks, hillbillies and holy rollers who had no place in the modern world. (This portrayal, by the way, was not wholly inaccurate in the case of some of the people Mencken and Darrow met in the celebrated Scopes "Monkey Trial" in Tennessee in 1925.) These throwbacks would fade, modernists believed, or be classified in history as relics of a passing world. The events of the next fifty years, in which the heirs of these "throwbacks" separated from "corrupt" mainline churches and built their own empire of sophisticated alternative institutions, proved these expectations to be misguided to say the least.

Now, at a time when fundamentalisms form in Sikhism and Buddhism, in Hinduism and Islam, secular rationalists are still tempted to dismiss them as cultural Neanderthals. Yet the fundamentalist movements keep proliferating, many of them with young, educated, and sometimes prosperous members—some of those members armed with books of scripture, others simply armed. The religions which have been most successful, it seems, have been the least secular in their message. They have been not ecumenical, but particular and even exclusive, and have attracted millions to what may be called a tribal view of the world. They have not been interactive so much as impelled to set new boundaries.

*Although they reject many of the values that modernity has brought, fundamentalists do not reject modern scientific means. Haredi Jews in Israel and the United States, for example, are known as connoisseurs of the latest communications and electronics technologies, often using them to refine their rituals of observance.*

Fundamentalists do not entirely reject Enlightenment-based modernity, however. They like many of its products—rapid transportation, telecommunications, electricity, medical science—but are wary of the values that seem to accompany these technological and scientific marvels. One such value of secular modernity is the superiority of human reason to all other means of knowledge, including religious revelation (that is, knowledge revealed to chosen people through extraordinary or supernatural means). When people agree that only rational discourse is permissible in a society, something of even greater value is lost, say the fundamentalists. This something is actually an intangible reality called spirit, an animating force that cannot be comprehended by human reason alone but is nonetheless as important as reason, intellect, and emotion in accounting for human behavior. To deny spirit, to act as if it is simply irrational and thus ignorable, is to threaten the very humanity of the person and of society. Fundamentalists would restore spiritual considerations to a central place in public and private discourse and would do so directly, by basing many of the laws and customs of society on the sacred scriptures or traditions which they believe to be the most authoritative guide to the Spirit who inspires all human goodness.

In thus depicting fundamentalists as defenders of the spiritual and restorers of the religious in societies, we must note an important qualification, one which touches upon the question of motivation. One may fairly ask whether fundamentalists pursue a program of "restoration" because they are genuinely concerned about the dehumanizing effects of materialism and the displacement of religion, or whether this program is no more than a means of achieving their real goal, namely, the attainment of power and privilege for themselves.

In response to this basic question of motivation, two observations are in order. First, posing the question as a choice between two alternatives may be misleading: human motivations are complex and overlapping. That is, fundamentalists may seek power for themselves, not only to redress an injustice done to them by "irreligious" people, but also because they sincerely believe that society would be better off were it run, or at least heavily influenced, by people of explicit religious convictions who are willing to act morally and politically on those convictions. Second, one must respect the distinction between leaders on the one hand and the rank and file membership of movements on the other. These two types of participants in fundamentalist movements may have different and even conflicting interests. In certain situations leaders or elites within a religious movement may emphasize doctrines or moral codes that reinforce their own status and privileges within that community. In manifesting this "elective affinity," as sociologists call it, between doctrine and office, leaders of fundamentalist movements may in fact reinforce their elite status and veer away from the will of the community.[2]

Certainly fundamentalist leaders exercise a special kind of authority over their followers, and this kind of authority is best explained if we consider the notion of freedom, another value associated with the Enlightenment. Fundamentalists have much to say about freedom and its proper interpretation. Freedom should not mean license to do anything one chooses in the name of self-fulfillment, fundamentalists argue; this notion leads only to libertarianism, and ultimately to the decay of a once moral society, because individuals are encouraged to indulge their desires in undisciplined, sometimes promiscuous, behavior. In such a culture, pornography thrives and life itself becomes cheapened. *Authentic* human fulfillment, as fundamentalists define it, depends upon the existence of conditions in society by which it is possible to pursue the divine will. Laws must perpetuate those conditions by protecting the rights of religious people to raise their children in a safe and moral environment and by restricting practices and people who would undermine the religious character of society. Only in obeying God's commandments, then, is one truly free to find happiness.

As we have seen, the natural and perhaps most insidious result of the Enlightenment mentality, fundamentalists believe, is its philosophical expression, known as modernism. *Modernist* and *modernism* are terms referring to the agents or proponents of secular modernity, whether these agents be liberal churchmen or religious scholars who want to read the Bible or Qur'an in such a way as to accommodate evolutionary theories of human origins, or philosophical systems which replace revealed norms and doctrines with modern ideologies like Marxism.

It is important to note, however, that fundamentalisms arose in response to the challenges of modernity that came from agents *within* the religious communities. These religious modernists were seen as the most menacing enemies of the faith because they were the link to the vast changes and secularizing tendencies of the world outside; they were also capable of manipulating the religious symbols and practices of the community from within. We will return to this point later, but one illustration may convey it succinctly. An ambassador to Iran during the 1979 revolution commented in a recent conversation upon an appointment he had with Ayatollah Beheshti, a leader of the revolution, to protest the taking of the American hostages. Do you realize how profoundly you have angered the American people and how bellicose they are toward Iran as a result? the ambassador asked. The ayatollah seemed unconcerned, and responded that the real purpose of the hostage-taking was to smoke out the traitors within the new Iranian regime, who would reveal themselves as such by their vocal opposition to the hostage-taking policy. By "traitors," the ambassador realized, Beheshti meant especially the moderates who did not thoroughly approve of the Ayatollah Khomeini's brand of revolutionary Shi'ism. If the taking of hostages further widened the gulf between the infidel Americans and the Khomeinists, all the better, but the first "great Satan" to be defeated was the one at home, not abroad.

This kind of attitude sets fundamentalists apart from other religious people who are worried about the effects of modernity and reluctant to embrace it uncritically. When agents of secular modernity threaten *conservatives* like old-time Baptists, the conservatives simply try to keep it at bay. Orthodox Jews see modernism coming and try to ward it off by wrapping themselves in a religious and cultural cocoon; traditionalists like the Amish try to keep the modern world at arm's length by resisting its pluralism, relativism, and seductions. *Fundamentalists*, however, *fight back*. That is their mark. They want to reclaim a place they feel has been taken from them. They would restore what are presumed or claimed to be old and secure ways retrieved from a world they are losing. Fundamentalists will do what it takes to assure their future in a world of their own defining.

"What it takes" may mean trying to convert others to the fundamentalists' worldview. It could also mean the attempt to pass laws and amend constitutions in order to get their programs put on the books. In extreme cases, though never yet in mass movement form in the United States, fundamentalists might make war against the modernists, attack the intruders, or engage in terrorism against the infidels. It is such aggressors who make the headlines and taint the term *fundamentalist* for the less militant.

Whatever else they share, fundamentalists around the globe have in common one feature: their very existence and astonishing appeal took the modern world by surprise. In the first two decades of this century, such movements were not expected to develop; they were not expected to keep growing at the century's end, and they were not expected to be so imitative of modernity even as they were rejecting it. This most surprising characteristic—the ways in which fundamentalisms draw on certain modern patterns of thought and behavior in an attempt to defeat secular modernity—will become clearer as we discuss their innovative tendencies.

## The Inventiveness of Fundamentalisms

Fundamentalist movements do not arise in liberalisms. An individual liberal, of course, may make the turn. The restless daughter of a mainstream Protestant couple can give her parents at least figurative fits after a Campus Crusade roommate converts her. She may come home at Thanksgiving prepared to win "born again" recruits from the family, or to reject those who resist her proselytizing and judgment. The son of Egyptian parents who no longer (or never did) practice the Five Pillars of Islam may find a missing element of identity in the Muslim youth organization sponsored by a local branch of the fundamentalist Muslim Brotherhood. Such a person initially acts in isolation, without support from friends and relatives. But he or she gravitates toward a new family, a fundamentalist movement, that emerges from institutions and social environments that are not liberal but conservative and traditional.

Such fundamentalist "families" are not content to overlook what they perceive to be an assault on their values or way of life. Their catalog of menaces is long. In America these come in the forms of the teaching of evolution in public schools; the "higher criticism" of the Bible, which fundamentalists see as having led otherwise reverent scholars to treat the Scripture like any other ancient text; the recognition of pluralism, which has led the United States Supreme Court to rule against school prayer in public schools; Court decisions, like *Roe v. Wade*, which have violated fundamentalist doctrines about human life; atheistic communism (in Cold War days); and, perhaps most of all, television, invading the intimacy of the home with its mix of sex and violence and its demeaning of traditional values. All these, taken together, represent a threat to the social and personal identity, to the very being, of conservatives who become fundamentalists, and they intend to do something about it, to fight back against the threats and invasions. They have had to react, to create a contrary world, even if only to stay together and to have something to transmit to their children. They invented fundamentalisms.

In America, at the turn of the century, many Protestants were moved to defend their cherished ways. They were patriarchal and thus abhorred the feminism of the 1920s. They were puritan and scorned the world of hip flasks and flappers. They were purists and preached against modernist tamperings with doctrines. They came to uphold the literal inerrancy of the Bible in order to claim an absolute hold on absolute truth.

As one glances elsewhere in the fundamentalist world, however, it becomes clear that in different cultures there are differing threats. Gush Emunim (which will receive extended attention in a later chapter) thinks that the United Nations and the Muslim world jeopardize the land of the Messiah, the nation of the Chosen People. Even the Israeli government or the American allies, they insist, cannot be counted on. So these Jewish fundamentalists, to whom the Rosenblums were drawn, turn to Torah and other ancient writings. They claim that the God of Israel has forever deeded the Land of Israel, with precise boundaries, to his children. But they must fight for it. Jewish fundamentalism has to do with story and law and then moves into practice.

In the Islamic world, which receives most notice on a worldwide basis and to which we shall give attention in some detail, still another framework appears. Scriptural inerrancy is not the battleground; all Muslims already believe that the Qur'an is simply the word of Allah uttered through the Prophet Muhammad, and all lines of all its *suras* are perfectly true. Modernity therefore threatened on other fronts. It was manifestly luring the young away from Shari'a, Islamic law. Therefore, both Shi'ite and Sunni Muslims, seeing their old ways jeopardized, retrieved the most shocking (to outsiders) themes and practices from the past and gave them a new prominence. These fundamentalists lifted past rulings or doctrines out of their original contexts and reinterpreted them radically in order to make a stand and to recover lost ground.

For example, there is a common perception among many Muslim religious scholars (*ulama*) that Muslims in Western or Westernized societies are being seduced by modern novels and confused by the notion of freedom of speech that prohibits the censoring of immoral or even slanderous works of art. What better way to dramatize the situation and its moral implications than by invoking the sacred laws of the seventh century against apostasy and sentencing Salman Rushdie, a prominent British novelist and a former Muslim, to death by execution? Rushdie wrote *The Satanic Verses,* a novel which featured a highly insulting, and to Muslims, blasphemous portrayal of the Prophet. His case made for a marvelous object lesson for confused Muslims who were wondering what was permissible and whether the old standards still held true. And if Ayatollah Khomeini's *fatwa* (religious ruling pronounced by a learned Islamic jurist) calling for the punishment of death violated international laws and British sovereignty, all the better: the ways of the West are not our ways, the Khomeinists declared.

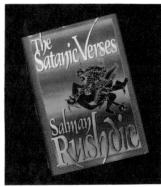

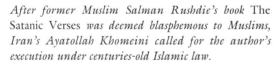

*After former Muslim Salman Rushdie's book* The Satanic Verses *was deemed blasphemous to Muslims, Iran's Ayatollah Khomeini called for the author's execution under centuries-old Islamic law.*

A flair for the dramatic, crisis-provoking action, a staple of fundamentalisms everywhere, perhaps never proved so useful as it did in inciting the uproar surrounding "the Rushdie Affair." The fatwa against the novelist has not been revoked at this writing.

It is relatively easy to locate the fundamentalist groundings in the three faiths called the Religions of the Book, precisely because Islam, Christianity, and Judaism each possess clearly defined canons of scripture and decisive commentaries. The adherent can reach to such canons for doctrines, stories, or laws. There, they are told, they will find a place where arguments can be settled authoritatively and claims staked out. In Hinduism, Sikhism, and Buddhism, however, this kind of authority is more difficult to ascertain. These are cases in which fundamentalist inventiveness extends to the construction of fundamentals—of "doctrines" from vast bodies of teaching, of "scriptures" from epics or historical accounts, and of "founders" of contemporary movements from mythical or legendary figures.

The Hindu world recognizes a vast and indefinitely bounded expanse of sacred writings—the Vedas (*veda* means "knowledge"), composed over the course of millennia (between 1400 and 400 B.C.E.) but never officially canonized or standardized and presented to the faithful as binding upon them. It is difficult to pin down any scriptural inerrantists in Hinduism, but this does not prevent contemporary Hindu activists from drawing on the Vedas, and upon ancient legends and epics, in various ways for political and religious purposes. In 1990, for example, Hindu activists belonging to the one-million-strong Rashtriya Svayamsevak Sangh (RSS, the National Union of Volunteers), formed the vanguard of protestors who stormed a mosque in the North Indian town of Ayodhya. These Hindu militants sought to demolish the mosque, a symbol of sixteenth-century Muslim and Mughal dominance in the region, and replace it with a temple of the Lord Rama, a Hindu deity celebrated in the ancient chronicle *Ramayana*. The Hindu "fundamentalists" insisted that the Lord Rama's birthplace was the very site on which the Babri Masjid Mosque stands—a site still very important to the thousands of Muslims who live in the region. Riots ensued, with loss of Hindu and Muslim lives. Nonetheless, the issue was capitalized upon by the leaders of

the Bharatiya Janata Party (BJP), the Hindu political party closely associated with
the RSS.

Hindu "fundamentalism" defines itself over against other fundamentalist-
like movements of South Asia, including Muslim organizations like the Jamaat-
i-Islami of Pakistan and the Jammu Liberation Front of Kashmir. Another
opponent of Hindu dominance in northern India is the company of militant Sikhs,
who have been intensely active in the Punjab since the early 1980s. Part of the
militants' strategy for claiming the high ground of Sikh orthopraxis consists in
highlighting minor themes in the Sikh sacred scriptures, the Granth Sahib
(compiled in 1604 by the fifth Sikh guru, Arjun, ensconced in the Golden Temple
of Amritsar, and canonized by the tenth guru, Gobind, in 1699). Finally, the
Hindu majority of India is also concerned with state policy toward Theravada
Buddhists in the war-torn island nation of Sri Lanka. There the Sinhalese Buddhist
nationalists who justify violence against the separatist Tamil Hindus of the north
invoke a historical and nationalist experience that is seldom filtered through the
lens of Buddhist ethical traditions or correlated to classical texts written in Pali
from the sixth to the third centuries B.C.E.[3]

## *Selecting Fundamentals: The Choice to Scandalize*

Fundamentalists consistently retrieve and stress those teachings or practices from
the past which clearly do not "fit" in an "enlightened" and "sophisticated"
modern society. Just when the liberal Christian feels comfortable with the church
toning down the references to the supernatural (such references, liberals worry,
may appear to be rooted in superstition, ignorance, or psychological fears or
needs), the fundamentalist comes along stressing the doctrine of the birth of
Christ to a virgin, or the traditional belief in the actual physical resurrection of
Christ, or the expectation of his imminent return "on clouds of glory." Just when
modernist Muslims attempt to present Islam as a religious faith that respects
human rights and follows due process of law, along comes a regime calling itself
Islamic and stoning adulterers, executing apostates, and imprisoning dissenters—

all in the name of Islam. Just when Zionists establish the State of Israel on secular principles, radical religious Jews raise a hue and cry that the Zionist state is ultimately religious, that it is, in truth, the land promised to Abraham by God in the Torah.

The "just when" element to this pattern is not accidental, but intentional. Fundamentalists act when they see the faith being undermined. They deplore the secularizing of lands or movements that they believe are sacred at the very core. In acting (or reacting), then, fundamentalists stress the very beliefs or practices they see being ignored or eclipsed or de-emphasized. The doctrines or rituals being de-emphasized are often the ones that would embarrass people who wish their religious life to be congruous with their life in the modern world—a world increasingly skeptical about miracles, prophecies, heaven and hell, and other experiences that lie outside the realm of ordinary experience. But for fundamentalists, this is precisely the point: religion ought to be extraordinary. It ought to upset our expectations. It ought to be *scandalous.*

Fundamentalists may be sensitive about the treatment they receive, but they do, all of them, intend to scandalize outsiders. The Greek word *skandalon* means something one trips over, something that entraps. Christian fundamentalists choose to emphasize doctrines like the Virgin Birth or the premillennial Second Coming of Jesus, the ending of our world as it is and the beginning of his consequent thousand-year rule. Shi'ite Muslims have in recent years stressed the traditional belief in the return of the Hidden Imam, who will usher in an era of divine justice. Jewish fundamentalists of two broad camps who differ on many other points will agree, and insist to nonfundamentalist Jews, that the advent of the Messiah and the time of redemption are nigh.

The insistence on holding fast to such beliefs at a time when they are threatened by the attitudes of outsiders suggests that the believer is not entirely rational, and this is precisely the point that fundamentalists wish to make. They are not mere rationalists. They are not bound by the Enlightenment covenant that dictates that all acceptable forms of knowledge and discourse must fall within the framework of secular rationalism. That form of discourse is limited, fundamentalists of all faiths agree, and has failed miserably at comprehending the world and producing just and equitable societies. One need only look at vast stretches of the Third World, underdeveloped societies poorly served by ruling elites who have hoarded the riches of secular modernity but left their people in poverty.

A radical critique of secular culture is required; what can be more radical than posing a different system of thought, a different epistemology? That is precisely what fundamentalists do. They catch the attention of the rest of us by scandalizing (or amusing) us with preposterous claims about virgin births or hidden imams or personified books. But the "show" carries a lesson: there is another way of imagining the world, of understanding human destiny, of tapping the enthusiasms, hopes, and talents of modern individuals. That way will scandalize, amuse, perhaps even persuade, the unbeliever because it relies on a knowledge given from above and certain to confound merely human imaginings. The scandalizing way must be studied, and lived, for it alone offers the hope of true human prosperity and fulfillment.

## Selecting Fundamentals: The Need for Absolute Authority

In the foregoing discussion we have portrayed fundamentalisms as protest movements of a particular kind. That is, they are movements of resistance against liberal or "enlightened" models of modern society. Liberals are at least nominally tolerant of different ways of believing and acting, and so admit the possibility of many different, equally valid expressions of religious faith and identity. Fundamentalists see in this approach a recipe for confusion and disorientation. Once one allows various formulations of religious identity, one is on a slippery slope leading finally to relativism—the notion that no belief is absolutely true because all beliefs are bound by the limitations of time and space. Closely related to relativism is pluralism—the notion that the presence of many different expressions of belief is in itself a good thing. Soon, to the dismay of fundamentalists, any notion is permitted of God, virtue, morality, family loyalty—matters which are intimately linked, one to the other, as fundamentalists see the matter.

*The strong lines of authority characteristic of fundamentalist movements stress uniformity of behavior, a distinctive dress code, and male leadership. Here, several hundred future ministers listen to Professor Bruce McAlister in the preaching class at Bob Jones University.*

Given this analysis of modern society, fundamentalists have formulated their own ways of constructing society, which stand in stark contrast to the ways of the secular modernists. In presenting their alternative model(s) of society, fundamentalists insist that the past provides texts or events upon which one can rely for authority with absolute confidence. But it is distracting, indeed impossible, to stress the whole past and give everything equal emphasis. In their battle against modernism and relativism, they strategically and quickly reach for the basics, those fundamentals which will hold their people together, keep others at a distance, and help decide who is in and who is out of God's kingdom. Fundamentalists retrieve the experiences, practices, and beliefs of the past which the liberal might find most objectionable—and they emphasize these as being essential to the identity of the religious community or group in question.

Fundamentalists do this not only to scandalize outsiders, as we described previously, but also to pose a challenge to fence-sitters, to the undecided who have not yet committed themselves by pledging their ultimate allegiance. They want people to declare themselves, and so they pose the alternatives as dramatically as possible. In so doing, they also make a bid to increase the authority of their own leaders—an authority that must be seen as absolute and unquestioned if it is to be effective in countering the erosive tendencies of secular, tolerant, pluralist expressions of the one true faith—as each fundamentalist believes his or her faith to be.

When, for example, progressive Catholic leaders in nineteenth-century Europe and the United States sought to portray Roman Catholicism as a force for liberalism, democracy, and material progress, Pope Pius IX reacted by fiercely condemning these movements and the values they embodied as being absolutely inimical to authentic Catholic identity. He also judged it wise to go on the offensive by bolstering his claim to absolute authority over the church. The primacy of the pope over an ecumenical council was a contested medieval doctrine that did not generate great enthusiasm from many of the liberalizing bishops and priests of the day. All the more reason, then, in the fundamentalist view, to convene an ecumenical council, Vatican I, in 1869, and to persuade its members to elevate the doctrine regarding the pope's power to dogmatic status, making it a litmus test of Catholic identity. In this sense Pius IX called the question by proclaiming the dogma of papal infallibility. His bishops were thereby forced to declare their loyalty and to close ranks—or else be considered heretics, renegades who would choose their own will in defiance of the manifest will of the Church Universal. The vast majority of churchmen closed ranks, although a schism did occur.[4]

In other cases, fundamentalists seek to establish new lines of authority within the religious community because they judge that the traditional authorities have been corrupted by compromises with nonbelievers. Thus these fundamentalists retrieve prophetic teachings that are then used to undermine tepid clergy rather than to scandalize nonbelievers. For example, Sayyid Qutb, a leading thinker of the Egyptian Muslim Brotherhood, retrieved the seventh-century concept of *jahiliyya*, describing a state of pre-Islamic ignorance or paganism, to characterize the state of Egyptian and Muslim society during the reign of Gamal Abdul Nasser. In the view of Qutb and Muslim Brotherhood founder Hasan al-Banna before him, the first (if not only) ones to blame for this state of ignorance and disgrace were the ulama, the religious scholars supposedly entrusted with the guardianship of the righteous community; they had failed miserably by giving in to the lures of colonial and postcolonial Westernization, and allowing laxity in morals. Thus, Qutb and other Muslim Brothers urged, the privilege of interpreting Islamic sources should no longer be confined to the ulama.

In either case, whether fundamentalists are bolstering clerical authority or replacing it with an innovative alternative, they select fundamentals with one eye on the implications of these teachings for the question of authority within the religious community.

## Selecting Fundamentals: The Will to Rule

Fundamentalists also reach for fundamentals that will help them to seize power over others. Precisely for this purpose, they often choose doctrines that seem nonfundamental in the eyes of many who do not sympathize with them.

The Sikh religious tradition in the Punjab, for example, was not identified with violence for the first four centuries of its existence. To the contrary, the religious teachings of the gurus laid great emphasis on the pursuit of peace and harmony. There were, however, exceptions to this general rule, exceptions that were to be invoked only in times of mortal threat to the Sikh community. As we mentioned, these minor themes in Sikh teachings have been increasingly invoked by radical Sikh leaders since the early nineteenth century. These leaders have sought to bring about Sikh rule over the Punjab region, to refashion the Punjab as the Sikh state of Khalistan.

In the late 1970s and early 1980s a charismatic leader of these radicals, Jarnail Singh Bhindranwale, claimed that Sikhs must fight back furiously against non-Sikhs and the Indian state that supposedly empowered outsiders to exploit the Punjab economically, or else lose everything they hold dear. To the traditional Sikh symbols Bhindranwale added the sign of the revolver and the motorcycle— the new emblems of Sikh identity in an age of militancy. Bhindranwale was a charismatic figure whose authority was enhanced by the sense of crisis surrounding him. He helped to foster this sense of crisis by reconstituting an order of "pure" Sikh warriors, and by dramatic acts of defiance against the Indian state, including the terrorist acts that led to his martyrdom in 1984, when Indian state security forces stormed the holiest Sikh shrine, the Golden Temple at Amritsar, where Bhindranwale had taken refuge. Nonfundamentalist Sikhs were and are dismayed by the violence in the Punjab, which continued in ever greater intensity in the years after Bhindranwale's death.

In Israel, Gush Emunim scandalizes others by deriving from ancient scriptures what international law and pragmatic alliances today deny them: a mandate for their land claims. The members quote Rav Zvi Yehuda Kook (1891–1982), the son of Rav Abraham Isaac Kook, the twentieth century's first chief rabbi in Palestine: "The Land was chosen even before the people. . . . The chosen land and the chosen people comprise one completed, divine unity, joined together at the creation of the world and the creation of history. They comprise *one vital and integral unit.*"[5] By quoting this kind of teaching, Jewish fundamentalists in Israel defend their claims to hegemony over territories that are contested by Palestinians who have lived there continuously for centuries.

One element of the traditional religious imagination that some fundamentalist groups make central to their self-understanding is eschatological, or end-time, thought. "Visions of the end" drive fundamentalist militancy in the case of Gush Emunim, for example, where there is an understanding that the religious settlers are God's vanguard, God's instruments for ushering in the age of redemption. As if to hasten this process, in 1984 core members of the Gush joined a Jewish underground in a plot which, had it been successful, could have led to a major international conflict. On Temple Mount, as Jews call the hill in Jerusalem which was the site of the ancient temple, stand two of the holiest Muslim shrines in the world. Muslims consider the hill, which they call al-Haram al-Sharif, to be the site of the Prophet's mystical night journey to Jerusalem and, from there, to heaven; but fundamentalist Jews believe that the Muslim shrines, the al-Aksa Mosque and the Dome of the Rock, must be destroyed so that the temple may be rebuilt in preparation for the Messiah. Thus the Jewish radicals of the underground planned in 1984 to blow up the shrines in order to pave the way for redemption.

Obviously a very sharp line can be drawn in the fundamentalist world, a line where good and bad, true and false, right and wrong get bartered and defined. Closely associated with the end-time thought of fundamentalisms is the embracing of a dualistic worldview which sharply divides the world into God's versus Satan's, Good versus Evil. The dualisms are extreme for a reason: they help fundamentalists see the enemy clearly and without flinching. They also motivate fellow defenders by pointing to a gross evil which impels the enemy to do the intruding. If there are shades of gray between light and darkness, or degrees of moderation between good and evil, there will be confusion in the battle. The Evil One may be embodied in the United States, the West, the evolutionists, or the other side in one's own denomination. Whoever it is, there must be no sympathy for this force, no vagueness about reasons for response, no motive to negotiate or to let the guard down.

Many fundamentalisms contain views of the outcome of history that shape their expression of meaning in the here and now. They may borrow from the Hebraic world the concept of a messiah and often add to that the notion of a millennium (though they may not be literal about the concept of a thousand years). This means that they see the meaning of history focused in a person and a sense of motion. In Shi'ite Islam this messianic figure is the Hidden Imam. For Jews, the figure of the Messiah in the words of the ancient prophets is variously interpreted and regularly invoked. Christian fundamentalists speak of Jesus Christ as the Saviour, who becomes the impeller of his followers into the world of action and the one who will lift them to himself in the final decisive battles at the end of history and the beginning of his thousand-year rule. When the Hidden Imam is revealed, when the Messiah comes, or when Jesus Christ comes again, the balance sheet of history will be evident. The remaining evil which has haunted the faithful will be finally defeated, and justice will have its sway. Such beliefs characterize the peoples who derive from the figure of Abraham and, one might say, the city of Jerusalem. They are somewhat more diffuse and ill-defined in Buddhist and Hindu religious circles, where other teachings are used to impel people to action.

The fundamentalists' ideological insistence on a dualistic view of the world means that they spend a great deal of their time and energy setting boundaries

between themselves and outsiders. These boundaries, which mark off the elect
from the reprobate, the chosen from those left behind, are expressed by the
distinctive dress, strict social and moral codes, and general behaviors of fundamentalist group members. Fundamentalists are different from nonfundamentalists. This difference is reinforced not only by scandalous doctrines, but by
scandalous patterns of living.[6] For example, Muslim women offend and dismay
feminists within and outside the *umma* (worldwide Islamic community) by
donning the veil and chador willingly and by defending the Islamic marriage
contract, as practiced in Pakistan and Iran, which presents a woman as a
commodity to be acquired, or dispatched, largely according to the will of a man.
The chapters on Jewish, Christian, and Islamic movements discuss these scandalous
behaviors and codes and their use as markers of group identity in some detail.

# The Imitation of the Enemy:
# Fundamentalisms as Modern Movements

When we look at fundamentalist movements within their historical contexts we
see an irony which, some scholars say, may ultimately prove their undoing.
Despite rhetoric invoking a bygone era and reliance on dualistic and apocalyptic
imaginings of the world, twentieth-century fundamentalism, in all of its forms, is
a modern phenomenon. The modern nature of these movements explains a good
deal about their radical and innovative character, but it also threatens to divest
them of their original source in the powerful experience of religion.

Why is this so? Fundamentalists are shrewd and careful observers of
modernity, and they adopt its useful features while imitating its powerful processes. These processes, however, include the manipulation and repackaging of
complex arguments and traditions for political or purely economic ends. Much
has been written about modern communications, and the sensibilities that
accompany them, as leading to the trivialization of moral and political discourse
in Westernized societies.[7] When activists of any kind (even sincere defenders of

the faith) tailor a religious tradition's teachings to fit narrow political objectives, invariably the risk arises that a richly layered worldview may be lost entirely in a more or less crass sociopolitical ideology. Too much imitation of modernity, too much innovation, even in the cause of defending the faith, may threaten the one element of religious fundamentalism that prevents it from deteriorating into a mere ideology, namely, the religious element—the reverence and respect for the transcendent referent in all human endeavor.

Because they are alert reactors but not reactionaries, inventors more than preservers, fundamentalists are very much at home with the world around them. If television is what assaults the traditionalist community, fundamentalists seize television's techniques and excel in the use of the medium. American Protestant fundamentalists and televangelists have shown how well this can work. So have Muslims in the Middle East. Let Westerners subvert Islamic villages with the secular sounds of cassettes and transistor radios—the ayatollahs will fight back with revolutionary cassettes of their own.

The use of the mass means of data-gathering, accounting, disseminating, broadcasting, and communicating by fundamentalists suggests an at-homeness with modern technology. Most religious liberals and humanist philosophers have, on the other hand, greeted such communications technology warily if not critically. In the spirit of Jewish theologian Martin Buber, who stressed the importance of "I-Thou" as opposed to "I-It" relations, many liberals have been suspicious of the ways technology "uses" people, dehumanizing them, robbing them of spiritual freedom, making them objects. Even faith, they have feared, might become a consumer item, a commodity; prospects for conversion would be manipulated and deceived; mechanization might substitute for community in circles of faith. What Protestant thinker Paul Tillich called "technical reason," it was feared, would prevail at the expense of the distinctively human.[8] Certainly radio, the cinema, and television were prime carriers of the virus called modernity. Reactive movements, one would have expected, would be extreme and intense in their opposition to them.

Anything but that. Modern religious fundamentalisms rose concurrently with mass media of communication in the electronic era, and they took over the centuries-old technologies of printing and added to them the new instruments of more rapid broadcasting, using them efficiently and exuberantly. Fundamentalists were quick to see that these instruments were precisely the means for ending their isolation. Traditionalists, like Orthodox Jews or the Amish, might do what they could to live at some remove in literal and figurative ghettos, segregations which were both chosen and imposed, but fundamentalists have by and large not chosen to stay at such a distance. Signals coming from the modern media were reaching into their enclosures, captivating the minds of their children. They had to react, and they have done so.

Earlier in this century, Shi'ite and Sunni Muslims, Zionist Jews, and conservative Protestants artfully used the emergence of mass media to their advantage. Sometimes they figuratively "jammed signals," or set out to limit the effectiveness of the media. But more often they used these instruments to portray the evils of the scientific and industrial worlds which made such media possible.

It is hard to find a fundamentalism that has not used radio, television, rapid mailings, or other such technical devices to gather groups into a movement. The Ayatollah Khomeini used inexpensive cassette recordings made during his Parisian exile to penetrate Iranian villages with Shi'ite revolutionary ideas. Sunni Islamic fundamentalist movements in Egypt and elsewhere efficiently employed radio. Fundamentalist-like evangelicalisms and pentecostalisms in Latin America make progress against traditional Catholicism by using local television and radio stations in urban and even sometimes some peasant village settings.

Just as fundamentalists have made use of modernity's main carrier, mass media, they also have appropriated the very heart of Enlightenment reason and rationalism. The near hysteria associated with some mass movement fundamentalist scenes on the Asian subcontinent, in the Middle East, and elsewhere, leads many to conclude that fundamentalisms are essentially antirational, opposed to reason. Some of them may be, but in those we have studied—and the sweep of them is vast—it is clear that fundamentalists often fight modernity by seizing the concept of reason and "throwing it back," using not unreason but a different modality of rationalism.

The familiar battle in the United States between fundamentalists who invented "Creation research" versus the biologists who take evolution for granted has not centered on faith versus reason—at least not in the view of fundamentalists. The struggle also has not meant emotion versus reason, though to some scientists the fundamentalists may seem strident and out of control. To watch fundamentalists in the courtroom is to gain a different impression. The "Creation research" anti-evolutionists, partly for reasons of complying with American strictures against mixing church and state but mainly for reasons having to do with their method, insist that their research is not faith-based. It may be congruent with revealed religion, as in the biblical book of Genesis, but the proponents of "Creation research" want to argue their case on the basis of the fossil record, common sense, and scholastic philosophy. The fact that all mainstream scientists reject such arguments does not mean that they are not intended to be based in reason; a different model of reasoning functions for the fundamentalist. As we shall see, the Protestant fundamentalists employ derivatives of Scottish Common-Sense Realist philosophy, a normative way of looking at science in early nineteenth-century America.

Fundamentalisms are, moreover, community-building movements in a time of modern individualist anomie on many cultural scenes. While for decades liberals have been *writing* about the need for strong communities to counter extreme individualism in societies where that has been free to develop, fundamentalists have *built* community. Agents of the liberal culture do not like the form these fundamentalists' communities take; they charge that people in them are drawn together as a result of strong impositions of religious authority, intense stimuli of the emotional and affective life, and sometimes manipulative appeals in the quest for identity. The criticism may be well taken, but one must observe that these communities are widespread and effective.

The motor and motive for the fundamentalists' reactions to modernity, it is important to remember, did not come from any new discoveries they made or new revelations they received. Fundamentalist communities may share many characteristics with so-called new religions, intense groups that the larger public stigmatizes as cults, but whereas "new religions" often depend upon the revelations of new charismatic leadership, fundamentalisms draw on the arsenal of inherited beliefs about the cosmos and ways of responding to the call of God in it. Some of these beliefs have national or political thrusts, but they are legitimated by the texts and codes of ancient faiths. It is in treating these ancient texts and codes as ingredients in a new sociopolitical recipe for cultural transformation, however, that fundamentalisms risk eroding the boundaries between themselves and the secular world that they have struggled so ardently to establish.

## Fundamentalism: A Working Definition

Drawing together the traits and elements we have discussed, we can say that fundamentalism is a distinctive tendency—a habit of mind and a pattern of behavior—found within modern religious communities and embodied in certain representative individuals and movements. Fundamentalism is, in other words, a religious way of being that manifests itself as a strategy by which beleaguered believers attempt to preserve their distinctive identity as a people or group.

Feeling this identity to be at risk in the contemporary era, fundamentalists fortify it by a selective retrieval of doctrines, beliefs, and practices from a sacred past. These retrieved "fundamentals" are refined, modified, and given new expression in institutions and political movements that often move beyond the confines and practices of a given traditional religion in the effort to keep it alive as an authentic way of life for modern people. The fundamentals are taught with great authority; by adhering obediently to them, believers will be able to resist the seductions of the secular world. Moreover, these fundamentals are accompanied in the new religious portfolio by unprecedented claims and doctrinal innovations. By the strength of these innovations and the new supporting doctrines, the retrieved and updated fundamentals are meant to regain the same charismatic intensity today by which they originally forged communal identity from formative revelatory religious experiences long ago.

In this sense contemporary fundamentalism is at once both derivative and vitally original. Fundamentalists do not intend to impose archaic practices and lifestyles or to return to a golden era, a sacred past, a bygone time of origins—although nostalgia for such an era is a hallmark of fundamentalist rhetoric. By selecting elements of tradition and modernity, fundamentalists seek to remake the world. Renewed religious identity becomes the exclusive and absolute basis for a re-created political and social order that is oriented toward the future rather than the past. The new world has been foretold in prophecy and unfolds, even now, under the watchful eye of God.

Such a world-building endeavor requires charismatic and authoritarian leadership, which fundamentalist movements rely on in nearly every case. These movements also feature a disciplined inner core of full-time staffers or organizational members, as well as a larger population of sympathizers who may be called upon in times of need. The inner core and sympathizers alike follow a rigorous socio-moral code that sets them apart from nonbelievers and from compromisers. Fundamentalists set boundaries, name and study their enemies, seek recruits and converts, and often imitate the very forces they oppose. What we shall call activist or interventionist fundamentalists, like Gush Emunim of Israel or Operation Rescue of the United States, seek no less than a comprehensive reorientation and reordering of society.[9]

This working definition and the broad comparisons we have drawn should not obscure the substantive differences between the various fundamentalist movements. The distinctiveness of each movement will become clear in the following individual portraits, beginning with the case of Protestant Christian fundamentalism.

## CHAPTER TWO

# FIGHTING BACK:
# PROTESTANT FUNDAMENTALISM IN
# THE UNITED STATES

Imagine that in 1959 someone sat on an American TV show and said, "I've had a vision! In the next thirty years, we will have murdered twenty-five million children in ways too barbaric to describe, sodomites will be parading in the streets, and politicians will be proclaiming Gay Pride Week. Your tax money is going to fund blasphemy and homosexual pornography. It will be illegal for a public school teacher to recite the Lord's Prayer or read the Twenty-third Psalm to her class, but that same teacher will be able to tell your child where to get a condom, and where to get an abortion, without your consent or your knowledge. There will be a cocaine crisis, and we will have mass murders going on in our country." Who would have believed it?[1]

Randall Terry is a new breed of Christian fundamentalist, but the anger and outrage he expresses in this impassioned description of an unsuspecting nation on the brink of moral anarchy could have been voiced by Jerry Falwell, founder of the now-defunct Moral Majority and of Liberty University, or by Bob Jones III, the president of the university in South Carolina which bears his family name. All three men, Terry, Falwell, and Jones, are fundamentalist Christians who have dedicated themselves to fighting back against the moral anarchy which, they are convinced, was unleashed with a special intensity during the 1960s but has always been present within sinful human institutions and structures.

While they agree that the problem lies in Satan's increasing power over American culture and that the solution lies in a return to the "traditional family values" and public virtues rooted in the Holy Bible, Terry, Falwell, and Jones also represent different forms of fundamentalism. Each adopts a different strategy in realizing the will of Jesus Christ on earth and defending the revealed fundamentals of the Christian faith.

Bob Jones III is the latest in a line of separatist fundamentalists—a line which stretches back past his grandfather to the first decade of this century, when the "come outers," as they were called, came out of the mainstream Protestant denominations, fleeing from them because they saw them as contaminated by modern heresies and liberal ideas. This wing of Christian fundamentalism has remained proudly—some would say stubbornly—separatist. They try to avoid sustained involvement with people who have not accepted Jesus Christ as Lord and Savior—people, that is, who have not been "born again" in the Holy Spirit.

When one is born again, she throws off the old, sinful person of her first birth and takes on Christ's sinless human nature. That nature will not be perfect in her, but it will orient her to the Second Coming of the Lord, an event which will make everything right. It is this event which separatist fundamentalists live for: the triumphant return of the Lord on clouds of glory is the *sole hope* for humankind. In the separatist view, no human efforts, even those made by a sincere Christian activist like Randall Terry, will hasten Jesus' coming. In fact, things will only get worse, society more corrupt, in the days before the Messiah returns to establish his thousand-year reign. Because separatist Christians believe that the Lord will return before the millennial reign begins, they are sometimes called *pre*millennialists.

What are the separatist fundamentalists to do while the Lord tarries? They are to retreat from the world, establish their own institutions, live by biblical fundamentals (as interpreted by leaders like Bob Jones), and try to remain pure and righteous even as they carry the good news to others who have not heard it or have heard it and rejected it. The separatist fundamentalists are soul-winners, but they are not activists in the political order. Involvement with earthly processes and politics would only lead to the defeat of the fundamentalist, for the earthly world is given over to Satan.

Jerry Falwell, a Baptist minister in Virginia, was once concerned exclusively with soul winning. In the 1950s he described his fundamentalism in terms very similar to those used by the separatists. His primary duty was to save souls for Jesus by preparing his congregation to receive the word of the Lord and accept Jesus. But Falwell changed as he and his congregation lived through the 1960s.

Assaulted by the developments of a decade that began with the abolition of prayer in public schools in 1963 and culminated with the legalization of abortion on demand in 1973, Falwell and many fundamentalist Christians like him decided that they could no longer remain passive. In their view, Satan, who had inspired the philosophy of secular humanism that was eroding the Judeo-Christian foundations of American schools, courts, and Congress, was threatening to ensure that there would be no future generation of American Christians to educate and nurture in the faith. So Falwell and others became activist fundamentalists. In the late 1970s and throughout the 1980s, they organized in political coalitions like the Moral Majority and the Religious Roundtable, and launched what proved to be a partially successful attempt to influence the course of American law and politics. Although political scientists have concluded that

*During the 1992 Republican convention, members of "The Religious Right" (such as broadcaster Pat Robertson, shown at right with Vice-President Dan Quayle) reemphasized their ties to the GOP and helped draft the party platform.* (Donna Binder, Impact Visuals)

the "New Christian Right" was anything but a political majority, it did develop a rhetoric of American exceptionalism and Christian family values, supported presidential and congressional candidates who endorsed these values, and looked with favor upon the appointment of conservative justices to the United States Supreme Court by presidents Reagan and Bush. The activists remained theologically premillennialist, although it was obvious from their behavior that they felt that the Lord needed a little help in clearing the threshing floor before he made his triumphant return.

Depending upon one's point of view, there are at least two ways to interpret Falwell's action in disbanding the Moral Majority in 1990 and returning to his Virginia base and to Liberty University. Detractors will say that Falwell and company were chastened by their lack of success in organizing Christian voters into a discernible power bloc; supporters will point to the rightward swing in American political and cultural norms in the 1980s and claim that the activist Christians achieved their goals. In either case, it is fair to say that the activists have not gone away; they have simply refocused their political energies on the local and state levels, even as they have won key positions on the national policy committees of the Republican party.

Randall Terry is an example of a new breed of activist fundamentalists who work on a local level in order to gradually, but dramatically, transform national policy. However, whereas Falwell and his generation of activists operated within the law of the land, Terry, and the members of the Operation Rescue movement that he leads, defy laws that they consider anti-Christian and therefore unjust. The law that has occupied the new activists' attention during the five years since they held their first "siege" in Atlanta in 1988 is the one permitting abortion on demand, codified in the 1973 Supreme Court ruling *Roe v. Wade*. Terry and his followers are militants; they are radical fundamentalists who, like the Gush Emunim settlers on the West Bank, seek to polarize a nation, creating a crisis of identity and thus an opportunity for radical decision on the part of the previously undecided. Terry is also battling for souls, but he sees that battle as necessarily being waged in the streets, at the steps of the abortion clinics blocked by "rescuers" who seek to "save babies."

*Randall Terry of the anti-abortion organization Operation Rescue rejects separatist fundamentalism in favor of social activism. By mobilizing protestors to block entry to abortion clinics, Terry is actively seeking to transform public opinion—and national policy.*

Terry sees Operation Rescue and the campaign against abortion as but the first step in returning America to its Christian roots and destiny. He sees himself as being in continuity with separatist fundamentalists in important ways, but he embraces a far different sense of his responsibilities to Christ while the Lord tarries. Says Terry:

> You know, I am an evangelist! I pick up hitchhikers, get 'em in my car, get 'em up to fifty-five miles per hour, and I preach the gospel to them! I mean, I don't talk to them about cultural reformation or abortion, or something like this. I say, 'Do you know Jesus? Are you a Christian?' So, that's me! That's part of me! I've stood on street corners and said, "Excuse me, everyone, can I have your attention?" And I preach the gospel of the living God to them! "Jesus Christ died for your sins. He rose from the dead on the third day and you can believe in Him and be forgiven!" So that's part of who I am. I believe in that. But where we part company with some wings of the church, the separatist wing of the church, is that they think that is it! That is the sum total of our duty as Christians to this generation. And I reject that!

Bob Jones III openly rejects the radical activist interpretation of the responsibilities of a fundamentalist. "This Moral Majority type of Christianity in America says, 'Let's elect good men, let's change the moral codes, let's change the laws, we'll have a Christian America.' Nothing could be farther from the mission of the church," Jones argues. "And to some people it sounds heretical for me to say that. But as I understand New Testament Christianity, it [commands us to] preach the gospel to every creature, get them saved, and then establish them on the foundation of the word of God, so their faith and practice is biblical."

At the heart of the debate among fundamentalists about the proper approach to "winning back America," then, is a diversity of opinion about the nature of the relationship between the Lord's will for true believers and the course of societal development. Randall Terry and the activist fundamentalists who challenge what they consider to be unjust and ungodly laws feel that true believers will be accountable to Christ if they fail to challenge directly a social and legal structure that promotes what is in their opinion the destruction of human lives and the corruption of souls. In the eyes of activist fundamentalists, Christ is calling for a prophetic response to the advance of an immoral society. For Bob Jones III and the separatist fundamentalists at the other end of the spectrum, engagement with the fallen world is both fruitless and morally compromising. The Lord has called true believers out of the mainline denominations and the public schools, away from the institutions and culture that corrupt the less vigilant Christians. Separatists pursue purity within a lifestyle based directly on biblical principles.

Jerry Falwell and other "new evangelicals," as they are sometimes called, represent a middle position on the spectrum of opinion on this question. Falwell began as a strict separatist but became an activist when he decided that the pursuit of purity was no longer possible in a secularized culture that was becoming more invasive and dominant each year. Penetrating community, home, and family through uncontrolled mass media, permissive legal rulings by liberal courts, and the libertarian advocacy of interest groups like the American Civil Liberties Union (ACLU), secular humanism threatened the young generation of Christians growing up in the world created by the 1960s. Falwell and members of the Moral Majority would actively intervene to oppose the encroachment of the secularists, but they would do so within the law and by manipulating the political system in their favor.

Standing just outside of this spectrum of fundamentalist opinion are well-known American religious figures such as Pat Robertson, Jimmy Swaggart, and Jim and Tammy Bakker, who are often mistakenly identified as fundamentalists. While these and other prominent or once-prominent televangelists share the biblical literalism and moralism associated with fundamentalism, they are pentecostalists rather than fundamentalists.

The theological orientation and heritage of pentecostals is different from that of fundamentalists and this leads to important differences on central questions such as the role that the Bible should play in ordering the Christian community and establishing the framework of moral life. Put simply, pentecostalists give a far greater weight to prophecy, speaking in tongues, faith healing, and other "spiritual gifts" than do fundamentalists. The pentecostal view of history as an unfolding and dynamic process is much more fluid than the fundamentalist sense that God has foreordained a precise beginning, middle, and (approaching) end to human affairs. Pentecostalists believe that the Bible is the inerrant word of God, but they remain open to the leading of the Holy Spirit in determining their next move. Fundamentalists are uncomfortable, to say the least, with the open-ended character of pentecostalism and feel that the Bible alone is perfectly sufficient in guiding Christian moral, religious, and political action. Writer Frances Fitzgerald caught this difference beautifully in describing the image of Jerry Falwell, hands folded across his chest solemnly and wearing a dark suit and a grimace rather than a smile, as he slid down one of the long water slides of the now-defunct PTL Heritage theme park that he took over briefly after the Bakkers went bankrupt. No self-respecting fundamentalist patriarch would enjoy such a silly divergence, especially one ennobled by the symbolism of the waters of baptism, which were on prominent display in the pentecostalist theme park.[2] Nor did Falwell support Pat Robertson's run for the presidency in 1988, despite their similar calls for a return to traditional moral values: a fundamentalist finds it difficult to entrust the future to anyone who is waiting for a new whisper in the ear from the Lord.

Having said this, it is important to note that pentecostalist preachers like Swaggart and Robertson (who disagree with one another on a number of issues, of course) do contribute in a powerful way to the momentum of fundamentalist-like social movements in the United States. After scandals destroyed the Swaggart and Bakker televangelical empires, and with Falwell disbanding the Moral Majority and concentrating his energies on Liberty University and other regional campaigns, Pat Robertson, the host of the still-popular TV show "The 700 Club" and patron of missionary efforts in Latin America, emerged in 1992 as the leader of the Christian Coalition, a grass-roots political network dedicated to advancing a conservative political agenda in local communities.

Robertson also resembles the fundamentalists in his adroit fusing of Christian apocalyptic themes and messianic expectations with political conspiracy theories and a rigorous moral critique of contemporary American society. As Soviet communism waned, fundamentalists and pentecostal political activists perceived a new enemy, a coming global threat of one-worldism inspired by New Age philosophy, which Robertson named and detailed in his 1991 bestseller, *The New World Order*:

> A single thread runs from the White House to the State Department to the Council on Foreign Relations to the Trilateral Commission to secret societies to extreme New Agers. There must be a new world order. It must eliminate national sovereignty. There must be world government, a world police force, world courts, world banking and currency, and a world elite in charge of it all. To some there must be a complete redistribution of wealth; to others there must be an elimination of Christianity; to some extreme New Agers there must be the deaths of two or three billion people in the Third World by the end of this decade.[3]

Although Robertson is a prominent evangelical Christian keeping the flame of religiously inspired political activism burning brightly, pentecostalists are not among the Christians who accept or who have accepted the term *fundamentalist* for themselves. Even within that group of self-proclaimed fundamentalists, which numbers twelve to fifteen million in the United States, a remarkable diversity exists which is rooted in the historical development of American evangelicalism.

# The Prehistory of Fundamentalism
# in the United States

The fundamentalists of recent decades have, by and large, not been historically minded; they have written few histories of their movement in the twentieth century, leaving that task to evangelicals, liberals, and even historians of secular outlook. But nonfundamentalists cannot hope to understand the present situation of fundamentalists without seeing the backdrop against which they developed. While most historians would place the roots of fundamentalism in the nineteenth century, believers are interested in a much longer story, which they tend to use as the plot for the basics of faith.

Leaders of American Christian fundamentalism would therefore say that the movement had its real roots laid down by a Creator God at the beginning of the world and time, several thousand years ago; at the very least, its beginnings reach back to the Bible, God's chosen means of revealing himself and informing the world about his plan for its salvation and about a set of commands which he expected to be fulfilled. Since the inerrant Bible said that one could lay no other foundation than the one laid in Christ's name, the New Testament, which witnessed to Jesus as the Messiah, was and is the determinative document.

Most fundamentalists did not fuss much with history between Biblical times and the recent past. They may have admired the early Christian fathers who developed doctrines and creeds designed to preserve, protect, and set forth biblical faith, but most of them saw in the Middle Ages the development of new doctrines and a departure into heresy and corruption of the old truths. They might pay respects to Martin Luther, John Calvin, John Knox, or other heroes of the sixteenth-century Protestant Reformation—these reformers were considered heroic because they rescued and restored biblical fundamentals after denouncing and breaking from the Roman Catholicism which dominated the Christian expression in Western Europe at that time—but the great figures of the Reformation were honored not as inventors but as restorers, not as innovators but as preservers. After all, once the fundamentals were clearly set forth, as they were only in the Bible, how could someone add to or change anything without ruining the purity of the original?

Thus, when American Protestant fundamentalism took rise informally in the late nineteenth century and formally in disputes after World War I, its leaders, after paying respects to the era of the Protestant Reformation, rejected much of what had taken place in recent history, in Protestantism specifically and in the Christianity that surrounded them.

The fundamentalist leaders of the turn of the century agreed that what was being professed was increasingly at odds with the true faith. Jewish fundamentalists, faced with a similar problem, insisted on a special interpretation of the history and mission of Jews or of Israel; Islamic fundamentalists, blessed with a sacred scripture that all believers adhere to literally, took doctrines for granted, whether in Shi'ism or Sunnism, but insisted that they be applied systematically. Protestants, however, made their case on the centrality of a few doctrines, with certain codes of behavior seen as issuing from adherence to these doctrines.

The fundamentalists of the early twentieth century could draw upon certain historical elements in consolidating their vision of America and American religion. Protestants in America, for example, had always looked with pride to the Puritan and other Protestant colonial pasts that had led to revolution, independence, and the making of the Constitution. They saw national heroes, especially George Washington, as Protestants, however heretical such Enlightenment-influenced founders may have been, and it was undeniable that the Protestant clergy had taken a leadership role in spreading the spirit of nationalism, supporting the new nation's armies, providing a moral structure, passing the laws of the land.

The more assertive clergy had begun to worry after the middle of the nineteenth century lest Catholics flooding in from Ireland after the potato famines crowd or even overtake Protestant capitals like Boston, New York, and Philadelphia; they saw the need for a united front that transcended sectarianism. Some of them saw the need for bogeymen; thus hoping to keep outsiders at a distance and insiders together, they pointed to atheists, infidels, agnostics, and scoffers wherever they looked, and exaggerated the importance of these extremely small minorities. But statistically none of these nonbelievers stood much chance against Protestants who, in effect, had their empire. If Protestants wanted to ward off the Catholic, the infidel, the barbarian, and win the West and the world for Christ, however, they had to stay together.

Yet stay together was precisely what they could not do. There were distinctive ways of baptizing or determining how God's grace came which had divided them all along. They had disagreed over mission strategies in the eighteenth century, over how to win "the Indian" to Protestantism, yet culturally they always saw themselves as custodians of a single national empire, as stewards of its symbols, as motors for the spread of its ideals around the world. They had to stay together to fulfill these goals.

In the nineteenth century some Protestants called themselves postmillennialists, because they believed they should spread the mission so far, press the moral cause so deeply, and certify the doctrines so doggedly, that the world would become a place of prosperity and peace so attractive that Christ could come again and bring the world to perfection. Not all these missionaries used the language of millennium, but most of them thought that the Kingdom of God was being realized around them and that they had to help God complete the task of forming and reforming worlds. Again, they needed to stay together for that purpose.[4]

Problems bigger than those posed by Catholics, infidels, and barbarians began to appear in the late nineteenth century, however. In America, Protestantisms for the most part had come to depend on their ability to monopolize, to "run the show," and increasingly they found it hard to run the show, not because of other Christians, but because of a world of change. Great cities were growing, and they were not founded on a covenant surrounding a single church with its high tower. Great cities attracted vice and the vicious, and these could not be controlled in the way they could be by revival meetings held on the equally lawless small-town frontier. The public press and the literary world gave notice to people who not only did not care for the ways of Christ but undercut them.

The philosopher Alfred North Whitehead once said that one must write history with attention to both brute forces and ideology. American Protestants faced modernity first as a brute force, made up of non-Protestant immigrants, distracting inventions, devilish immoralities (like alcoholic beverages and drunkenness), political corruption, and alluring means of communication which seduced people from the church. As for ideology, it took three main forms after the Civil War, and all of them threatened the conservative Protestants and led them to react and innovate. The first of these is often overlooked, but in recent decades its role in determining "the fundamentals" stands out ever more. In academic terms, there arose a battle over philosophies of history.

## *The End and the Philosophy of History: Premillennialism*

One cannot comment on the meaning of history without knowing beginnings and endings, just as one cannot summarize the meaning of a person's life without knowing how that person started and what became of her at the end of her days.

The late nineteenth century was a time when many vied to describe the end, and thus the meaning, of history. The modernists used the language of evolution, progress, socialism, and science—all seen as rivals to the plot of biblical fundamentals. A few, a very few, invoked prophets like Karl Marx from Europe, but his was too heavy an ideology for export to America; his solutions—class warfare, permanent revolution—did not match American problems. A few more dedicated themselves to the organization of society on socialist lines, but they were also ineffective; in their peak political year, 1912, they drew only about 8 percent of the vote. Americans were not in the mood for ideology. They were a practical people who dreamed. They needed an ideology based in what they could observe in the empirical situation.

The doctrine of progress proved to be an ideology that one could see in action out the window. Where once there had been sailing ships, rivers, stagecoaches, and corduroy roads, now there were steamships, canals, railroads, and eventually automobiles. Where once there had been painstaking custom work, American factories were making possible the spread of luxuries to common people. Whereas before transactions were minute and petty, now great corporations were bringing in efficiency. Protestant reformers always saw the negative developments, but most of the people wanted the products of the mines and factories and were ready to pay the spiritual price modern progress demanded.

The conservative Protestants joined the reformers in noticing the underside of modernity. It occurred to them that the doctrine of progress and its effects were rivals to the ways of God and the realms of faith. They did not think things were getting better and better. Indeed, there was so much devastation around them that they became convinced the world was choosing the wrong view of the future.

Even worse, the celebrators of progress came from right within the Protestant house. Progressives, modernists, promoters of a "social gospel," were distorting the biblical message that it was necessary to be rescued *from* the world and were making people too much at home *in* the world. These proponents of the social gospel were not even content with the world's pace of progress; they wanted to hurry progress along and to say that it was God's instrument in their hands. To conservatives this looked like a sellout. Nowhere had the Bible said that the world would make progress. Just the opposite. Jesus and the apostles had prophesied an early end to the world. Before that end there would be dire events: men's hearts failing them for fear, wars and rumors of war, signs in the heavens and on earth. These were not marginal or accidental features of the Christian message, they were fundamental. These conservatives did not all agree on details, but they did agree that earthly progress was not part of the divine scheme. Divine intervention was.

Bob Jones, Jr., the separatist fundamentalist leader of the university in South Carolina which bears his name, comments:

> You see, most of our great denominations today have gone a long way from the Bible. Their philosophy is a philosophy of compliance. "Let's fit into society." Our business is not to fit into society, our business is to change society. And we can only change society as we change *individuals* in society. *There is no such thing as a social Gospel.* That's a joke! There's only the Gospel of the grace of God, and it's an individual

*Bob Jones, Jr., and Bob Jones III favor a separatist approach in lieu of the high-profile political involvement that characterizes the "Religious Right."*

Gospel. Whosoever comes, whosoever believes. The Lord's message is always a message to the individual.

Now it happened that through the middle decades of the nineteenth century there were new parties, sects, and movements in England making similar moves, moves which were to influence early twentieth-century American thought. For example, an evangelist named John Nelson Darby was founding a group known to some as Darbyites and to others as Plymouth Brethren. He left the Church of England in 1828 and by 1840 was leading his own faction of Brethren. He invented or discovered or rediscovered—it depends on who is telling the story—much of the approach called dispensationalism, a key feature in much of fundamentalism. In this teaching, he divided history into precise sections, or dispensations, in each of which God ruled differently. Darby dubbed his own era "the age of the church," in which people failed to live up to God's demands. Darby attacked almost everything about the modern era of the church. To him only hope would be drastic action on the part of God.[5]

The action would mean a new dispensation, at the beginning of which Jesus would "rapture," or gather up the faithful. Associated with such an event were other prophesied events: Israel would be restored, great tribulation would come, there would be a battle of Armageddon, and in the midst of the devastation,

Christ, now returned to earth, would begin a thousand years of rule. Darby drew these teachings from the most visionary, dream-filled, symbolic books of the Bible, like Revelation, and astonished his critics by applying them literally to world affairs. One hundred and fifty years later his ideas sound contrived, arcane—even silly—to nonfundamentalists, including other Christians. It is hard to penetrate his worldview. Yet he and his colleagues propagated it so successfully in the mid-nineteenth century that it still provides the mental framework for tens of millions of Christians today.

What became of Darby and the Plymouth Brethren? The Brethren exist, but more as a network than as a denomination; they have exercised their influence in existing denominations. The Brethren also had the good luck to find a kindred spirit in Dwight L. Moody, the greatest American revivalist of the second half of the nineteenth century. Moody commuted across the Atlantic, picking up and reinforcing ideas about the millennium. Moody, himself a generally buoyant personality, showed by his outlook that dispensationalism did not have to be an expression of personal pessimism.

Dispensationalism was a philosophy of history which motivated believers to want to rescue others from damnation before the Second Coming. Fundamentalist pioneers looked around at moderate Protestantism and saw a decline of interest in saving souls. Moody rescued souls, and as he did so he and his colleagues helped spread premillennial views so effectively that many followers came to believe that such a view of history had always been around. They joined Moody and people more extreme than he in taking the prophecies of Daniel, Ezekiel, and the Book of Revelation literally.

The explicit preaching of a literal second coming of Christ thus became one of the fundamentals. Premillennialism became so prominent in a set of meetings, particularly the Niagara Bible Conferences, held from 1883 to 1897, that it occupies a privileged place among the Christian anticipations of "the end of history."

It only takes a little imagination to see how powerful premillennial ideas were and can be in fundamentalism. Do you seek a distinctive identity? Here is a teaching which separates you from other Christians, Protestants, and even

*"Premillennial" fundamentalists believe in the imminent return of the Messiah, at which time Jesus will "rapture," or gather up the faithful. As this bumper sticker implies, these believers see themselves among the chosen who will be whisked away at the Second Coming.*

evangelical conservatives. Do you need the feeling of being inside? With dispensationalism, you can read the newspapers with a knowledge and perception denied other believers who have no guide to apparently plotless or contradictory events. Do you want to turn modernity against itself? While everyone else adheres to class revolt or economic progress or other ideologies which can be tested and, inevitably, seen to fail, you can be motivated by an outlook which cannot be tested because the outcome depends upon the mysterious purpose of God.

Premillennial beliefs impel the elect of God into action on his behalf. "The Bible says if a watchman sees the enemy coming in, and doesn't warn people so that they get up and fight the enemy, then he's to blame and the blood of those people will be on his hands. If however, he gives a warning, and they stay in bed and get slain in their bed, then their blood is not on him because he's done his duty," Bob Jones, Jr., says. "I think any Christian who neglects the opportunity of winning men to Christ is going to be accountable to God for the fact that they are lost." Christ's commands to convert the world are taken literally, and believers are inspired by the need for haste, since time is running out.

One can see how this component of fundamentalist belief gives a certain advantage far beyond the strength of their numbers to fundamentalists in denominational battles. They are energized to focus on a single point while moderates flounder and liberals live with ambiguity. The end goal is in sight for fundamentalists, for they have read of it in the Bible and are assured of attaining it.

## *The Beginnings and the Philosophy of History: Creationism*

As with ends of history, so with beginnings. Most nonfundamentalists know that fundamentalists have opposed and still oppose the theory of evolution. Even at the end of the twentieth century there are legislative and court battles over "Creation research" in public schools. Why oppose evolution? Given a fundamentalist outlook, there were and are many reasons. For one thing, the teachings of those who led up to and those who followed British scientist Charles Darwin, and most of all Darwin's disciples, represented the leading edge of science, the world's knowledge apart from God. In 1896 the founding president of Cornell University, Andrew D. White, who liked religion but hated theology, wrote a book entitled *A History of the Warfare of Science with Theology in Christendom*, and fundamentalists thought it important to take up the battle for theology or faith from the Christian side. They opposed all science which they thought threatened the domain of God (as opposed to practical science, which might improve living); evolution was the most obvious teaching on that front.

In the case of evolution, we can again see that what we are calling a philosophy of history was at stake. Fundamentalists were, and still are, engaged in warfare over the meaning of life and the origin of humans. Throughout the early years of the twentieth century they saw evolution sweep the citadels of faith, the colleges which Protestants had founded, the literary and intellectual worlds which fundamentalists had once dominated. In the teaching of evolution they saw a threat to their own most cherished beliefs: that humans inhabited a world created suddenly, perhaps literally in one week, by God; that humans themselves were all descended from a single pair, Adam and Eve, who were subjects of divine creation and were made in the image of God.

The Darwinians taught that humans had evolved from other, "lower" species, that we had animal ancestry, and that whatever was special about us in matters of brain and speech, mind and soul, had simply developed as these progressive species adapted to the environment. But how would people be held responsible if they had not been made in God's image? How to explain a "Fall"

*Charles Darwin's theory of evolution is unacceptable to fundamentalists, who cannot reconcile the progressive development of species with the biblical account of creation.*

in the Garden of Eden, a fall into sin, if humans were emerging as a higher form of animal life? How could human beings think of themselves as noble if they were merely an animal species that survived as the fittest but were not unique? How would nations and armies be prevented from working out their bloody will against others as a certification that they were the fittest?

Worst of all—and here is where fundamentalism found its impetus—some Protestant insiders, as we have noted above, began adapting. Evolution is God's way of doing things, said Henry Ward Beecher, a liberal cleric on a rescue mission for his cause. If people have evolved from lower species, he argued, let them be seen as continuing to evolve, perfecting their environment, fulfilling history, moving beyond views of human nature which led them to feel fallen, condemned, limited. Charles Darwin's view of natural selection had not prevailed in the late nineteenth century; the preferred American version of evolution was one named after the theorist Lamarck, which stressed purposive and ordered progression. That being the case, evolution could be seen as a working out of the promises of God, a sign that God chose to work not transcendently, from outside the world, but immanently, through its natural processes. Even some conservatives were mild theistic (God-centered) evolutionists at the time when Lamarckism reigned. When the concept of Darwinian natural selection began to gain adherents, reactionaries could no longer tolerate any part of it. Liberals, of course, were committed, and were ready to surrender or utterly revise those elements of their faith which did not match the new style of evolutionary thinking, no matter what that did to their concept of God.

The moderate, we have seen, is the enemy of the fundamentalist. There is little chance to reinforce individual or group identity in a world of moderation. In the American Protestant case, fundamentalist identity was confirmed by taking the opening chapters of Genesis literally. This meant insisting on the miraculous, instantaneous creation of Adam and Eve in a young universe. It meant the story of a Garden of Eden, a fall, a plan of redemption set forth in the scripture.

The pioneers of fundamentalism, even before their movement had a name, had a certain advantage. The Genesis story was stamped on the minds of most of the nation's populace because it had been taught to them from childhood. It provided the imagery for believers' thinking about who they were. Most of them did not think deeply about "the fossil record," the evidence of development scientists claimed to see. Instead, believers were ennobled by the sense that they were specific creations in the image of God and that fallen though they were, they could be restored—indeed, they *had* been restored—when they believed in Jesus, who obviously was not a descendant from monkeys but the Virgin-born Son of God, as their rescuer and redeemer. Most believers had no trouble, then, with the literal truth of accounts in the Bible, and those who became fundamentalists had no problem appealing to them.

Meanwhile Protestants who were going to college and university, moving with the general scientific and literary currents, found this literalism increasingly embarrassing. They welcomed the experiments and the authoritative voices of celebrity preachers and professors who made things come out right between church and world, faith and reason, theology and science. Some of these preachers were Presbyterians and Baptists who taught at denominational colleges; more of them moved into the state universities, which were more congenial laboratories for progressive science and evolutionary theoretical thinking. A kind of class- or education-based schism developed, though not all anti-evolutionists were poor or ignorant. The reactionary parties that became fundamentalist even had some academic bastions (such as much of Princeton University well into the twentieth century), but in general they were losing the lay elites to the newer scientific worldviews.

While colleges and universities became one battleground, higher education was still the province of the few in the early decades of the twentieth century; there are plenty of stories of how a young Protestant lost his faith when a cynical evolutionary scientist beguiled him at the university, but for most people the battle was to be fought elsewhere. Since taxpayers were required to support public elementary and secondary schools, those schools became an even bigger combat zone. On one side ranged the biology teachers, textbook writers, and progressive educational administrators. On the other were the preachers, many of the parents, and not a few of the legislators who appealed to both.

The most familiar test case occurred in Tennessee in 1925, where the state legislature had passed an anti-evolution law. A teacher named John Scopes was encouraged to test the law, and was supported in the inevitable subsequent trial by the American Civil Liberties Union and other such agencies. The evolutionists secured the services of a secular-minded lawyer named Clarence Darrow; the anti-evolutionists had as their champion the politician William Jennings Bryan, who made this cause his reason for living in his final years. Bryan, a former perennial presidential candidate and a peace-minded secretary of state, was convinced it was on the principles of Darwinian survival-of-the-fittest ideology that the Germans thought they could try to dominate history by waging World War I. He also thought he saw destructive moral effects of the teaching in the America of the 1920s, so he lined up literal interpretations of the Bible against illicit, immoral, ungodly, and even illegal, evolutionary theory. As those familiar with American history well know, he won the trial, but fundamentalists got a bad name for obscurantism and folksy ignorance, and the image of hillbillies and backwoods inhabitants stuck.[6]

## *The Central Authority: An Inerrant Bible*

While believers were determining that the ends and beginnings of history are literally depicted in the Bible, a parallel and perhaps even more decisive issue was arising, one that had to do with the Bible itself. If Ezekiel, Daniel, and Revelation gave fundamentalists their texts about endings and Genesis about beginnings, how could they be assured that the Bible was right? Could it be relied on? After all, modernity taught suspicion and modernists were constantly exposing ancient documents as flawed or fraudulent. What about the Bible itself?

Enter here another set of imported thoughts. If premillennialism came as a positive weapon from England and evolution as a negative assault from there, it was Germany that provided the threat to the Bible and Scotland that produced the response. Of course, most fundamentalists do not think in these geographical or historical terms; they simply accept a truth as being the truth, preached by their preachers, accessible to all right-minded lay readers of the Bible. But it is important and helpful to understand the international transmission of ideas that influenced American Protestant fundamentalism.

Germany had a rightful reputation in the nineteenth century for being host to radical ideas on Christian soil. Its universities were homes to generations of intellectuals who, brought up in Christian faith, began to adapt that faith to the modern philosophies associated with names like Hegel and Kant. Often they did this to rescue an intellectually credible faith from the jaws of atheism; sometimes they came to be atheists themselves. Most German philosophical theology was utterly unwelcome across the spectrum of American Protestantisms, but one instrument usable both for rescue and destruction was in place by the end of the century at Harvard, Yale, Chicago, and Union Theological Seminary, among other institutions. These prestigious theology schools and literary departments of the United States began to employ the "higher criticism of the Bible."[7]

The very phrase put its practitioners at a disadvantage in the appeal to the hearts and minds of the laity. Criticism to most people meant not analysis of texts but carping, undercutting, negative and destructive activity. The Bible critic, however, saw himself (and in those days all the critics were male) as an honest searcher for truth. Who could believe in all those biblical miracles? What about the immoralities depicted in the Bible, and the image of a warrior God who committed genocide? How to have faith when biblical stories did not match, when teachings contradicted each other, when errors abounded?

"Lower" critics of the Bible simply tried to find the best texts among the ancient manuscripts. There were no autographs, nothing to authenticate a text as from the hand of an apostle or a prophet, but there were countless parchments from the early Christian centuries, and it was important to produce the best text. Few of the faithful fretted about the biblical texts; they were sure that a provident God gave them in the manuscripts that survived the truth they needed to be saved.

"Higher" criticism was another matter. The higher critic of the Bible was not, for example, satisfied with the traditional naming of authors. Who was Mark? Did Mark write the Gospel of Mark? Who was John? Jesus' beloved disciple or a second-century author who claimed his name? Who wrote Revelation? If it was not the same John who wrote the Fourth Gospel, what did this do to traditional concepts of authorship? The higher biblical critics said that the latter portion of the Book of Isaiah came from a hand other than that of the early chapters, yet Jesus quoted the later chapters and called them Isaiah. What did this mean for the belief that Jesus, being the Son of God, was all-knowing? Why did he not serve as a higher critic himself and correct the misunderstanding of people in his day who thought that if something was in Isaiah it was by Isaiah?

Critics went on to examine the background of the books of the Bible, to surmise how they came to be written. They studied the beliefs of ancient communities, the texts that came down from Babylon. They saw startling parallels between a Babylonian genesis story and the biblical one; what did this mean for the uniqueness of God's revelation? Behind the first three Gospels they discerned a common source they called "Q," and then saw special and sometimes contradictory sources. One Gospel placed Jesus' cleansing of the temple at one point in his ministry and another at a different time. The conservatives thought this meant two temple cleansings; the liberal commentators and higher critics were ready to say that it meant one shadowy remembered incident told two different ways by two schools of gospel writers whose accounts did not match.

All these notions were profoundly upsetting to ordinary believers after the turn of the century, who were already suffering through many adjustments to modernity and its attacks on their traditions and ways of life. The people in the pew could not identify with the intellectual struggles for consistency and respectability. Desperately eager for authority in an unstable world, they listened when ministers waved a whole Bible before them and said simply, Thus saith the Lord! Implied or even added explicitly was the message: And don't let the modern biblical critics raise questions! When the congregations in these nascent fundamentalist churches responded favorably to claims of surety and attacks on critics, the attacking ministers banded with others to defend the positions they shared. They did so with a tenacity and fervor which gave them an advantage over Christians who were open to many modern influences.

If the critics relied on a philosophy, so too did the conservatives. The Bible itself was too ambiguous about its own authority. For example, while Jesus and his contemporaries had the "canon," an authorized set of Hebrew scriptures or Old Testament writings, they did not have the New Testament at all. Nor did the New Testament canon get set until two centuries later, and when it was set, it came not from direct revelation by God but from tradition, from actions by church councils, by practice. It was important, however, for Protestants to assert, against the Bible critics, that the writings of the New Testament all came from the apostles whose names they bore. But on the face of things, it was not a convincing claim, nor did the Bible clearly call itself inerrant. It spoke of the Word of God as having authority and that it would not mislead. It said that Scripture could not be "broken," or gone against, but there were no verbs in the original Greek which meant what modern fundamentalists claimed and needed: an unassailable declaration that these scriptures were without error.

Scotland came to the rescue, or at least a school of thought associated with Scotland, although few fundamentalists-to-be of the 1890s and few fundamentalists of the 1920s knew the source of the doctrine they used for support, or cared. (It was left to their elites to grasp and apply such a philosophy, their preachers to mediate the results, and the people to put to work the teachings based on it.) Mention to today's fundamentalists that their view of the Bible is based on Aristotelian-Ramist-Baconian-Scottish-Common-Sense-Realist philosophy and they are likely to have no idea what you mean.

Scottish Common-Sense Realism—what did it mean? During the Enlightenment, when major thinkers professed skepticism, including mistrust of the senses, a number of Scottish intellectuals, many of them moderate clerics, counterattacked. A pioneer was Thomas Reid (d. 1796), who taught at Aberdeen. In his work he fought the whole range of modern philosophies: those of Hume, Descartes, and others. Reid believed these philosophies taught that the mind was a kind of mediator between actual things as they are, and ideas, which had a separate reality. In Reid's view, reality could be known by instant and immediate "judgments of nature." This is the case, Reid said, because God made human minds to grasp reality directly. The result was "the common sense of mankind," which could not be called into question or become the object of suspicion. He held this truth to be self-evident, a phrase that serves as a reminder that many of our nation's founders held to elements of Reid's philosophy that a century later were regarded as obsolete.

Reid's successors, including Dugald Stewart of Edinburgh (d. 1828) brought this line of thinking into the nineteenth century. He stressed what Francis Bacon had taught: the value of inductive reasoning based on observation. This school of thought came across with teachers from Scotland and England who found employment in schools and as tutors in homes of Americans; it was part of the foundation of the American Enlightenment and was widely accepted.[8]

When the Bible was challenged, ultra conservatives at Princeton and elsewhere applied this "Common Sense" philosophy to the scriptures in defense. What did this mean for the Bible? The Common-Sense realist said that one could have a direct experience of God through the only clear instrument God chose, the Bible. If one thinks of God as provident and loving, this God must be seen as informing his creatures of his will. He does this through his word. God being God and thus being perfect, infallible, without the capability of erring or imparting error, his will as expressed in the words of the Bible must be perfect, infallible, and inerrant. The human dimension might remain in the Bible's grammar and rhetoric, but in no matters of historical, geographical, scientific, or natural fact could there be anything more than an appearance of error. The appearance might exist because the original manuscripts were lost, but common sense assured that God would not let anything so accidental as ancient library fires lead to confusion about his word or will. More likely apparent contradictions would be resolved by more study.

The inductive method thus turned the Bible into a book of facts. Theology meant studying, ordering, lining up, and expounding those facts. This fact-centered approach had an appeal in practical, empirical, science-minded America and made it possible for certain kinds of scientists then and now to be fundamentalist. In a sense they need have but one miracle: the belief that God chose to impart the divine will through a book. From there on, everything made sense and provided authority.

There is little wonder as to why in dictionary definitions American fundamentalism was and is connected more with a belief in biblical inerrancy than with premillennialism and anti-evolution theory, the other two important basics. While there might be arguments among fundamentalists over millennial teachings and while the record of opposition to evolution keeps changing, one needed to say only one word to rally conservatives in what has been called "the battle for the Bible"—*inerrancy*. It became more a weapon than a doctrine—a shibboleth and rallying cry, a summons to arms.

Bob Jones, Jr., identifies fundamentalism with the notion that the Bible as written and transmitted is the one authentic source of truth for all Christians and should be the authoritative guide for all human behavior:

> You see, there are four marks of a fundamentalist. In the first place, a fundamentalist needs to *believe* the word of God; that the Bible doesn't contain the word of God, but *is* the word of God. I don't set my mind to choose what it is and what it isn't. The Bible is the word of God. A fundamentalist has a calling to *proclaim* the word of God. That is, to reach man with the word of God, with the gospel of the word of God. Whether he's a preacher or whether he's a layman, he's supposed to be a soul winner. And then a man has to be willing to *defend* the word of God whether it's pleasant or whether it isn't pleasant, whether it costs him something or whether it doesn't cost him anything. But it will always cost him. And then finally, a man, to be a fundamentalist, has to *obey* the word of God. Those are the four-fold requirements of the

fundamentalist. To believe the word, to defend the word, to proclaim
the word, and above all, to obey the word. That's where people fall down
these days. They say, "I believe the Bible is God's word," but they don't
bring themselves under the authority of the Bible.

## *The Choice of Doctrines: Literal and Scandalous*

One more element was added to the original fundamentalist package: the concept
of the literal interpretation of the scriptures. William Jennings Bryan was to say,
after hearing all the right doctrines in the creeds of moderate churches but finding
the reciters of creeds referring to their attachments as "symbolic" or "spiritual"
or "sacramental," that such attachments meant the sucking of truth out of every
doctrine, that only literalism could save it.

Literalism helped American Protestant fundamentalists complete their
program. Recall that we mentioned the need for fundamentalisms to scandalize,
in the root meaning of that word. That is, they must embrace teachings that
outsiders will trip over or fall into as traps should they want to transgress the
sacred boundaries of the faithful, and that insiders will use to reinforce each other.
Fundamentalists revisited certain of the biblical stories and stressed the offensive,
embarrassing, and scandalous (to modern minds) elements.

For example, one of the four Gospels says that Jesus was conceived through
the activity of the Holy Spirit without the agency of a human father and that Mary
as a virgin gave birth to him. Moderates and liberals may "spiritualize" the story,
or not make much of it while professing that Jesus was unique among humans
and that a veil of mystery is drawn across his birth. Fundamentalists relished the
proclamation that, indeed, they believed in a literal virgin birth. Something in the
physicality of semen and fetus and an unbroken hymen as being part of their faith
in divine intervention, much as it might repel the moderate or the outsider, was
attractive as literal truth for those inside the circle.

Something of the same physicality appears, secondly, in the literal teaching
of the "blood atonement" of Jesus. All Christians believed that something

mysterious took place in the transaction called the Crucifixion, the death of Christ as a sacrifice. But the fundamentalists made much of the biblical notion that Jesus was sacrificed by God the Father to satisfy desire for vengeance against a human race whose sins Jesus bore. There is no question but that there are biblical texts favoring such an interpretation, but fundamentalists made it central. Do you believe in the substitutionary blood atonement of Jesus? became a test of membership in the elect.

A third scandalizing physicality alongside semen and blood was corpuscles, an image which the fundamentalists stressed with the phrase "the physical resurrection of Jesus." Before belief in a literal second coming, there had to be faith in the fact, attested to in an inerrant scripture, that Jesus was physically resurrected. Where there had been a dead body on the verge of decay, the corpuscles (the very cells of that body) were revitalized and the body was quickened. Most Christians believed in some sort of event called the Resurrection, and that more was involved than a change in the psychological state of the disciples who professed to have seen Jesus after his death, but they "spiritualized" it and thus, in Bryan's terms, "sucked the truth" out of what the literalist believed. Talk about Jesus being the first fruit of a "New Creation," as Paul the apostle wrote, was less worthwhile or fulfilling than the question, Do you believe in the physical resurrection of Jesus? answered affirmatively.

Belief in inerrancy, a virgin birth, a substitutionary blood atonement, physical resurrection, and a literal second coming may have embarrassed moderates and liberals who were trying to get at the "essence" of Christianity while yielding on some of the "facts," but fundamentalists did not care what moderns thought. Indeed, they believed their own "literal" truths better matched the inductive modes of science, and that they could convert more successfully across radical boundaries than could moderates, who lacked their motivation and rhetoric for converting.

## *How Fundamentalists Organized*

Fundamentalist parties organized interdenominationally at the Niagara Bible Conferences, at Princeton Seminary, and within Presbyterian, Baptist, and other mainstream churches, which saw themselves as the custodians of American values. In the second decade of the twentieth century wealthy laymen paid for the publication and distribution of a series of pamphlets called *The Fundamentals,* a name which obviously helped implant the idea of fundamentalism during the 1920s and beyond. After World War I, everything seemed up for grabs in the Protestant world. It was a time of social and cultural unsettlement. Landmarks were eroded and folkways upset; skepticism and cynicism reached many; worldliness was attractive in the climate of the times. And liberals endured as a powerful force that held control of most seminaries, some mission boards, and other agents of "denominational machinery."[9]

While the Scopes trial of 1925 brought the fundamentalist beliefs about evolution and literalism to the attention of the nation and showed that fundamentalism could be a political force involving state legislatures and courts, for a time the main battles had been within the church. Year after year three-way battles formed. One wing was frankly liberal and sometimes even radically modernist. The reactive party, prompted to fight back, was frankly evangelical and sometimes even radically fundamentalist. In the middle were the moderates, whose hearts were with the evangelicals, whose heads were with the liberals, and whose instincts were to keep the peace, not rock the boat, not give in to extremes.

The fundamentalists were firm in their purposes, and they recognized that the moderates and conservatives were not allies. In 1920 Curtis Lee Laws, editor of the Baptist *Watchman-Examiner,* surveyed the field and rejected the term *premillennialism*. New realities demanded new names. "We suggest that those who still cling to the great fundamentals and who mean to do battle royal for the fundamentals shall be called 'Fundamentalist.' By that name the editor of the *Watchman-Examiner* is willing to be called." Willing? Eager. So were others, who joined the forces. Secular America looked on as newspapers carried stories of these battles royal. Pundit Walter Lippmann, himself in search of a new "religion of the spirit" to face "the acids of modernity," surprised his liberal and modernist kin by seeing more integrity in the fundamentalists.

In such a mix, fundamentalists found that the very techniques they used to get themselves together (like the World's Christian Fundamentals Association, organized in 1919, or the Bible Baptist Union of roughly similar vintage) worked against their ability to control denominations. They did not know how to manipulate the machinery of public opinion. They wanted to scandalize, but it was moderates they offended and drove off, leaving the moderates (and thus also the liberals and modernists) in power.

The fundamentalists gradually found themselves so ostracized or frustrated that many of them left to form new denominations. Some of them, once they began to be precise about what was fundamental, became so precise that they fell into the pattern that afflicts many movements: schism. While liberals were always ready to accommodate one more voice, fundamentalists always had to purge the even slightly deviant one, lest authority be lost and identity eroded.

The American fundamentalisms of the 1920s were composed of white citizens. African-Americans often professed a conservative kind of theology and outlook, but were not attracted to hardline fundamentalism, with its European philosophical background. Also, these movements were largely Northern. They were born along the Niagara, in downtown Baptist churches in Toronto, Boston, Minneapolis, New York; in the Moody Bible Institute in Chicago and in-numerable conferences and publishing ventures. In any cast of "top ten" fun-damentalists of the earlier period, only one was vividly Southern: J. Frank Norris of Fort Worth, master rhetorician and organizer.

Why, then, one might ask, was fundamentalism typed as a redneck, hillbilly, backcountry movement? In the 1920s, the American South, as in the Southern Baptist Convention, was deeply conservative. Southerners were traditionalists; they often resisted Northern and European intellectual innovations. Original fundamentalism was not needed on such soil, as geographically protected Southern rural people met only their own kind, for the most part, and escaped many of the threats of modernity in the early part of this century.

Formal fundamentalisms developed decades later, as "Dixie" became "the Sunbelt." Northerners brought their versions of battles to the South, and mass media helped spread the fundamentalist message. The "fundamentalist takeover" of the Southern Baptist Convention, always an innately conservative body, did not occur until the 1970s and 1980s.

## *The Silent Period*

After 1925, the focal year for fundamentalist defeats in the denominations, their leaders kept their organizations going, not exactly as an underground movement, but as an unnoticed one. While mainstream Protestantism suffered some sort of malaise during the Depression, coasting in the culture of decline, fundamentalists reacted. Liberal Protestants gained access to free radio time when radio became a new instrument for entertaining, informing, and appealing. But fundamentalists began to *buy* time, and by the early 1930s their Old-Fashioned Revival programs and *The Lutheran Hour,* a semi-fundamentalist program, swept the ratings. While liberals kept drawing the notice of *Newsweek* and *Time,* the new weekly news magazines, fundamentalists started publishing houses, tract societies, and journals of their own, and began to outsell the liberals who shared their congregations and audiences with other moderns. While liberals kept letting modernity erode their bastions in the universities and liberal arts colleges, fundamentalists established Bible colleges which disdained the liberal arts and imparted biblical knowledge and missionary skills.[10]

During World War II, militant fundamentalists, under Presbyterian schismatic Carl McIntire, formed the American Council of Christian Churches to oppose the ecumenical (Protestant) World Council of Churches. At about the same time slightly more moderate types organized the National Association of Evangelicals. To moderates and liberals this last, conservative organization looked like fundamentalism in new guise, and some elements in it were. Neo-evangelical members wavered on inerrancy, and there was some variation of opinion (but not much) on premillennialism, but they had no trouble with virgin birth, substitutionary atonement, or physical resurrection and literal second coming.

To a person, however, they had trouble with the face fundamentalism wore. They were convinced that fundamentalists were misplacing the scandal of Christianity. Nonconverts and others who might be attracted to conservative evangelical witness were being alienated by the brusque manners, the militancy, the shocking intentions of the McIntire types. The neo-evangelicals coalesced with tidied-up, intentionally better mannered second-generation fundamentalists who found their own more moderate ways to have greater potential for converting the world, exemplifying the love of Christ, and loving God with their minds. They found a national figure in Billy Graham, a set of intellectual homes in historic Wheaton College, the new Fuller Seminary, and the like. They started respectable journals like *Christianity Today* and began to overtake and replace mainstream Protestantism in publishing.

The evangelicals also drew the wrath of fundamentalists. In the angry literature of fundamentalist stalwarts, evangelicalism drew more fire than did modernists. After all, modernists were so far beyond the pale of true Christianity that they could not deceive others. Liberals were sellouts to secularism, as any fool could see. But evangelicals professed the right doctrines in the wrong way. They knew they ought to separate, but refused to do so. Billy Graham knew all about the Antichrist being the pope, yet he welcomed the Catholic, Episcopal, and United Methodist bishops to his stage during campaigns—and turned converts over to the "church of their choice," even if it was not fundamentalist-evangelical. Evangelicalism was now the voice of the deceiver. Keeping fundamentalism and evangelicalism apart may be a difficult task from a distance, but it is not hard to see the difference in the rhetoric of the pure and separatist fundamentalist.

American fundamentalists also distanced themselves from another party that came to prominence in mainstream America after mid-century: pentecostalism, known in some circles as charismatic movements. Born out of Wesleyan holiness impulses at the turn of the century, the pentecostal movement was conservative and traditional in many ways. But, as we noted earlier, it included belief in the direct involvement of the Holy Spirit, an involvement which issued in "speaking in tongues," miraculous healings, interpretations of prophecy, and the like. Pentecostalists came in many varieties, and most could subscribe to the fundamentalists' fundamentals, yet fundamentalists were suspicious of them. Fundamentalists like to have everything set in order, reliably placed, and fixed. Pentecostalists keep things eruptive, interactive, and capable of being revised by a new visitation of the Holy Spirit.

The movements went their separate ways, though they could join in matters having to do with personal and familial values, or single issues in politics. The pentecostalists might be condemned for speaking in tongues; major Baptist leaders like Jerry Falwell silenced pentecostalists who came to their colleges and kept them from leadership posts; pentecostalists often regarded fundamentalists as too rigid, not exuberant witnesses. But the two groups, along with the evangelicals, often found validity in a common political front which became particularly strong in the 1960s and 1970s, as we shall see.

# The Second Wave: Fundamentalists in Political Coalitions, 1979–1992

During the moderate Republican and liberal Democratic presidencies of Dwight Eisenhower and John F. Kennedy, and early in the tenure of Lyndon Baines Johnson, liberal Protestants, Catholics, and Jews often united to back the United Nations, assented to the Supreme Court decision *Brown v. Board of Education,* and rallied around the civil rights cause. They might be "Cold Warriors," fighting off the threat of the Soviet Union, but they were also anti-McCarthyite, refusing to see a need for purges of everything to the left of them. This informal coalition of moderates and liberals from the churches and synagogues joined the War on Poverty, backed the Peace Corps and the Job Corps and VISTA, and supported interfaith agencies. Suspicious of militant secularism, they often found allies in friendly nonbelievers who shared their social concerns. The Reverend John

Courtney Murray, a Jesuit priest, spoke of these religious activists as "conspirators"—literally, "breathers together."

In the spring of 1965 an observer might have prophesied that this coalition would continue to dominate the religious-political scene. Then came sudden change. The United States Supreme Court, in 1962 and 1963 decisions, outlawed school prayer, and thus seemed to some to be carrying on a godless assault on an institution which fundamentalist religious forces had once regarded as the domain in which they were strongest, the public school. By 1965 the reactive forces began to gather to bring about a constitutional amendment to "put God back into the schools."

In 1965 President Johnson committed troops to Vietnam, and the nation fell into discontent, dissent, and disarray. That summer the Watts area of Los Angeles was torched by angry blacks who were, in effect, setting their own houses on fire. Newark burned. Detroit burned. The civil rights theme of integration was gradually replaced by calls for separatist "black power." The Catholic church did not make easy and elegant adjustments to post–Vatican II life after 1965, and was torn over ethnic and ideological themes. Mainstream Protestantism underwent a steep decline after having coasted into prosperity in the 1950s. The assassinations of President Kennedy and his brother Robert and of Martin Luther King, Jr., suggested radical instability in the world.

More was to come. Feminists organized, often in opposition to traditional biblical understandings of gender roles. Hippies and radical youth protested the war and their parents' culture. In 1973 the Supreme Court ruled in *Roe v. Wade* that abortions in some stages were legal, thus providing reactionaries with the best claim yet that godlessness and the devil were ruling in high places, legitimating murder. A conservative president failed conservatives, thanks to Watergate. Some felt they must become more radical in their fundamentalism.

In 1980 Jerry Falwell looked back on the two previous decades of American history and summarized the diagnosis of many fundamentalists in a manifesto for political activism entitled *Listen, America!*:

We must reverse the trend America finds herself in today. Young people
between the ages of twenty-five and forty have been born and reared in
a different world than Americans of years past. The television set has
been their primary baby-sitter. From the television set they have learned
situation ethics and immorality—they have learned a loss of respect for
human life. They have learned to disrespect the family as God has
established it. They have been educated in a public-school system that
is permeated with secular humanism. They have been taught that the
Bible is just another book of literature. They have been taught that there
are no absolutes in our world today. They have been introduced to the
drug culture. They have been reared by the family and by the public
school in a society that is greatly void of discipline and character-
building. These same young people have been reared under the influence
of a government that has taught them socialism and welfarism. They
have been taught to believe that the world owes them a living whether
they work or not.[11]

Our Founding Fathers separated church and state in function, but never
intended to establish a government void of God. As is evidenced by our
Constitution, good people in America must exert an influence and
provide a conscience and climate of morality in which it is difficult to
go wrong, not difficult for people to go right in America.[12]

The second wave of highly visible fundamentalist politicking and cultural
presence thus came in the late 1970s and early 1980s. With the election of Ronald
Reagan to the presidency in 1980 it was suddenly clear that a "New Christian
Right" had emerged. While they could not agree on theology and the ethos of
church life, fundamentalists joined conservative evangelicals and politically
minded pentecostalists, arguing that American culture had become so corrupt
that they had no choice but to react and try to take history into their hands.

Once a Bible-believing, soul-winning separatist who shunned non-evan-
gelicals and who had harsh words for Catholics and blacks, by the late 1970s Jerry
Falwell saw the necessity of forming coalitions with both groups and with others
who shared a sense of moral outrage at the dismantling of traditional values. He

and his associates felt that if they did not stand up against an aggressive government in this generation, there *might not be* another generation of believers.

Since the 1920s fundamentalists had been building a system of private schools, Bible colleges, and publishing houses to complement and extend the work of their churches across the country. By the 1970s upwardly mobile, urbanized Southerners, many of them newly entered into the middle class, were enriching the coffers of these churches and supporting institutions, which were thus natural resources for fundamentalist political organizers. "Nowhere was this surfeit of organizational power more apparent than in the television ministries," Nancy Ammerman writes of the 1970s. "Television is an enormously powerful medium for raising money, and evangelists were constantly being pushed along by the sheer power of the resources available. They not only raised money to stay on the air and preach the gospel; they also raised money for whatever enterprises their imagination and charisma could create and sustain."[13] When the money rolled in, prime-time preachers built quasi-denominational complexes of institutions like Pat Robertson's Regent (formerly CBN) University, and Falwell's Liberty University.

Jimmy Carter, "the evangelical president," was a strict adherent of the traditional Baptist belief in the separation of church and state and disappointed many fundamentalists by taking foreign and domestic policy positions that were at odds with their own. Nonetheless, 1976 was dubbed by the media as "the Year of the Evangelical," and the national spotlight turned to fundamentalists and to a discussion of the nation's moral roots. Boosted by this growing interest in their preliminary foray into the national debate over welfare, defense, women's rights, and a host of other social issues, fundamentalists organized politically in 1979. Pastors of huge "superchurches" forged alliances with conservative political organizers Richard Viguerie and Ed McAteer in forming the Moral Majority, billed as a nonpartisan political organization. Also established at the time were conservative religious political groups like the Religious Roundtable, the American Coalition for Traditional Values, and Christian Voice.

These organizations pursued a full range of political activities. They circulated newsletters, conducted seminars, registered voters, lobbied Congress, and supported conservatives running for office. "No public office or bureaucratic position was too low; as political organizers, they realized that their crusade must begin from the ground up," Ammerman explains. "And like the network of independent churches on which they built, Moral Majority activities were often out of public sight, varying in form and emphasis from one location to another."[14]

The numerical strength of the movement was inflated somewhat by the media and by the fundamentalist publicists, and Falwell took generous credit for early conservative political victories:

> In America today, pro-moral people have been the sleeping giant. We have been lulled to sleep after eating and drinking our fill of the good life, which our forefathers bequeathed to us by founding our nation on sound, Judeo-Christian principles. Liberal forces such as the abortionists, the homosexuals, the pornographers, secular humanists, and Marxists have made significant inroads in the giant's house and have carried off much of our goods. Now that sleeping giant has awakened and we have come to our senses, but unless we are more agile than our liberal opponents who have had a head start "down the beanstalk," we risk suffering the same fate as the giant of the fairy tale.

> I believe we not only can, but we must win this race! We have already won some significant battles along the way. These include the virtual burial of the Equal Rights Amendment after its quick ratification by all three of the required 38 states; the passage of the Hyde Amendment which cut off tax money for welfare abortions and the upholding of the amendment's constitutionality by the Supreme Court; the crushing defeat of the television networks' attempt to denigrate the airwaves with gratuitous sex and violence, through the efforts of the Coalition for Better Television; the support of creationism bills in half of the 50 state legislatures requiring that the scientific evidence for creation be taught alongside the scientific evidence for evolution in public schools and, of course, the mighty effect in the 1980 elections caused by the mobilization of millions of heretofore uninvolved pro-moralists, born-again Christians, and religious people in general.[15]

The strategy of the fundamentalist activists was to establish institutions and agencies that would neutralize the efforts of organized liberals. For example, the Moral Majority formed a Legal Defense Foundation, which was designed as the conservative counterpart to the American Civil Liberties Union, which, Falwell said, "has done so much damage to this country in the last decade." It also attempted to establish fifty state chapters at the precinct level "for the purpose of effecting legislative and moral change from the grassroots up."[16]

But several things happened to take some of the limelight away from the fundamentalists. For one thing, counterforces appeared. Liberals regrouped in agencies like People for the American Way to block the fundamentalists on paths where these reactive innovators were showing their skills. Second, fundamentalists began to learn that they were better at cultural than political revolt. They had access to Ronald Reagan and the White House, but none of them (and few evangelicals or pentecostals) were appointed to high positions. They did not get the desired support from him for the constitutional amendments they cherished. His own image as a family man was so ambiguous and contradictory that he did not remain the exemplar they thought he might be in 1980.

By 1984 it became clear that Republican politicians could not afford public identification with militant fundamentalists—it cost them more votes than it gained. The fundamentalists suffered stigma when their pentecostal cousins in televangelism—Jim Bakker, Jimmy Swaggart, and others—were exposed in sexual and financial scandals. They found themselves tainted by their alliances and coalitions. Being too close to Catholics on abortion made it difficult for them to contradict Catholic bishops on issues of peace and the economy. Being too close to Jews on Israel made it more complex to criticize secular (often read, Jewish) influence in the media. Putting energy into support for organizations like the Moral Majority distracted from efforts to keep the camp together.

On a number of fronts, however, the fundamentalists grew in strength in the 1970s and 1980s and remain very strong today.

# The Christian School Movement

Between 1965 and 1983, enrollment in private Christian (evangelical and fundamentalist) schools increased sixfold. By the end of this period the Christian school movement was educating 20 percent of the private school population in the United States, second only to the Roman Catholic parochial system. In addition, perhaps as many as a hundred thousand fundamentalist children were being taught at home. Robert Smith, executive director of the Council for American Private Education (CAPE), a consortium of religiously affiliated and independent school associations representing 90 percent of the private school population, estimated Christian school enrollment to be about 700,000 students in the late 1980s. Estimates indicate that between 15,000 and 18,000 Christian schools exist, with an average enrollment of between 100 and 150 students but ranging from 5 to 2,500 students.[17]

In the building of the Christian school movement, fundamentalists found political and legal intervention necessary, and so they established organizations to protect the rights and help sustain the growth of the schools. By 1982, the American Association of Christian Schools had existed for a decade and numbered 1,080 schools with 175,000 students. The Association of Christian Schools was larger, serving 1,728 schools and colleges with 320,950 students. These associations monitored legislation at the state and federal levels, provided legal assistance to new academies, offered school and teacher accreditation and professional training, and sponsored national competitions in athletics, academic debates, music, and Bible studies.[18]

The protection of parents' rights to educate their children without undue state intervention had been a cause célèbre since a Supreme Court decision of 1925 (*Pierce v. Society of Sisters*) established the legality of the religious educational alternative. Subsequently, religious groups flooded the courts with legal petitions at any sign of infringement of this right, resulting in an noninterventionist tradition that in many states led to remarkably liberal policies allowing the existence of an educational subculture of religious academies that do not submit to standards for state accreditation but instead follow only minimal state health and safety requirements. Fundamentalists whose children are not able to attend such academies have successfully challenged the public school system, as in the 1987 Tennessee court decision in favor of Christian parents' rights to censor educational materials used in public schools (*Mozert v. Hawkins County Bd. of Education*) and in the 1987 Alabama case that considered the question of secular humanism as a religion informing the public school educational philosophy (*Smith v. Bd. of School Commissioners of Mobile County*).

Meanwhile, fundamentalist educators in towns and cities across the country sought to create a "total world" encompassing every aspect of students' lives. Pedagogy and curriculum were rooted in a worldview in which history is *His* story: fundamentalist math, an entrée to the ordered and dependable processes of Creation; fundamentalist science, a lens by which to view a universe sustained at every moment by divine providence. The schools offer parents the opportunity to present their children with knowledge that is in harmony with their beliefs. A number of publishers provide complete curricula for the schools. Among the most widely used are the materials of the Accelerated Christian Education (ACE) series, which stresses memorization and factual information and has proved successful in preparing students for standardized tests. A mother in a Northeastern city explained why she wanted her daughter in the church's academy: "I think she is going to have less options thrown at her in a Christian school than if she was in a public school, where there might be a few more things that she might have to choose about. I would rather control her environment as much as possible while she is young, until she is old enough to be let go."[19] Many parents seem to share this attitude, and private schools that control the students' environment while correlating academic material to Christian scriptures have become an important part of the fundamentalist way of life.

## Creation Science and the Battle Against Evolution

The decades-long fundamentalist battle against evolution was revived in the 1960s. Today it is an international movement based in the United States but

*A biology lab at Bob Jones University, where science professors must adhere to a university policy which states that "anything that fails to fit the biblical framework must be rejected as erroneous." At BJU, "creation is taught as a matter of biblical revelation and evolution is taught as a matter of man's speculation about origins. Neither is scientific because of the impossibility of human perception of these events," explains Dr. Joseph Henson, chair of the natural sciences department. The university claims a success rate of more than 90 percent in placing its premed students in medical schools.*

growing today in the countries of the developing world. Activists focus their attention on local school boards in the 1990s; federal judges in the 1980s were generally unconvinced by the argument that creationism is a form of science to be taught alongside evolution in the schools.

The new wave of creationism began in 1963, when Henry M. Morris, a hydraulic engineer at Virginia Polytechnic Institute and author of *The Genesis Flood,* organized the Creation Research Society and recruited Christians with postgraduate degrees in the natural sciences, medicine, and engineering. Society members make a statement of faith avowing the historic accuracy of the Genesis account of Creation, the fixity of created kinds of species, and the universality of the Flood. The *Creation Research Society Quarterly* is the major publication of the society, which also formed a textbook committee that in 1971 published a volume for use in high schools, *Biology: A Search for Order in Complexity.* In 1972 Morris established the Institute for Creation Research (ICR) on the campus of Christian Heritage College in San Diego. Funded by private donations and fundamentalist churches, by 1984 ICR's thirty staff scientists were sending information and newsletters to seventy-five thousand supporters and had published dozens of creationist books and monographs, with sales of over one million copies. ICR spawned summer institutes, a graduate school, a library, a museum, a press, hundreds of public lectures, and expeditions in search of fossil anomalies and Noah's Ark.[20] The goal of the ICR scientists is to fortify scientific creationism as the source of the natural knowledge required to validate biblical creationism. In the early 1980s, laws favoring the teaching of biblical creationism were passed in Arkansas and Louisiana, and the issue of its scientific character was eventually addressed in court.[21]

The creationists were undaunted when they lost the court battles. Historian James Moore writes:

> Despite the failure, to date, to achieve legislative sanction, fundamentalist creationism in North America retains all the vitality of a well-heeled popular movement using advanced technologies—film, television, video, computerized direct-mail promotions—to commend its cosmos as genuine science to a culture still largely impressed with claims to scientificity. From lacking scientific credentials or having amateur status at best, they have acquired the insignia of professionalism and, with these, the poise and self-esteem to pursue their politico-religious aims regardless of temporary setbacks. Already, for example, in the wake of the Louisiana ruling, fundamentalist experts have been hard at work in the history and philosophy of science, seeking to strip creationism of its religious connotations by classifying it among theories of "abrupt appearance" or by distinguishing it as "origin science" as opposed to "operation science."[22]

## *The Role of Women in Fundamentalism*

Fundamentalism was strengthened as a social movement in another way in the 1970s and 1980s. Women took a new leadership role, especially in the battle against feminism. "If one of the achievements of the feminist movement is this escalation of female participation [in political action], paradoxically this very success has also meant the increased involvement by women opposed to the goals and values at the core of feminism," writes Rebecca Klatch.[23] These women of the New Right contended that there was more than one definition of liberation and charged that the feminist movement threatened to undermine the real power that women exercise in a patriarchal society.

Fundamentalists, men and women alike, believe that society is patriarchal by the will of God. "God's word says that the man is to be the head of the home, and frankly as a woman I delight in that," says Beneth Jones, the wife of Bob Jones III. "I would hate to have to make the decisions for the home that he has to make. And I'm very thankful that I can lean on my husband and submit to him." Women like Beneth Jones, who keep the patriarchal system intact, believe that it is the best—the only—way to ensure that the traditional family remains strong. Behind their reassertion of patriarchy is a social critique that holds feminism largely accountable for the breakdown in family structures.

Klatch points out that the women of the New Right were divided into two groups: the "social conservatives," represented by figures like Phyllis Schlafly, whose motivations were religious and who led the antifeminist charge; and the "laissez-faire conservatives," women whose protest was based in economic conservatism rather than in religious belief. The social conservatives spoke of moral decay and focused on social issues such as the proposed Equal Rights Amendment, busing, abortion, homosexuality, and schooling, while the laissez-faire conservatives focused on economic issues and promoted tax reduction, the free market, and welfare cutbacks. Both groups were opposed to Communism and "Big Government," the social conservatives fearing atheism and secular humanism, respectively, the laissez-faire conservatives fearing the threat of these forces against capitalism and individual freedoms.

The rhetoric of fundamentalist women matched that of fundamentalist men on most issues, but it was the women who spoke with the greatest authority on the threat that seemed most dire to all fundamentalists: the assault on the traditional family. "Until the close of perhaps 1950 America was accepted as being a Christian nation," Virginia Bessey argued at a 1982 Family Forum conference. "We had a definite standard against which we could measure our whole existence, our actions, our laws, and our lives, a set of Judeo-Christian principles that had not changed to fit the times or convenience's sake." For fundamentalists this was a golden age.

> This country was then very much family-oriented. Though divorce, living together outside of marriage, abortion, homosexuality were not uncommon then, they were at least seldom defended in theory. There were moral absolutes that were recognized; and agencies of public expression, including the media and school system, honored these values. Then, unfortunately, over the last twenty years this Judeo-Christian moral consensus has been threatened, challenged, and often times shattered.[24]

Feminists have been the agents of change for the worse, such fundamentalist women believe, by propagating myths about the oppression of women in America. "The claim that American women are downtrodden and unfairly treated is the fraud of the century," says Schlafly, insisting that females are in a favored position in America. "Let me clue you in—it's a great advantage being female." "I get away with things I could never do if I were a man!" says another fundamentalist activist. "You know, I get in to see corporate leaders; I get through to people on the phone. I'm sure that it would be a lot easier for some of these men to brush off another man than to brush me off. I just think that it's a great advantage. I'm so glad I'm a woman. There's not a thing in the world that I wanted to do that I couldn't do."[25]

The wave of political activism brought with it, then, a new generation of fundamentalists, trained in Christian academies and universities or on the job in the political trenches. This generation was prepared to organize at local and state levels after the efforts at the national level seemed exhausted in 1990, the year Falwell disbanded the Moral Majority.

## *Denominational Control and Institutional Growth*

An enduring effect of the most recent wave of fundamentalist activism is felt today in the independent and affiliated Protestant churches, especially in the South and the Midwest, which moved closer to fundamentalism as a result of the organized lobbying and political efforts of shrewd church leaders. In the 1980s fundamentalists, proclaiming biblical inerrancy to be the touchstone of Christian orthodoxy, won major victories in the Missouri Synod of the Lutheran Church and in the Southern Baptist Convention.

Beginning in the 1960s, fundamentalist Lutherans opposed "liberalizing tendencies" and targeted Concordia Seminary in Saint Louis as the source of these tendencies. At the 1969 convention Lutheran fundamentalists waged a successful campaign in support of the presidential candidacy of J. A. O. Preus, who launched investigations of Concordia. Preus and his followers insisted that the inerrancy of the Bible is the foundation of the historic Lutheran creeds and began a campaign to expel moderates and liberals from the leadership of Lutheran education and mission efforts. The moderate dissidents formed a separate denomination, the Association of Evangelical Lutheran Churches.

At the same time, Southern Baptist fundamentalists started a newspaper, the *Southern Baptist Journal,* the pages of which emphasized dispensational premillennialism and the need for Baptists to adhere strictly to the inerrancy of Scripture. Some propagandists suggested that an oath affirming this doctrine was the sine qua non for church leadership. The fundamentalists charged that Southern Baptist seminaries, colleges, and missionary boards were being infected by a virus of liberalism and social activism that only served to weaken the body of the church in its efforts to proclaim the gospel and win souls for Christ. In part the fundamentalists' efforts were a mode of resistance against the loss of cultural hegemony: they often depicted the Northern migrant to the Bible Belt as the culprit behind the liberalizing trend. "Their rising levels of income and urbanization gave them resources and opportunities for mobilization that had not been there in earlier eras," Ammerman writes. "Southerners were both more concerned

*The education wing at Preston-wood Baptist Church in Dallas (membership: 8,000) closely resembles a modern suburban shopping mall—complete with atrium, fountains, artificial trees, and park benches.*

and more able to fight to defend the orthodoxy they remembered."[26] They cut off funding for the targeted institutions and gave support to the unofficial seminaries and missionaries untainted by the denomination's liberal drift.

A Texas judge, Paul Pressler, turned the denomination's constitutional structure to the fundamentalists' advantage. He and fellow Texan Paige Patterson exploited the president's power to change policy by influencing the election of seminary trustees. Pressler and Patterson also organized a small group of prominent pastors who took on the task of recruiting support for the fundamentalist takeover in their states. In 1979 fundamentalist pastor Adrian Rogers was elected president of the convention, beginning an unbroken string of fundamentalist victories. By appointing only strict inerrantists who enforced their policy guidelines in the denomination's institutions, fundamentalists put their stamp on the nation's largest Protestant denomination; by 1987, denominational agencies were firmly under their control. The fundamentalists—who today prefer to be called conservatives—forced moderate seminary presidents, professors, and editors of church publications from office. The convention publishing house initiated a commentary series based on strict inerrancy, and missionaries de-emphasized education and focused their energies on evangelism and starting new churches. And, in what many nonfundamentalist Baptists, including members of the American Baptist churches, saw as a departure from the historic Baptist tradition, Southern Baptist social agencies abandoned the defense of the separation of church and state, and downplayed social programs combating hunger, racism, and violence. The focus of denominational activity shifted toward the issues of abortion and school prayer and the political agenda of the New Christian Right.

Even as church conventions and overarching agencies adopted a fundamentalist orientation toward their historic missions, individual fundamentalist and conservative evangelical churches, some of them independent and others affiliated with a convention, grew in size and developed into cultural and religious mini-empires in the 1970s and 1980s. Today the superchurch, or megachurch, constitutes a world unto itself—but it is a world that takes many of its institutional cues from modern culture.

*First Baptist Church in Dallas, which claims more than 20,000 members, offers a less formal "Seekers' Service" every Sunday in addition to two traditional worship services. At the Seekers' Service, the minister preaches in shirtsleeves, hymn lyrics are projected on an overhead screen so that hymnals are unnecessary, and skits are performed to help illustrate the day's lesson. Here, two "families" of actors (the hip Smiths and the smart-but-nerdy Joneses) guess at answers to the question "How do you cope with fear?" in a chancel rendition of the TV game show "Family Feud."*

Fundamentalist and evangelical megachurches attempt to purify and then absorb the style and substance of the secular institutions familiar to modern Americans. Prestonwood Baptist Church, just north of Dallas, impresses the visitor with its sprawling mall of goods and services, a concept (and architectural style) adopted from the secular economy. Worship services at First Baptist Church of Dallas are innovative and imitative, providing a combination of teaching and entertainment for the TV generation. On 12 April 1992, for example, the 9:30 A.M. worship service for young adults—also known as the Seekers' Service—was advertised in the bulletin as a "Family Feud Instrumental" and featured a mock game show, modeled after the popular television show, in which two "families" (played by members of the congregation) compete to answer a series of questions.

In the First Baptist version, the game was an exploration of human fears and the appropriate Christian family responses to these fears; competing groups strove to identify the correct scriptural citations addressing the problems of contemporary families.[27]

The Seekers' Service is modeled, writes First Baptist pastor Joel C. Gregory, on activities at the Willow Creek Community Church, an independent evangelical megachurch in South Barrington, Illinois, thirty miles northwest of downtown Chicago. Willow Creek is the nation's largest congregation, with a weekly attendance of fourteen thousand. "This church has recognized the crucial role of convenient parking in attracting the unreached and the unchurched," Gregory writes. "As First Baptist approaches the opportunity for significant leaps in growth related to our new worship service and Sunday School configuration, we must continue to address the parking challenge." With an annual budget of $75,000 for parking control, 652 parking cones, a huge parking complex lettered and numbered airport-style, and a massive staff of volunteer parking helpers, Willow Creek has indeed solved the parking problem—and also signalled the scope of its ambition to attract new souls for Christ. Its streamlined worship services emphasize music and preaching but are, ironically, low on doctrinal content. First Baptist may not imitate Willow Creek in this latter regard, however, as it can draw upon the experience of senior pastor W. A. Criswell, a veteran of doctrinal wars, and upon supporting institutions like the Dallas Theological Seminary, which trains teachers, preachers, missionaries, and biblical scholars dedicated to spreading the fundamentalist gospel of biblical inerrancy.

## Recent Changes and Fundamentalist Prospects

Ten years after this second wave of fundamentalist political activism, some of the "Sunday soldiers" among them folded their tents, left the scene of celebrity status and public battle, and headed for home to mend fences, regather and re-equip the faithful, revise their projections, and plan new strategies. They devised new organizations to perpetuate and even intensify old strategies. Operation Rescue, for example, is a largely fundamentalist operation which has engaged in radical protest. Citing the precedent of American civil disobedience in other causes, they block entrances to abortion clinics and harass people who seek access. Operation Rescue's Randall Terry understands his duty to Jesus in religiopolitical terms. "We are supposed to be extending the borders of the kingdom of God," he says. Activists of Terry's persuasion are "going into the culture with the crowned rights of King Jesus! This is His world!"

Others, like high school biology teacher John Peloza, believe that there is a conspiracy to cover up the existence of what he and other fundamentalists call "a state-sponsored religion." "It's called The Religion of Humanism, with evolution being the primary tenet of it," Peloza argues. "And it's being promoted in the public classroom, and despite the Constitution that prohibits the establishment of a particular religious view."[28] Peloza fights back by teaching "creation science" in his public school biology class. "Now of course, it comes out as though I'm attempting to promote my religious view, but I believe that's a smoke screen. I believe that's an attempt to divert the public from the real issue. And is the real issue, evolutionism, science? Or is it a religious belief system?" Peloza believes that the Bible is the inerrant word of God. "I'm a student of the Bible as well as a student of biology. And my responsibility is to—to teach the truth in the classroom," he says. "And I believe that there's a major deception occurring in our public education system today. And that's the myth that evolution is a scientific theory that can be substantiated with scientific evidence. I have found that it is not."

Still others continue the battle to have only textbooks that they have approved in schools, books that meet their standards in libraries. Fundamentalists have worked against the National Endowment for the Arts, complaining that some art at least partially subsidized by this governmental agency is obscene. Jim Corbett, a high school teacher who is a critic of activist fundamentalism, sums up the concerns of many like him. "What's at stake here, it seems to me, is what kind of society are we going to have," he says. "Are we going to let religious fundamentalists of any ilk make public policy based on their religion?"

Some of these fundamentalist organizational moves are instinctive, some planned. Though media coverage might suggest otherwise, it is hard to remain fundamentalist in America. There are options, such as evangelicalism, which allow one to be doctrinally consistent yet behaviorally more open. In the face of stigma, many of the young become ex- or post-fundamentalist, rebelling or drifting off. Worldliness comes with success, and it is hard to maintain the fundamentalist witness when it produces bestsellers and celebrities.

It is equally important to note that there are not fewer firm fundamentalists in the United States than there were a dozen years ago. They have not lost their vision or resolve. They might be regrouping, or looking for new names, but they have not yielded on the fundamentals that empower them.

"Fundamentalists definitely want to change the world in their image," says Dennis MacDonald, a former student at Bob Jones University and a biblical scholar. "They would not say they want to transform it in their image, but want to transform it for Jesus Christ because humankind is worthless on their own. It is the world, they are of the flesh, and humankind can never attain salvation by themselves. Therefore there's this urgency—their blood is on you unless you get out and evangelize."

Fundamentalists are finding new fronts. Often they are part of a permanent coalition through which local, state, and national candidates can prevail. During the 1992 Republican convention, for example, the leaders of "the Religious Right," including Jerry Falwell and Pat Robertson, demonstrated the enduring influence of Christian fundamentalism and conservative evangelicalism by winning decisive battles to determine the content of the national party party platform. They are likely to share in some "wins" in Supreme Court decisions and legislative actions. They will not stop aggressive recruitment or working for conversions. They will not desert Israel, and will continue to play an important role in geopolitics.

Having patented the term *fundamentalism* and then having unwittingly and perhaps sometimes unwillingly exported and shared it with other religions, how do American Protestants match the marks we have seen when comparing fundamentalisms? On their own terms, American fundamentalists are religious idealists, convinced that their purposes are the purposes of God. They rely on authoritative sacred texts: The Bible says. I believe it. That settles it. Their beliefs and behavior "scandalize" those who want religion to match the norms of secular rationality and liberal religious culture. They are firm in their belief that the world will end or be transformed by a millennium.

We saw fundamentalisms as needing enemies. These enemies American Protestant fundamentalists find in liberal and ecumenical Protestantism, and in secular humanism. They demonize these opponents and see them as instruments of the Evil One. They work to establish and protect boundaries for members. Without being identified in Yellow Pages or yearbooks, they know each other and know they belong. Missionary zeal they never lack: they send more and more outspoken missionaries overseas at a time when mainstream Protestants talk about interfaith dialogue.

Fundamentalism arose in the crises of post–World War I America and reemerged, this time as a cultural and political force, during the battle over values in America in the mid-1960s and after. Some fundamentalists wish to completely replace the existing polity; more of them want back what they presume was their domain, but purged and purified. Their approach to modernity is selective. They disapprove of much, but are at home with many inventions, such as mass communications technology.

Doctrinally, they engage in selective retrieval, picking and choosing from a presumed past and an assured text what will do most to ward off modernity. When other ways of running governments, clinics, schools, or churches fail, or are seen to fail, they find their moment to strike. They serve people who want to reclaim a world they have lost, or have been told they have lost. They are militant, though in the American prospect there is no reason to believe they would move to terrorism or radical social discontent, since they have much at stake in the survival of America, and, as fundamentalist nationalists, they are highly patriotic.

If they were to weaken in their resolve or begin to moderate, so that they no longer fill the fundamentalist niche in the American spiritual and political ecology, it is likely that a new charismatic leader or set of leaders would rise and form a new movement, again devoted to fighting for the Lord, fighting back against modernity, fighting in the name of the fundamentals.

## CHAPTER THREE

# GUSH EMUNIM:
# A FUNDAMENTALISM OF THE LAND

During the mid-1970s a band of several hundred skullcapped and bearded young men with assault rifles on their shoulders and rabbinic texts in their hands captured the imagination of the media, the general public, and many politicians in Israel. Gideon Aran, a sociologist at Hebrew University in Jerusalem, describes the early days of this band of Jewish activists:

> They spent their nights in the territories on the West Bank of the Jordan River conquered and administered by the Israeli Defense Forces since the 1967 war. There they skillfully outmaneuvered or attacked soldiers and compelled them to participate in an ecstatic Hasidic dance. Joined by their wives and numerous babies, they pitched tents as they repeated the sermons of an aging rabbi. In the mornings, they marched through Arab towns, waving Israeli flags, breaking windows and puncturing tires. Meanwhile, within the State of Israel proper, some group members convened with senior officials and conspired with tycoons, and others traveled hundreds of miles in a dilapidated pickup truck to recruit supporters, sometimes napping in sleeping bags along the road. They rebuked the nation for its moral shortcomings via the TV cameras, which were immediately attracted to them. They covered the public squares of large cities with placards, lay down in front of the vehicles of visiting foreign ministers, and shouted their anguish through loudspeakers to

disrupt the prime minister's daily routine. Between, and even during, these campaigns, they studied the Torah intensively and prayed with great devotion.[1]

These young men, ranging in age from twenty-five to forty, were well-educated, middle-class Israelis of Ashkenazic (European or Russian) background, closely associated with the Mercaz Harav Yeshiva, a school of traditional Jewish learning in Jerusalem. Around them formed the movement Gush Emunim, that today remains strikingly close-knit despite—or perhaps because of—its troubles during the years of the *intifada,* the uprising of Palestinian Arabs living side by side with Gush members and other Israeli settlers in the West Bank. (The intifada began in December 1987 and continues to the present day.)

The Gush is a tiny minority within the Israeli populace. Eighty percent of the citizens of Israel do not actively practice the faith of Judaism, that is, they are ethnic but not religious Jews. But even to say this is to introduce a distinction that is seldom hard and fast. When one is born to a Jewish family, invariably one is born into a culture informed by the experience of Judaism as a way of life—a way of life involving ritual, law, lore, and legend no less than politics, business pursuits, and family matters. Many if not all Jews feel a certain nostalgia, or at least hold a deep respect, for the traditional Jewish way of life, even though they may not have experienced it themselves and may not observe Jewish law and practice. Although they are a minority even among religious Jews in Israel, Gush Emunim members depend upon this respect for Judaism and attempt to transform it into active sympathy for their particular cause, the settlement of the lands promised by God to the Jews in the Torah (literally, "instruction," the first five books of the Bible, which set down the basics of Jewish law).

This strategy of exploiting the religious heritage of Israelis was evident from the formal beginning of the movement, in June 1973, when the Jewish activists who would shortly become core members of Gush Emunim pushed their way into the northern part of the West Bank, into the middle of the land they call by its biblical name, Samaria. This aggressive movement into an area heavily populated with Palestinians was in direct violation of the policy of the Israeli Labor

*New Jewish settlements under construction in the West Bank, spring 1992. After the victory of the Labor Party, led by Yitzhak Rabin, in the 1992 election, the construction of new settlements was suspended.*

government, but the "pioneers," as the radical Jews called themselves, were confident that no Israeli government would evacuate Jews by force from land that they perceived to be historically Jewish land.

In making this assumption, which proved to be accurate, the radicals were appealing not only to religious sympathies but also to the spirit of Zionism, a secular political movement begun in 1897 with the worldwide efforts of Theodore Herzl to organize a Jewish movement of return to Zion (the ancient citadel of Jerusalem, by extension the ancient Land of Israel as a whole) from the Diaspora, the scattered colonies of Jews outside Palestine. Zionism, which led to the creation of the State of Israel in 1948, was in some ways the culmination of a drive by nonreligious Jews to reinterpret Judaism as Jewish nationalism. The settlers of 1973 were deliberately imitating "the historical pattern of Pioneering

Zionism: an illicit minority action followed by majority recognition and gratitude."[2] They calculated, correctly, that government ministers, who did not share their explicit religious convictions, would nonetheless sympathize with their plight; after all, the ministers had themselves been "brash kibbutzniks" defying the British and the Arabs and trying to establish a Jewish state. The Labor government thus showed tremendous patience with the law-breaking settlers, and treated them, in the words of Moshe Halbertal, "like colorful, naughty, and idealistic youth rather than as what they really were: an energetic political movement with drastic methods and objectives that was beginning to impose on the government and the state a de facto annexation of the West Bank."[3] Thus began a controversial process of settlement of lands that the radical Jews believed God had promised to them, but that for centuries had been the home of Palestinian Arabs.

To Gush Emunim members, the de facto collaboration of the Zionist leaders with their expansionist scheme came as no real surprise. According to Rav Abraham Isaac Ha-Cohen Kook (1865–1935), the Ashkenazi chief rabbi of Israel whose visionary teachings about "the end of days" influenced future Gush Emunim leaders, political and cultural Zionism is, in its hidden essence, a crucial stage in the unfolding of redemption and the messianic process. In the Zionist movement, Rabbi Kook taught, God was beginning to fulfill his ancient promise to send a messiah, usually understood to be a human ruler descended from King David, to lead God's chosen people to victory and to establish a reign of peace and justice over all the earth. The first signs of redemption appeared in events such as the 1917 Balfour Declaration, in which Great Britain promised the Jews a national homeland in Palestine. Although they were unaware of it, Rabbi Kook taught, the secular Zionists possessed a sacred "inner spark," and were responding to a call from Heaven. "The wonder is performed before our eyes, not by the work of man or by his machinations, but by the miraculous ways of Him who is perfect in knowledge, the Lord of War, who bringeth forth salvation," Kook wrote. "This is certain—the voice of the Lord is heard."[4]

Rabbi Kook made a distinction between the subjective intent of the secular Zionists and the objective consequences of their action. As Aviezer Ravitzky explains the Kookist doctrine, a person may play a role in the advance of a historical process, and hasten it, without even being aware of the real meaning of the events or the eventual results of the process. "Thus a Zionist who regards Zionism as an entirely secular enterprise and wholeheartedly opposes the world of the Torah, the commandments, and religious redemption may in the last instance turn out to be someone who has taken part in a historical, cosmic process that differs entirely from his or her own objectives and goals. For that person lays the foundation for religious messianic redemption without having a clear notion of it."[5] Drawing heavily on medieval kabbalistic lore, Rabbi Kook held that "the Return to Zion" was an unconscious act of repentance and religious obligation on the part of the secular Jews, that in their heart of hearts the Zionists wanted the messianic enterprise to succeed.

This teaching was elaborated by Rabbi Kook's son, Rabbi Zvi Yehuda Kook (d. 1982), who proclaimed from Mercaz Harav Yeshiva that the secular Zionists had launched the messianic "Age of Redemption" by founding the State of Israel. The younger Rabbi Kook attracted a number of enthusiastic and devout young yeshiva students, the Pioneer Torah Scholars' Group, who came to be known as Gahelet ("the embers"). These teenagers studied the doctrine of Rabbi Kook the Elder, transforming it from "the esoteric and quietistic dogma of a small and marginal circle into a gospel which spread throughout Israel to serve as a platform for the ensuing activism," as Gideon Aran writes. "By adopting Rabbi Kook the Younger as their spiritual leader, members of Gahelet propelled him from the status of a forgotten, ridiculed figure at the margins of the Torah and Zionist worlds into an outstanding Israeli personality with a magnetic influence on a broad circle."[6]

Zvi Yehuda Kook searched for signs of the advance of the Age of Redemption in current historical events. "True Redemption" is revealed, he wrote, "in the progress of settlement of the Land, the revival of Israel in its Land, and in the continuing renewal of this settlement by the ingathering of the exiles . . . in the possession of the Land . . . [and] in our public devotion to its holiness."[7] Today, twenty-five years after he wrote these words, leaders of Gush Emunim continue to interpret the history of the State of Israel, and the founding of new settlements across "the Whole Land" promised in the Torah, as signs of the intensification of the messianic age. From his office at Gush Emunim headquarters in Beit Hadassah, Rabbi Eliezer Waldman, who was a candidate for a seat in Israel's twelfth Knesset, commented:

> We've been hearing, within the last half year, President Bush of the United States saying that he's going to create a "new world order." I cannot understand that. The whole thing of a human being thinking that he can determine and create world orders! There is only One who creates world orders and that is the creator, our God. And he has been creating a new world order for the last hundred years [in the Zionist movement]. There is nothing that can be more revolutionary as a new world order than the return of a dispersed people to its homeland. The renewal of Jewish life here in the land of Israel—there is no parallel to that in the history of mankind. *This* is the new world order and no superpower, even the president of the United States, will be able to deter this godly process.[8]

Gush Emunim's interpretation of history, and of the meaning of current political and religious events in the Middle East, exemplifies a common characteristic of fundamentalisms. Fundamentalists, as we have noted, find themselves in opposition to the post-Enlightenment definition of reality and reading of history. In response, they prepare and promote a counterdefinition and a counterhistory, informed not by "enlightened reason" but by "enlightened faith," not by secular logic but by sacred (in the Jewish case, kabbalistic, or mystical) lore. The Gush see the process of settling "the Land of Israel"—and displacing indigenous Arabs, where necessary—as a religious event ordained by God and ultimately beyond the control of human design.

The majority of Israelis, as we have said, do not see it that way at all; they differ among themselves strongly about the wisdom of pursuing a policy of Jewish settlement of lands taken by Israel in the 1967 Six-Day War against the Arabs. But Gush Emunim members, a radical religious minority even among the minority who are religious, are undaunted by being outnumbered. Although they cannot control the plan of redemption, they can influence its unfolding, for they are the agents of God, his instruments in bringing about the fulfillment.

# The Haredim

Other religiously observant Jews in Israel find this way of thinking to be presumptuous, misguided, and even dangerous. In Mea Shearim, a neighborhood of Jerusalem tightly controlled by its "ultra-Orthodox" inhabitants, religious Jews look down their noses at Gush Emunim and disdain its "pioneering spirit." They judge the Zionist State of Israel to be a folly of human arrogance and an abomination, and contend that religious Jews who are Zionists are misrepresenting Judaism by identifying it with a human, secular enterprise. To the ultra-Orthodox, also known as *haredi* Jews (plural, *haredim*), the messianic age is the work of God alone. Taking their cue from the prophet Isaiah—"Hear the word of the Lord, you who tremble [haredim] at His word" (Isaiah 66:5)— the haredim stand in awe of God's ways, which are never to be confused or conflated with the ways of earthly governments or movements. As we shall see, *haredim* is a general term that includes a number of diverse subgroups, each with a different charismatic leader and with an at least slightly different perspective on political and theological matters. But all haredi Jews agree that the appropriate response to God's revelation is devotion to it, and this devotion is best expressed by studying the word of God in the Torah and as it is elaborated in the Mishnah (the ancient code of Jewish law) and in the rabbinical commentaries, especially the Talmud.

To the haredim it seems that Gush Emunim has turned its back on a cornerstone of traditional Jewish religious sensibility, the belief that God will redeem his people in his own good time. Waiting faithfully on the Lord is an essential element of the true faith. "Notwithstanding the fact that they are religious and devout and uphold the commandments, the people of Gush Emunim seem to be impatient with God's 'incompetence' to ingather the exiles, and therefore they have taken things into their own hands," complains haredi

Rabbi Moshe Hirsch. "According to Jewish theology, however, taking divine things into mortal hands can only be catastrophic."

Indeed, the 300,000 or so haredim who live in Israel (an additional 250,000 are in the Diaspora, with major communities in the United States and Canada) did not migrate there to become part of the Zionist enterprise. Instead, they have separated themselves as much as possible from mainstream Israeli society by retreating into enclaves like Mea Shearim, where they can preserve the milieu of the eastern European shtetls of their eighteenth- and nineteenth-century ancestors. Haredi men retain the earlocks, long beards, and black garb of their forefathers; women dress modestly in the traditional style, avoiding contemporary and fashionable clothes. Ubiquitous posters in Hebrew and English warn visitors to Mea Shearim that they must respect the behavioral norms of the community; women in particular are admonished to dress modestly.

The relationship of the haredim to the Zionist government is complex to the point of being baffling to an outsider. On the one hand, the ultra-Orthodox enjoy certain privileges granted by the state, the most important being exemption from military service, which is compulsory for all other Israeli men. On the other hand, at times the haredim have had an openly adversarial relationship with the State of Israel. They have disturbed civil society by protesting at local cinemas and engaging in "defensive violence," usually stone throwing, against people who drive through the neighborhood on Saturdays and thus violate the Sabbath. Haredi Jews have also attempted to revise the Law of Return, which governs the conditions under which Jews may immigrate to Israel and receive full citizenship. The haredim have pushed, unsuccessfully, for a narrow definition of "who is a Jew" that excludes converts to Judaism who were converted by American reform and conservative rabbis. When they enter into Israeli politics, as various subgroups have done in the last five years with modest but nonetheless surprising success, most haredim do so not in order to support Israeli expansion in the West Bank but in order to defend and preserve (and perhaps extend) their own domestic privileges within Israel proper.[9]

The haredi subgroups differ among themselves on essential points of strategy in response to the "Zionist occupation" of Israel. Rabbi Hirsch is the

*Many haredim trek to the Western Wall for prayer, while others flock to synagogues in the neighborhoods of Mea Shearim. Unlike these "ultra-Orthodox" Jews, some radical Jewish activists feel that preoccupation with the loss of the Temple sidetracks Jews from their true destiny of regaining "the whole Land of Israel."*

"foreign minister" of the small extremist group Neturei Karta (Aramaic for "guardians of the city"). Neturei Karta is so vehemently opposed to the Zionist enterprise that it sent two members to advise the Palestinian Arab delegation to the third round of the Middle East peace conferences which began in Washington on 27 April 1992. Hirsch, who migrated to Israel from New York in 1955 at the age of twenty-one, describes himself as "a Palestinian who is a Jew fighting [the State of] Israel." "I chose to come to God's backyard to serve him in his Holy Land," he says. "That is different from coming here *en masse* challenging God as the Zionists are doing." By encouraging refugees from Africa and from the former Soviet Union to migrate to Israel, Neturei Karta believes, the Zionists are courting disaster by attempting to take matters into their own hands and denying full sovereignty to God. Hirsch maintains that the "dissolution of the Zionist state is a foregone conclusion. We hope it will be done without bloodshed or harm to any of its residents." He fully expects to be the minister of Jewish affairs should an independent Palestinian state come into being.

The Neturei Karta is at the extreme edge of ultra-Orthodox opposition to Zionism. A much larger haredi group, Eda Haredit, also opposes Zionism, but will not go to the length of cooperating with anti-Israel operations like the PLO. For Neturei Karta, however, "our war with the Zionist enemy is a theological war which cannot accept compromise." In this view the Zionists have brought increased suffering on the Jews and may even have been responsible in the divine plan for the Holocaust. "If the Jewish people persist in defying God, these consequences are very real. This is the most dangerous spot on earth."[10] The warning rings loudly today in a time of controversy over increased expansionism led, ironically, by other religious extremists, the Jewish settlers of Gush Emunim.

In many ways, then, these two groups of religious Jews, the haredim and Gush Emunim, are radically opposed. While both groups take a critical stance toward secular Zionism, the haredim reject it outright, while the Gush embraces it, seeking to manipulate Zionism and "exhaust its secularity." The haredim envision no scenario in which the Zionists would establish a true Jewish state. "If the management of Pepsi-Cola were to be Jewish, it would not make Pepsi a Jewish drink," explains Rabbi Hirsch. "The Zionist state, although ruled by Jews, is not a Jewish state. On the contrary it is diametrically opposed to Judaism and continues to vacuumize the souls of its subjects." This image is in stark contrast to the Gush notion that secular Zionists, possessing a hidden sacred spark, are the ones being transformed. Thus, while each group looks to sacred writings of the past and expects the Messiah to come in the near future, the haredim believe that this will be accomplished without human endeavor, while Gush Emunim members believe that the time of redemption will be hastened by human effort.

# Origins and Development of Gush Emunim

The Gush must know when to act, and knowing when to act depends on the proper reading of the signs of the times. This is evident when we consider how the formal organization coalesced in 1974.

In the 1967 Six-Day War, Israel achieved a stunning victory over the combined forces of Jordan, Syria, and Egypt, and took control of the West Bank of the Jordan River, the Golan Heights, and the Sinai Peninsula. Known in Gush Emunim's idiom as "the War of Redemption," this military operation had a profound impact on Israeli society. In less than a week Israel seemed to reverse its geopolitical fortunes and to demonstrate its moral, cultural, and military superiority over its Arab neighbors. (Islamic fundamentalists in Egypt, decrying the defeat of the Arabs, blamed it on the abandonment of Islam—and pointed with grudging respect to Israel, a state which had not renounced its own religious roots. In this instance, at least, the Jewish and Muslim radicals agreed with one another, and even many secular Zionists in Israel expressed their postwar euphoria in religious terms.)

With the "overnight" occupation of the West Bank, Jews came suddenly into possession of Judea and Samaria, the heart of the historic nation of Israel and thus an important stretch of the land promised in the covenant between God and Abraham described in chapter 15 of the Book of Genesis. (The covenanted land also includes vast territories that now belong to Jordan, Syria, and Iraq, but to date even Gush Emunim has left the conquering of that further horizon entirely to God.) Although it was ostensibly the result of a military and political action, the 1967 victory and ensuing occupation of territory inspired a wave of religious messianism in Israel. At the same time, there developed among secular Israelis a heightened sense of nationalism.

The disciples of Zvi Yehuda Kook proclaimed the true import of the victory: it confirmed the imminent advent of the Messiah. Dynamic leadership emerged in the persons of Hanan Porat and Rabbi Moshe Levinger, among others, who intensified their devotion to Torah study and conducted meetings

*The Israeli flag flies at the foot of the Cave of the Patriarchs and Matriarchs in Hebron, a shrine for all three Abrahamic faiths. An Arab worshiper enters the shrine* (below) *under the watchful eye of armed Israeli soldiers* (lower right and upper left). *For years Hebron has been the site of violent confrontations between Palestinians and radical Jewish settlers who seek exclusive identification with the holy places.*

of rabbis and yeshiva students from Mercaz Harav. "From this point on, the Jewish radicals had a cause—the Territories—in which to invest their religious energies and simultaneously develop their potential political powers," writes Gideon Aran. "Their theology, which was revolutionary in any case . . . acquired additional dimensions and an unexpected vitality and attractiveness. The integrity of the land, in turn, was accorded an intense significance, which raised its importance inestimably." The ideas and values discussed by these nascent activists in the wake of the war were "a pastiche of realpolitik, Zionist clichés, moral preachings and biblical injunctions, and citations from the Talmud and later rabbinic authorities."[11]

In this political climate, Rabbi Levinger and several Torah scholars and their families moved, at first rather surreptitiously, into the heart of the town of Hebron on the occupied West Bank. Hebron is of special significance to all Abrahamic faiths (Judaism, Islam, and Christianity) because it is the site of the Cave of the Patriarchs and Matriarchs, the burial place of Abraham, Sarah, and Isaac. By laying claim to the site, Levinger and his followers were also laying claim to its *meaning,* that is, to the Jewish interpretation of these legendary figures and their religious and historical significance. Today the settlement at Kiryat Arba in Hebron, supported by the Israeli government, still stands despite political opposition and despite constant threats from Arabs.

Five years passed, however, before Levinger's initiative was transformed into a full-fledged movement. The transition came not, as one might have expected, after a stunning Israeli military victory over its Arab enemies, but after the "defeat" in the October 1973 Yom Kippur War.[12] In addition to the military blunder which allowed their armed forces to be surprised by Egypt's penetration into the Sinai Peninsula, Israelis had to suffer the further embarrassment of a United Nations decision of 1974 which denounced Zionism as racism, bringing the Zionist enterprise to an ideological low point. In the thinking of the Jewish fundamentalists, however, this was precisely the time for Zionism to be rekindled by its religious center—a "center" that had been relegated to the periphery by the secular Zionists running the State of Israel. At a time when the confidence of the secular Zionists waned momentarily, the self-styled agents of God, confident in Zionism's hidden religious character and in its ultimate transformation and victory, seized the moment. Gush Emunim activists established an important settlement in Sebastia, an abandoned Ottoman railroad station located near the ruins of the ancient capital of biblical Israel and adjacent to a large Palestinian population. The group which settled there became legendary in the lore of the movement and even today its members retain a kind of moral superiority over others in Gush Emunim.

At about the same time, in the mid-1970s, members of the core group of the emerging movement began to recruit members of the religious Zionist youth movement B'nei Akiva, whom they encountered at rallies protesting Israeli concessions to Syria and Egypt. Moshe Halbertal, now at Harvard University, recalls:

> At the time I was studying in a yeshiva high school of B'nei Akiva, the youth movement of religious Zionism. The new pioneering perfectly suited our adolescence. It seemed like a legitimate form of rebellion, even a heroic form of rebellion, against the ossified and nostalgic elders who ruled the state and the society. And so most of my friends in B'nei Akiva joined Gush Emunim.
>
> They had another, less obvious reason for joining. With its messianism and its religious radicalism, Gush Emunim was a way for these young people to overcome a deep and double inferiority complex, about both the secular Zionists and the [Orthodox Jewish] believers who rejected Zionism. The ultra-Orthodox Jews accused religious Zionists of a lack of religious authenticity, of a spiritual spinelessness, since they had not stood firm against the temptations of a secular political movement that wished to define Jewishness on the modern basis of national identity rather than on the traditional basis of Jewish law. From the other side, the secular Zionists who led the effort to establish and to protect Israel, insisted that the contribution of religious Zionists had been minor and marginal. The religious Zionist party in the Knesset, the National Religious Party or NRP, offered no psychologically satisfying solution: before 1967 it shared the moderate politics of Israel's labor movement, and it was therefore perceived as a comfortable satellite to mainstream secular Zionism.[13]

Gush Emunim offered religious people who believed in the Zionist movement a way out of this dilemma. On the one hand, by joining the settlement movement in the West Bank, young Israelis in yarmulkes could claim to have inherited the pioneering zeal of the Zionists and to be transforming it along religious lines. On the other hand, the young Gush members could also respond to the criticism of the ultra-Orthodox rabbis who had rejected Zionism as ungodly and who also scorned the religious Zionists for presumptuously offering a blessing to Zionism. Indeed, the propagandists of Gush Emunim seemed to offer a solution to young Jews who wished to be the vanguard of Israeli expansionism while remaining explicitly religious. "Here was a new form of religious radicalism," Halbertal writes, "drenched in ancient biblical and modern mystical texts, which demanded dedication and sacrifice, and which was animated not by the rejection of Zionism but by the intensification of its spiritual dimensions."[14]

Among the early sympathizers of the Gush were the Land of Israel Loyalists, right-wing members of the underground during the pre-State period and representatives of the activist wing of the labor movement. Affiliated with the elite troops of the Israeli Defense Forces, they had founded kibbutzim and veterans' cooperative settlements. The core group that would form Gush Emunim discovered its affinities with several other groups and seized upon the opportunity to form coalitions. Torah scholars began to leave the yeshiva world and join settlement groups. At about the same time, veteran Israeli politicians of the right wing decided that the National Religious Party [NRP] was not an adequate political vehicle for their goals. During a February 1974 conference at kibbutz Kfar Etzion in the West Bank, the name Gush Emunim was picked up by the media, and the movement had its formal organizational beginnings.

From its inception to the present day, Gush Emunim's theology and messianic outlook has remained basically the same, even as the movement has matured from a spontaneous and unorganized outburst of messianic and mystical fervor into an institutionalized power bloc within Israeli politics. The road has not been without its treacherous turns, however, and the movement has suffered divisions brought on by disagreements about policy and the interpretation of historical events, policy and history being intimately connected in fundamentalisms of many kinds.

The external event that brought on the biggest crisis within the movement is known to insiders simply as "Yamit." The Gush was violently opposed to the historic Camp David peace treaty signed by Menachem Begin, Jimmy Carter, and Anwar Sadat in March 1979, for it called for Israeli evacuation of the Sinai. The NRP proved ineffective in blocking the treaty, and certain Gush members, including Hanan Porat and Rabbi Eliezer Waldman, approached Rabbi Kook the Younger, who lent his support to the formation of a right-wing political party, Tehiya, in 1979. Despite scoring some important political victories, including the approval of a 1980 law formally annexing Jerusalem and naming it the capital of Israel, the Tehiya party, with only three seats in the Knesset after the 1981 elections, was unable to halt the Israeli evacuation of the Sinai. Marching under the banner of the "Movement to Halt the Retreat in Sinai," Gush Emunim took its stand at Yamit, a Jewish settlement in the northern Sinai. The fundamentalist activists believed and behaved as if a miracle would occur to cancel the retreat. It did not. Yamit was bulldozed, and the protestors were disgraced—although it required months of effort on the part of twenty thousand Israeli troops to clear the settlers out. The return of land seized "for God's purposes" was not just a bitter blow to the messianic worldview of the Gush, it was completely unthinkable.

Yamit occasioned an unprecedented soul-searching among the leading Gush Emunim activists. Some concluded that they had failed because they had acted without first building support among the majority of Israelis, while the more radical members concluded that the defeat was a sign that God was calling for even more dramatic initiatives to hasten the redemption. Meanwhile, out of disappointment with the failures of the movement to influence Israeli policy, many Gush supporters left the settlement movement and returned to traditional Torah studies. In 1982 Rabbi Kook the Younger died, and the movement seemed to be in disarray.[15]

The sense of internal crisis deepened when the movement came under the criticism of a respected elder rabbi and head of an important Gush yeshiva, Yehuda Amital. He announced that the defeat at Yamit, followed by the strong Gush support for the Israeli incursion into southern Lebanon to destroy bases of the

Palestine Liberation Organization (and, eventually, the Gush believed, to regain Jewish territory), was the result of a mistaken obsession with the land. In their interpretations of the *halakha* (Jewish law), the Kookists had stressed three elements, Amital reminded the Gush Emunim radicals: equally sacred were the People of Israel, the Torah of Israel, and the Land of Israel. By unduly focusing upon the land, the Gush were jeopardizing the safety of the people and the integrity of the Torah, he warned.

These controversies led to a radicalization of Gush Emunim. The radicals did not leave the movement, but they did join a newly formed Jewish underground. By 1984, members of the underground were being held responsible for a number of terrorist acts designed to exacerbate the tension between Israelis and Palestinian Arabs. These terrorist acts included the 1980 planting of bombs in the cars of two Arab mayors, the 1983 killing of three Palestinian students in an Islamic institute in Hebron, and most significantly, a 1984 plot to blow up the Dome of the Rock, Islam's sacred shrine, on the Temple Mount in Jerusalem. Members of the underground, which included high-ranking Israeli army officers

*From this vantage point on Mt. Scopus in Jerusalem members of the Jewish underground plotted to blow up the Dome of the Rock, Islam's sacred shrine* (upper right). *The conspirators were discovered before the shrine was damaged.*

and heads of large and respected Jewish families, had stolen explosives from a military camp in the Golan Heights. Twenty skilled Israeli reservists, equipped with Uzis, special silencers, and gas canisters, were prepared to storm the mount, and kill the guards if necessary, in order to plant twenty-eight precision bombs designed to destroy the shrine without damaging its surroundings. Had it been successful, the bombing would undoubtedly have led to a profound crisis and an Arab-Israeli confrontation of unpredictable magnitude. The plot was uncovered during the interrogation of twenty-seven members of the underground who were caught in the process of wiring five buses with explosives on 27 April 1984. The buses were scheduled to carry Arab passengers.

That the radicalization of influential segments of Gush Emunim had caused a change in the movement's overall attitude toward Palestinian Arabs was apparent in other ways as well. In the 1970s Gush members had called simply for Israeli annexation of the occupied territories. After Yamit, there were more settlers, including members of Rabbi Meir Kahane's Kach party, demanding the forced evacuation of Palestinians from the land (a policy referred to euphemistically as the "transfer" of Arabs).

Radicalization led in turn to a major rift in the Gush Emunim movement, when the leaders were forced to respond to the fact that some of their associates had participated in the terrorist acts of the underground. Most were truly shocked to learn that fellow activists had resorted to violence of this sort. The image and public standing of the movement, which had portrayed itself as the best hope for the nation, plummeted.

Over the next eight years, up to the present day, two camps have vied within the Gush for supremacy. The radicals, led by Daniela Weiss and Rabbi Levinger, among others, have argued that Jewish settlers in the West Bank must take security matters into their own hands because the government of Israel is not doing enough to protect them from violent Arab reprisals. When the government punished the underground and other Jewish activists, the radicals maintain, it only served to embolden Arabs to accelerate their own terrorist acts. In 1987, Gush Emunim radicals staged a fierce retaliatory raid on the Arab refugee camp of Kalkiliya, where a settler car carrying a family had been firebombed. Gush

*Several hundred thousand Arabs live under Israeli rule in Gaza, along the Mediterranean coast.* (Left) *Street scene in an Arab refugee camp;* (below) *Gaza's main market is closed and shuttered, a victim of the* intifada.

leaders, Weiss among them, also threw stones at the Israeli soldiers called in to quell the riot. This act, beamed over Israeli television, was too much for the moderates of Gush Emunim. Led by Hanan Porat, they staged a sit-in at the movement headquarters in Jerusalem to protest the radicals' actions. But the movement did not formally splinter.

The fortunes of the radical camp were buoyed, ironically, by the outbreak of the intifada in 1987. In the eyes of an increasing portion of the Israeli public, the Palestinian uprising in the West Bank and Gaza seemed for a time to exonerate the settlers, whose militance now seemed somewhat justified in the face of organized Arab violence. Yet the intifada brought new hardships, anxiety, and fear to the settlers, and served to isolate them from most Israelis, who avoided passing through the territories. The frustration of the radicals increased as it became apparent that the Likud government led by Yitzhak Shamir was not going to take measures to crush the Palestinian uprising—although the level of violence and abuse on both sides of the conflict increased dramatically after 1987.

In the context of the intifada, the rift dividing Gush Emunim widened. Rabbi Yoel Ben-Nun, a leading moderate and an original founder of the movement, suggested that the original hope of cajoling the government of Israel to annex the entire West Bank was now no longer feasible; to the dismay of the radicals, he forged links with leaders of the Israeli peace movement and recommended a territorial compromise with the Palestinans. In 1989, after a wave of Gush-inspired settler vigilantism, including the murder of an Arab bystander in Hebron by Levinger, Ben-Nun announced that he was leaving Gush Emunim because it was dividing the nation. Levinger, his main opponent within the movement, was proclaiming that the time had come to accelerate the process of redemption by open and systematic acts of violence against Arabs.

The Gush seems to have survived the storms of controversy. "Both sides came to realize that their mutual interests and shared beliefs were much greater than their disagreements," Ehud Sprinzak has observed. Both the extremists and the moderates within the movement recognized that "there was still no substitute for the original Gush Emunim, a settlement movement committed to Eretz Israel [the Land of Israel] in its entirety and a loyal representative of the mundane interests of many thousands of settlers."[16]

Some proponents of the Gush would even argue that it is thriving, buoyed by the influx of Jewish immigrants from the former Soviet Union and by the aggressive policies of Housing Minister Ariel Sharon and a right-wing Likud coalition, formed in the elections of 1990, that promised to build seven thousand additional housing units in the West Bank with the capacity to absorb at least twenty thousand settlers. The election of Labor Party leader Yitzhak Rabin as Israel's prime minister in June 1992 jeopardized government support for the settler movement, however, for Rabin had campaigned against Shamir's (and the Likud Party's) open embrace of the "Land of Israel" ideology promoted by Gush Emunim and others on the radical right. Furthermore, Rabin promised to suspend the establishment of new settlements in the territories and endorsed the possibility of territorial compromise with the Palestinians. Gush Emunim activist Daniela Weiss acknowledged after the election that "from an ideological point of view, there has been a deterioration" but predicted that the new political opposition within Israel would, as it had in the past, serve only to strengthen the settlers' resolve. "There is room for all sorts of initiatives, maneuvers, and imaginative solutions," she said. "There is a very active element among us, and imagination works harder when there is pressure."[17]

An even more important explanation for the tenacity of Gush Emunim lies in its organizational structure and its "invisible realm," the vast links the movement enjoys to the mechanisms of state support.[18]

## Why Gush Emunim Endures

Today a Jew does not need to join the Gush in order to live in the West Bank—at least 75 percent of the 100,000 settlers there are not Gush members—but each settler must contend with the organizational resources and influence of the three thousand families who form the core of Gush Emunim and who run its secretariat and Amana, its official settlement center. Gush members fill hundreds of paid official positions, control large development budgets, and maintain much of the regional and municipal infrastructure of the West Bank. Thus the movement's influence far outweighs its numerical force. The movement at its core is homogeneous, but it is not democratic; even within the inner circle there are hierarchies of influence and status, determined in part by the personalities and accomplishments of the members, and partly by the degree to which various members have internalized the Kookist doctrine and mystical lore. Even as radical and moderate ideologues argue vehemently about issues such as the appropriate response to the intifada or the morality of the procession of young enthusiasts who escorted Rabbi Levinger to jail after his conviction in the death of an innocent Arab shopkeeper, the real day-to-day business of the settler movement proceeds like clockwork.

To become a member of Gush Emunim, one is usually born into the neighborhood, so to speak. The fourteen-year-olds who lifted Zvi Yehuda Kook to prominence later established the first illegal settlements and now appear as the graying eminences of the movement. They came from the same neighborhoods, schools, summer camps, and army units. The core families know each other personally and share patterns of behavior, and even a common folklore, that set them apart from outsiders. Gideon Aran has observed these families closely:

> Activist-believers favor certain literary genres, specific dress codes, and a particular brand of humor. A distinct type of beard, for example, is an inseparable feature of a Jewish radical's appearance. Linguistically Gush Emunim is recognizable in a particularly revealing inflection and vocabulary: a rare mixture of talmudic-based Yiddish expressions uttered with an Ashkenazic-Diaspora accent, along with a native Israeli vernacular borrowed from the lexicon of the Israeli Defense Forces, filled with expressions of heroism, advanced technology, and simple congeniality. Gush Emunim runs on its own schedule (for example, it tends to turn day into night); it has a particular taste in interior decoration and music, and reflects a typical range of livelihoods, not to mention a specific repertoire of books, children's names, and other identifying features. One can easily identify typical Gush Emunim patterns of family and interpersonal relations, techniques of recruitment and conversion, mechanisms of decision making and social control, and the like.[19]

If one is not born into the Gush "family," it is possible to become a member in a number of ways, including Aliya (migration to Israel) followed by a conversion to Gush lifestyle and belief. A battery of psychological tests awaits those who seek membership, and it usually takes years to penetrate the inner core of the movement.

This procedure has not intimidated American Jews like Michael Lighter, who moved his family to the West Bank in 1984, and who rivals the native Israeli settlers in his dedication to the cause. "The bottom line is that when you are doing something that is you, that is a living expression of your grasp of life, then everything becomes easy and exciting," Lighter says.[20] "There's nothing here that falls out of the realm of writing history. This is what's going to be written about in Jewish history books, one or two hundred years from now, not [the story of a] kosher pizza shop opening in lower Brooklyn." Lighter possesses a strong sense of personal destiny as interwoven with the national destiny of Israel. "If my great-grandmother, who lived in the stench of the Russian pale some two hundred years ago, was given the opportunity to be in Israel for just five minutes, she would have given everything she had just to breathe the air and see the trees," he points out. "I was born in a generation that saw the rise of my people to a modern country absorbing Jews from one hundred and twenty countries, putting it all together and making it work. That couldn't be done without a very intense passion for this people and for this land."

The role of women in Gush Emunim is also noteworthy. Like the men, who studied in Israel's best universities and in the Mercaz Harav Yeshiva, many of the women have also been educated religiously, in their own "seminaries." Women are in many ways the real heart of Gush Emunim. The settlers depend upon women who, because they are defending their homes and children, articulate the earthly goals, aspirations, and values of the movement with great power. "You have to understand that I am a religious person. I have been religious for my whole life. I always live as a religious person, and truly that is the source of my life," explains Esther Karish when asked about her motivation for joining the movement. "We believe that to live in Israel, to found the state, to settle in Judea and Samaria, this is all part of our religion. Zionism is a part of our religion." Esther objects to media characterizations of the Gush. "I think that most of the people in the world picture us as warlike, fighting for everything. Fanatics to a large degree. First of all, we are human beings. We live ninety-nine percent of our lives like human beings—as Jews, as religious Jews—and as Israelis." Who would not defend her right, and her children's rights, to live securely in their home? she asks. "We are going to the demonstration and we bring the children because we really feel that this is a battle for our home. This is our right, to express our aspirations and opinions."

We note here the similarities between Jewish and American Christian fundamentalists when it comes to defending the family—and involving the family in a countercultural lifestyle. In both cases women are the real leaders in this effort. Separatist Christian fundamentalist women and haredi women share a willingness to participate within a patriarchal society almost exclusively through a life of domestic responsibilities. In the case of some haredi groups, women even cede a measure of authority of the upbringing of children to the male head of the household. But in the activist Jewish and Christian fundamentalist movements, as we have seen, women assumed leadership roles in defending the patriarchal system from assault during the 1970s and 1980s.

Although male rabbis form the innermost core of the Gush leadership, for example, some women have emerged as their allies and even as spokespersons. Daniela Weiss is one such charismatic leader, and her story is particularly instructive, for it reveals the spirit of the movement no less than the rifts and developments that it has endured in twenty-plus years of formal existence.

Weiss describes herself proudly as a fanatic—extremism in the defense of God's commandments is no vice, she says, echoing the formulation of the nineteenth-century American abolitionist William Lloyd Garrison—and she speaks with the zeal of a true believer. Her histrionics, carefully orchestrated for the camera and the tape recorder, nonetheless strike the listener as based in sincere religious conviction. The mother of five young children, she wants them to grow up in the movement. "I do not give anybody that does not think the way that I think the opportunity to say what he thinks to my children," she asserts. "I want my children to be exposed to the complete conviction that this land [the occupied territories] is only Jewish land and I will not for the sake of superficial openness expose them to other views. I am very far from tolerant."

*Daniela Weiss, a pioneer in the settler movement and prominent activist allied with Gush Emunim.*

Weiss's credentials as a bona fide messianist are beyond dispute. She has risked her life and health several times in service to the settlers' cause. From her home in the strategically important Elon Moreh settlement in "Samaria," she describes the source of her confidence. "When I see what I see now from this window, the green of the leaves, the blue of the sky, the white of the clouds, the flowers, I tell you that the colors are getting more and more beautiful and I see that it comes in harmony with the growing and strength that the State of Israel is getting," she exclaims. "I feel that there is such harmony around me and it is exactly what I read in the holy books. This is Messiah. This inner full feeling of happiness."

Recognizing her personal appeal and considerable charisma, the leaders of Gush Emunim in 1984 named Weiss the secretary-general of their newly revived secretariat. She immediately became "the darling of the Israeli media,"[21] and she worked strenuously to rebuild the image of the Gush, which had been tarnished by the discovery of its participation in the terrorist activities of the Jewish underground. Portraying the movement as the vanguard of a cultural revival of Israel, she wooed the public as well as the founding fathers and leading intellectuals of Gush Emunim. Under her leadership the Gush established a council of ten people to handle the day-to-day affairs of the movement, and named a council of fifty "wise men" to examine spiritual and educational issues and recommend long-term strategies. The more formalized structure was designed in part to eliminate unrecognized groups like the underground and to provide an element of stability to the movement in difficult times.

The trial of the Gush members implicated in the 1984 plot to destroy the Dome of the Rock proved a stumbling block for Daniela, for she basically agreed with the radicals' interpretation of the historical event of Yamit: it was a warning from God that the Gush must become more aggressive in securing "the Whole Land of Israel." She, too, vowed that "Yamit cannot happen again, Yamit will never happen again." The defendants on trial may have gone too far, but in Daniela's judgment the blame lay with the government, which had abandoned its sacred duty to protect the land. Shortly after her appointment as secretary-general of the movement, and despite her impressive initial organizational and public relations successes, Daniela alienated the moderates within Gush Emunim by leading sit-ins and rallies against the government and on behalf of the convicted Jewish terrorists. In 1987 she was on the front lines of the Gush activists who terrorized the residents of Kalkiliya and clashed with soldiers of the Israeli Defense Forces.

The spirit of defiance and religious zeal which continues to motivate Daniela Weiss also inspires her friends in the settlements, who consult with her daily by telephone to plan the next rally. In Beit-El, a Gush settlement thirty minutes northeast of Jerusalem, Emuna Elon admits that she and her family entertain doubts about the wisdom of their devotion to the movement. "Well, of course there are doubts with everyone. We are only human. We're never able to know for sure that we are doing the right thing," she admits. "But when I have doubts about the road I have chosen, I open our holy books. Books that were written long before I came into the world. I open the Bible and I see that what I am doing is what the prophet said would happen, what the Creator commanded us to do." Elon also takes heart from the recent wave of immigration and the Likud government's decision in 1991 to increase settlement construction, even in defiance of the United States Secretary of State James Baker, who tied U.S. loan guarantees to Israel to the suspension of new settlements. "When I see the cities of Israel fruitful, as the prophet Ezekiel said, I see people of Israel gathered and coming from the four corners of the world, just as the prophet said," she says. "And then I understand what processes are coming to pass. God's program is being implemented and I am acting in that plan."

# Are They Fundamentalists?

Some observers hesitate to describe Gush Emunim as fundamentalist. The activist Jews of the settler movement are certainly religious radicals or extremists, these people acknowledge, but their brand of religious Zionism should not be described as a revival based on any so-called fundamentals of the Jewish religion, since this would impugn the integrity of Judaism. Besides, such critics say, Gush Emunim is not really based on a literal reading of an authoritative text; instead, it is an innovative movement empowered by a series of rather questionable—some would say, sloppy—readings of Jewish texts and inspired by the mystical-messianic thought of a turn-of-the-century Talmudic scholar, Rabbi Kook, rather than an ancient rabbinic sage.

Furthermore, the argument continues, Kook himself was influenced as much by the German philosopher G. W. F. Hegel as he was by traditional Jewish thought. Following Hegel's dialectical understanding of history, Kook reinterpreted the Jewish messianic traditions which envisioned the coming of the Messiah as a preordained rupture in time that would radically overturn historical reality. Kook held that the "Age of Messianic Redemption" was the end point of history's dialectical progress, in which secular Zionism and traditional Judaism alike would be transcended by a new reality. His followers were the bearers of that new reality. Due to its embrace of Kook's "Hegelian Jewish mysticism," Gush Emunim is the first messianic movement in Jewish history that is not centered around a figure who claims to be the Messiah. Instead, the messianic expectation is centered on a process, namely, the resettling of the ancient Land of Israel. There may be setbacks such as the Camp David accords and the disaster at Yamit—and the 1992 election of Rabin, an opponent of the settlers' movement, to the office of Prime Minister—but the process itself is inexorable and its conclusion inevitable.

How could such a movement be "fundamental" to traditional Judaism in any sense of the word? No, the argument concludes, these Jews are too modern, innovative, and un-literal to be called fundamentalist.

Of course, these critics are correct if fundamentalism is identified exclusively with a literal reading and application of sacred texts or traditions and with an earnest return to the basics of traditional faith. And one can understand why Orthodox Jews resent outsiders who identify extremists like the Gush, whom they detest, with the religious heritage that they seek to uphold. Devout Muslims and Christians have similar reactions when their respective religious traditions are represented to the general public by extremists who seem to them to distort the basic messages of the faith.

As we have seen, however, modern religious fundamentalism is not to be confused with traditional religion, although it often cloaks itself in the language and authority of traditional faith. Fundamentalists are playing a different game. To take them at their word, fundamentalists are striving to defend their interpretation of traditional religion and to preserve a place for it in contemporary life. To do so, they must adopt some of the ways of their secular adversaries. But even if Daniela Weiss believes herself to be a "defender of God," and claims that she is standing up for the true fundamentals of Judaism, it is also clear that she is a thoroughly modern and innovative leader, one who is more than willing to appropriate Hegelian philosophy, medieval kabbalistic lore, "relevant" history and scriptural citations, the technology of the cellular telephone and the Israeli media, and anything else that might give her an advantage over the secular (or traditionally religious) opponents of her campaign to hasten the process of redemption.

This is the irony of fundamentalisms. Their powerful appeal is based in part on a claim that they are the defenders of an ancient faith, but their presentation of that faith is selective, partial, highly polemical and creative, and thus not truly traditional at all. Fundamentalists create something new out of the raw material of the past, the opportunities of the present, and the possibilities of the future. Ironically, they most resemble secular ideologues and politicians in their selective and calculating memories and invocations of the (national) past. Fundamentalists are at least as concerned with bringing material progress to their people as they are with restoring spiritual pride and "authentic" religion.

Eliezer Waldman, an American rabbi who migrated to Israel, boasts openly about this civilizational project. "We've come back here [the West Bank] to create Jewish life, human progress, settlements, modern technology, medicine, social services, [on] every inch of Jewish land which cannot be—but which theoretically would be—yielded to Arab rule." Displaying more than a hint of racism, Rabbi Waldman argues that Arab rule of the territories "would invite terror and regression to the area," that the Gush "have come . . . to bring progress, human progress, to this area."

Like fundamentalists in other religious traditions, and in other crisis situations, Gush Emunim displays a religious fervor that can actually be comforting to people who are looking for an anchor in the maelstrom of contemporary society. Knesset member Avraham Burg disdains the Gush, but understands their appeal. "Fundamentalism . . . in the Jewish world is an immediate response of a group of people in times of uncertainty," he remarks.

> People say, "We don't know what will happen about employment, about security, about the future of the state of Israel with all of these new changes in the world and the crisis in the Gulf and the wall falling in Berlin and the Ethiopians are coming, and the Russians, and we don't have employment for them." With Israel in a time of uncertainty and turmoil [the Jewish fundamentalist] is saying, "Trust me, I have a direct line to the divine Lord, I can tell you what will happen tomorrow, I am Gush Emunim. Support me." He is actually saying, "I am a fundamentalist and I have the ultimate answer to the period of uncertainty."

Presenting themselves in this way means that fundamentalists are intensely and openly pious. The Gush outdo even Orthodox Jews when it comes to strict observance of certain religious precepts. Beyond the customary fasts on Yom Kippur and the Ninth of Av (the anniversary of the destruction of the Temple), for example, they observe at least four additional fast days a year. Gush faithful conform to norms which are not stipulated explicitly in the Torah, and enforce the separation of the sexes in education and entertainment beginning in early childhood. The Gush also emphasize the need for the detailed, comprehensive knowledge of these norms, which is only provided by rigorous study. Students, some of whom may spend eighteen hours a day in the yeshiva, count the number of pages they devote each day and week to the Gemara (the Babylonian and Jerusalem Talmuds). Children attend a *heder,* a class providing strict religious instruction. In addition to interpretation and elaboration of religious law, Gush Emunim expands the scope in which it is applied. Not only domestic matters but also business decisions and civic and political behavior, are to be conducted according to talmudic regulations. Gush members also look to their rabbis for guidance in voting.

Because fundamentalisms are driven to engage the powers that be, they may take on the trappings of power themselves or find themselves engaged in the building of kingdoms of this world, but they understand this activism as being in service to the essential calling of the faith tradition. Asked if Gush Emunim is a form of world-transforming fundamentalism, Rabbi Waldman provides, perhaps inadvertently, an eloquent expression of the ways in which fundamentalists understand themselves to be true believers. "I don't know what you mean by fundamentalism," he says. "You can express it as you wish, but why go to high concepts, abstract concepts?" Instead, he says, describe it this way:

> I am a believing Jew. I believe in what God told us in the Bible. I believe in the visions of our prophets. I believe in the Jews coming back to their homeland and being redeemed and becoming a great nation and bringing the blessings to the nations of the world. I believe that everything that has happened here in Israel, including the Jews coming back, including the miraculous falling down of the walls in the Kremlin, of hundreds of thousands of Jews coming back here, which was such a surprise. I believe that God brought us back to Judea and Samaria just as He has brought us back to the Galilee and the coastal plains. I believe that God expects us to perform that important command of settling the land and bring back Jewish life to the land. If you think that is fundamentalism . . .

From the 613 *mitzvot,* or religious commandments, referred to in the Torah, the Gush select one—*avodah,* or "service" to the holy nation of Israel—and elevate it to a controlling principle by which all other laws are to be interpreted. They seek to revive dormant or irrelevant traditionalism and to transform traditionless secularism through the energy of a common national avodah in the holy land. As we have seen, they pursue these twin goals by reinterpreting the teachings of the past and blending them with modern philosophies in "a sort of cultural alchemy," as scholar Michael Fishbane has termed it.[22]

For these reasons the acknowledged experts on Gush Emunim do not hesitate to present the movement as a brand of Jewish fundamentalism. The Gush manifests "obsession with authenticity in response to the challenge posed by drastic change in social environment, and a reliance on ancient holy writ as a source of authority and a guide to behavior, with a tendency toward unequivocal, binding interpretation," Gideon Aran writes. Gush members make a "sharp distinction between the collective of the elect, pure, and faithful, and all others, who are considered infidels and the embodiment of evil incarnate"; they take "an oppositional, if not hostile, stance towards the prevailing culture, the religious establishment, and other religious groups." The Gush is "authoritarian and absolutist, with a strong emphasis on moralism." Ehud Sprinzak draws on the comparative definition of fundamentalism to describe the Gush and calls it "the most effective social movement that has emerged in Israel since 1948." Political scientist Myron Aronoff sees the Gush as "a charismatic, messianic, religious, political, revitalization movement" which has become institutionalized. That seems to be as good a definition as any of what we are calling fundamentalism in this book.[23]

As soon as once-traditional religious people encounter modernity and its dazzling array of philosophical and material choices, they cannot escape what sociologist Peter Berger has called "the heretical imperative."[24] He refers to the inevitable necessity in the modern world of reconstructing personal and group identity by drawing, at least in part, on "heretical" contemporary sensibilities as well as ancient texts—on Hegel as well as Torah, to cite the case of Gush Emunim.

The heretical imperative causes twentieth-century religious revitalization move-ments like Gush Emunim to appear at once as both "fundamental" and religiously questionable or even deviant (that is, as ersatz Islam or Judaism or Christianity).

To understand the paradox that fundamentalism entails, we must recog-nize that the very act of designating fundamentals automatically places the designator at great remove from the time when religion thrived as a whole way of life, before the pluralism of modern societies led to the elaboration of countless distinctions and the establishment of innumerable variations on major religious themes. To identify *any one thing* (for example, the Land of Israel) or any one set of beliefs or practices (the commandments dealing with the land) as being fundamental or essential to the faith is to diminish the other elements of what was once an organic whole. In the case of Gush Emunim, 612 mitzvot are subordinated to the one that concerns its members the most, politically and spiritually—the injunction to settle the land.

Before the acids of modernity started eating away at the structural supports of traditional religion—at the belief systems and prescientific worldviews, for example, within which the existence of a law-giving, all-powerful, transcendent deity made perfect sense to most people—religion was experienced as an integral and homogenous whole. This was true especially in local communities, which were for all intents and purposes "the world" to most people. Before the eighteenth-century dawning of the Haskalah, or Jewish Enlightenment, the values of the European Enlightenment and secular education had not yet posed a decisive challenge to the Jewish communities in western and eastern Europe. In those halcyon days the local community, the extended family, and the officials and laws of the local if not the national government conspired to reinforce the tenets of faith and conduct.

But the Enlightenment did intervene, and Judaism, along with other faith traditions, entered a prolonged period of adjustment and creative adaptation that has culminated in the rise of movements like the Gush at one extreme and the haredim at the other.

Moses Mendelssohn (1729–1786), like his fellow *Maskilim* (enlightened ones) did not consider the Torah to be a revealed source of eternal truths—those truths were accessible to human reason—but, instead, a revealed source of Jewish laws and a polity that no longer existed in the eighteenth century. Thus Jews were free, he argued, to obey the civil laws of the modern state as good citizens; religion was a private and inward matter. Another development that preceded and accompanied the Haskalah was the rise of Hasidism, a spiritualistic, pietistic, and charismatic movement begun in eastern Europe by Israel ben Eliezer, the Baal Shem Tov, of Podolia and elaborated by his successor, Dov Baer, the Maggid of Mezerich in nearby Volhynia. Hasidism, with its emphasis on mystical prayer and spiritual ecstasy, appealed to impoverished Jews of the Diaspora and posed a challenge to the strict legalism of traditional rabbinic Judaism as it was institutionalized in the yeshiva world of Lithuania and elsewhere. Rabbinic Judaism's greatest defender at the time was Rabbi Elijah ben Solomon (1720–1797) of Lithuania, also known as the Gaon (eminence, genius) of Vilna. One of the last giants of talmudic rabbinism, the Gaon of Vilna resisted any deviance from medieval Jewish norms and stood as a model of traditionalism. But even this staunch traditionalist incorporated the new learning of the secular sciences in his lifelong study of the Torah and relied on his own disciplined reason rather than on the opinions of earlier authorities.

In the nineteenth century the post-Enlightenment adaptations continued in the work of Abraham Geiger (1810–1874), a leading proponent of Liberal-Reform Judaism, a movement which attempted to modify or even eliminate those features of Judaism which alienated Jews from Gentiles. On this basis Geiger opposed Orthodoxy and promoted a rational, ethical faith in one God, supported by the historical and "scientific" study of Judaism as an evolving civilization. Geiger's adversary was Orthodox rabbi Samson Raphael Hirsch (1808–1888), who rejected biblical criticism and denied that Judaism had evolved in an historical process. Rabbi Hirsch presented Judaism not solely as an ethical message but also as a "national religious consciousness" with a mission to all the nations. In the late nineteenth and early twentieth centuries these developments continued in different directions in the thought of influential European Jews such as Franz Rosenzweig and Martin Buber, both of whom expressed their complex relationship to the Jewish heritage in terms of the secular philosophical categories of the age.[25]

*Rabbi Meir Kahane's Kach party advocated the "transfer" (explusion) of Arabs from "Greater Israel." His followers still command attention after his assassination in New York in 1990. Here, an Arab man in Jerusalem hurries by graffiti that reads "Rabbi Kahane, we will remember you."*

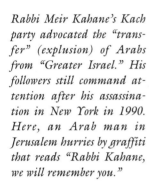

Twentieth-century movements like Gush Emunim are a tapestry of the various strands woven into Judaism by the adapters in response to the Enlightenment. Rabbi Kook the Elder, for example, was a Hasidic Jew who had also studied in the older rabbinic tradition at the Volozhin yeshiva; it is no surprise that he was a complex man who blended in his own person and work elements of Hasidic mysticism, traditional religious messianism, and rabbinic traditionalism.

Fundamentalist groups like Gush Emunim, or the late Rabbi Meir Kahane's Kach party, move into a vacuum caused by the breakdown of traditional religion and the inability of any mass movement to replace religion's central defining role in the Jewish community. When Gush Emunim presents itself as the new orthodoxy, however, and condemns its religious opponents on the left for drawing upon Western democratic values, the Gush "flatter themselves," says Jewish scholar Moshe Halbertal. "Their controlling ideas are not as rabbinic or as authentic as they think. Ultranationalism, the deification of the state, and the organic conception of land and people are not traditional Jewish categories. They have their roots in the West, too." Halbertal is even stronger in condemning Kahane's retrieval of the biblical account of Joshua's expulsion of the Canaanites from the land and presenting it as the Jewish paradigm for treatment of the indigenous Palestinians of the present day. Halbertal calls this type of fundamentalism (he does not use the word) "a really diabolical deformation of Judaism for political purposes."[26]

Given the long history of Jewish adaptation after the Enlightenment, however, it is perhaps unrealistic to expect or to demand a strict literalism from contemporary religious figures who seek to conserve and revitalize elements of traditional religion. It is impossible to recapture a naive attitude once a religious community has passed through a period of profound social and intellectual testing. By saying this we do not mean in any way to justify or excuse the lamentable attempt of Kahane's movement to cloak racism in the garb of biblical Judaism. We simply note that fundamentalisms of many types arise and thrive when traditional religion is severely weakened or absent, and when the plausibility structures—the worldviews within which certain beliefs are plausible—that once supported traditional faith have broken down. The forced reconstruction of those structures, even by sincerely intentioned fundamentalists, is unavoidably arbitrary and artificial to a degree.

Given the invasive nature and pervasive presence of post-Enlightenment secularity, the real question is not whether the fundamentalists are really representing "the old-time religion"—clearly, they are not—but whether *any* form of contemporary religious life can truly do so.

# The Haredim as Fundamentalists

To explore this question we must look briefly at those who fear just the type of absorption and compromise which, they believe, has sullied the orthodoxy of fundamentalists like the Gush and led them to so many erroneous conclusions (like support of secular Zionism). Haredi or ultra-Orthodox Jews seek to defend traditional Judaism from erosion and thus they separate themselves from outsiders and from Israeli culture as much as possible. They are a pure remnant, an elect people who alone have remained true to the Torah and Talmud.

As we mentioned before, the haredim, like the Gush, await the Messiah. But they repudiate any efforts to hasten his arrival. Haredi Jews cling to the traditional concept of *galut* (exile); even in the state of Israel, the *erlicher Yidn* (virtuous Jews) are strangers in a foreign kingdom. Their real home is not of this world; it will appear when the Messiah ushers it in. In the interim, the virtuous Jew must obey the laws of the land (when they do not conflict with the prescribed religious observances) and defend traditional Judaism against its detractors and misinterpreters. Whereas the Gush innovate by elevating the sanctity of the Land of Israel above all other considerations, the ultra-Orthodox attempt to remain true to the complex whole of the Jewish law. Thus, because the law holds that human life is more sacred than land, many haredi rabbis, including Eliezer Shach of the Degel Ha-Torah party, have ruled that a government must give up land for peace if the exchange will save lives. The haredim see this as a straightforward presentation of the tradition, in contrast to the manipulative interpretations of Gush Emunim rabbis. They are upholding, one might say, the entire range of fundamentals of the ancient Jewish religion.

Who, then, are the real fundamentalists—Gush Emunim or the haredim?

The question does not yield a simple answer. Rather than choose one as the fundamentalist and one as the traditionalist movement, it may be more accurate to view Gush Emunim and the haredim (with all their subgroups) as two distinct trends within a larger modernizing process that is occurring in traditional Jewish religion in the late twentieth century. Even the ultratraditionalism of the haredim may be seen as a modern, twentieth-century adaptation of pre-Enlightenment patterns of Jewish religion. If we do see the two groups this way, we may compare them directly on questions such as end-time thought, orientation to political life, and preservation of traditional religion, three categories by which we have considered fundamentalisms in this book.

On the eschatological question—the question of their vision of the age of redemption, or "final things"—Jewish fundamentalists recall the patterns of their Christian counterparts. As we mentioned in the previous chapter, separatist Christians such as the faculty and students of Bob Jones University believe that the Lord Jesus will return any day to establish his earthly kingdom. But their

*A haredi Jew prays at the Western Wall while an armed Israeli soldier inserts a petition into a crack between the stones.*

Christian premillennial eschatology teaches that Jesus alone will bring this about: his followers will play no anticipatory role other than preparing themselves for his coming by remaining separate from the fallen, sinful world and preserving their literal belief in the fundamental truths of the faith. Whatever action they take is defensive, not programmatic.

This general orientation to the end times is shared, in its essence, by the haredi Jews. The Messiah is coming, but not as a result of any historical process that they can discern with certainty; in fact, they are forbidden to make predictions about the time and place. (It must be noted that Lubavitcher Jews in Brooklyn and Israel observed this prohibition in the breach when their ninety-year-old *rebbe*, Menachem Schneerson, seemed prepared to enter Jerusalem for the first time in April 1992, heralded by the cry that "Messiah is coming now!") Certainly, haredi Jews read the signs of the times, searching for clues that the prophecy is about to be fulfilled, but they do not see themselves as agents of that fulfillment and reject the teachings of Jews like the Gush who see in Zionism the harbinger of the age of redemption. Although they are called ultra-Orthodox, the haredim focus less on doctrine and more on behavior in accordance with the halakha. They remain ritually pure, studying the Torah in isolation from an unknowing outside world.

Continuing the analogy to American Christianity, the activist-believers of Gush Emunim remind the observer in some ways of the activist Christian fundamentalists, like Randall Terry, who believe that God is commanding them to "extend the borders" of the divine kingdom before Jesus returns. "Prepare the path of the Lord" is a slogan that makes sense coming from *post*millennialist Christians (Jesus will come *after* the thousand-year era begins), no less than from the pioneering settlers of Gush Emunim, who believe that they are active participants in the messianic age even now.

In such fundamentalisms the eschatological orientation of the group determines the ends and extremes of political activism. Thus it is not surprising that the Gush, who see themselves as active agents of the Messiah, are much more politically aggressive than are the haredim, whose increasing (and disproportionately influential) involvement in Israeli politics is primarily defensive. For example, while the politicians and Knesset representatives of the Gush-supported Tehiya party attempt to act as brokers of important debates on issues of real relevance to Israeli identity and national defense, such as the official policy toward Palestinians participating in the intifada, the representatives of the haredi-supported Shas party are most concerned with passing legislation designed to protect and reinforce the internal security of the ultra-Orthodox community within Israel proper. The haredim are less interested in official policy toward the Palestinians, although their leaders are capable of swaying significant blocs of Israeli voters.[27]

Finally, the comparativist recognizes fundamentalist patterns in both Gush and haredi appropriations of traditional religion. Gush Emunim's selective retrieval of Jewish law and prophecy, entailing as it does a significant departure from the canons of conventional messianism, are clear. But what is more surprising is the degree to which ultra-Orthodox Jews have appropriated not only modern means, but also modern sensibilities, in their defense against the erosion of a traditional way of life. Erosion has already taken its toll, however, as is evident from the defensive posture the haredim find themselves in, huddled in their enclaves, dressed in the garb and living the ritual life not of ancient Israel but of pre-Holocaust, nineteenth-century eastern Europe, the original home of the yeshivas that nurtured their forefathers and foremothers in the tradition.

But the fact that nurturing took place during the breakup of the shared worldview and customs of pre-Enlightenment Judaism meant that traditional Judaism would be divided into two broad camps: the Misnagdim, represented by the Gaon of Vilna and his followers, who stressed law and Torah study; and the Hasidim, led by the Baal Shem Tov and his followers, who stressed mystical prayer and emotional experience. What emerged from the eventual fusion of these two competing strands was truly a new face of Judaism. The "new" orthodoxy could no longer depend on the Jewish home and community to convey the tradition from generation to generation. In this situation, traditional Judaism became more text-oriented, more legalistic and inward-turning, than "traditional" Judaism had ever been. The number and scope of books on the application of Jewish law to modern conditions soared dramatically after the eastern European communities were displaced by World War II and Orthodox Jews found themselves once again on the run.[28] Judaism in this expression became stiffer, more formalized, and, like other fundamentalisms, more dependent on both institutional expressions (thus, the explosion of the "yeshiva world" in the twentieth century) and upon charismatic leaders, or *rebbes* (the Hasidic term for a rabbi who attracts a devoted flock of students). Second, it also became more schismatic. The practice of individual rabbinic interpretation of the sacred codes, accepted as a means of facilitating adaptation to the rapidly changing modern world, led inevitably to the splintering of the traditional intellectual community. We will see the same phenomenon splintering Islam in the twentieth century.

Today the results of that process are evident in the enclave mentality of the various sects within ultra-Orthodoxy, which compete with one another more than with the outside world. As we have seen in the case of the fundamentalist Christians who fled the political, social, and religious mainstream in America in the early twentieth century, the enclave mentality fosters the rise of religious fundamentalism. In the case of Judaism, it has led to the oppositional attitude of ultra-Orthodox Jewish separatists as well as to the radical politics of Gush Emunim. Both movements, like fundamentalisms elsewhere, demonstrate the difficulty of remaining traditionally religious in a secular and plural environment that is perceived to have its own inner dynamism and historical trajectory.

*CHAPTER FOUR*

# REMAKING THE WORLD OF ISLAM

The decade of the 1980s was one of civil unrest in Egypt. In 1981 members of the Jihad movement, incensed by the Camp David accords, assassinated President Anwar Sadat as he reviewed a military parade. Sadat, "the believer-president," had released Muslim fundamentalists from prison and tentatively encouraged their reorganization after he succeeded Gamal Abdul Nasser in 1970, only to "betray" the fundamentalists by refusing to accede to their most radical demands and, ultimately, by making peace with Israel. After Sadat was killed, the hoped-for Islamic revolution did not occur, but unrest continued on almost a monthly basis as groups of Muslim militants, bent on breaking the government's hold on public order, provoked violent confrontations with Egyptian security forces.

On 24 August 1986, to take one of many sequences as an example, members of Al-Jama'a al-Islamiyya ("the Islamic Group," hereafter referred to as the Jama'a) formed human blockades across the Cairo-Aswan highway. When traffic stalled, they raided trucks carrying beer and other alcoholic beverages and smashed the bottles on the roadside. As these Jama'a radicals had anticipated, Egyptian security forces intervened and pursued them to a local mosque. Many of the organization's leaders were arrested and later brought to trial by the state security prosecutor. The cycle of violence and retaliation had begun again.[1]

Like the many-headed Hydra of Greek mythology, the Islamic movement demonstrated that the decapitation of one threat would quickly lead to the rise of another. Following the highway incident, the Jihad organization began to recruit members from the large student population of the university in the 'Ayn Shams district of Cairo. In August of 1988, provoked by rallies and public disturbances, security forces threw a cordon around the Mosque of Adam, the Jihad's base of operations. The congregation built barricades of burning tires, set two police cars ablaze, and hurled rocks at the police, who responded with tear gas and water cannons, stormed the mosque, and arrested 105 militants.

Undaunted by the prospect of imprisonment, other members of the Jama'a planned a campaign against the tourist trade, a major source of "corruption" in Egyptian society. After burning a tourist bus at Cairo's al-Salam Hotel on New Year's Eve 1988, Jama'a members were apprehended carrying explosives to use in other assaults. These arrests only served to inspire another Jama'a militant, who tossed a grenade into a tent where a controversial play was being staged, wounding an Egyptian officer. In an act of calculated defiance to warnings from the government following this incident, the Jama'a founder, a blind 'alim (religious scholar; pl. ulama) named Shaykh 'Abd al-Rahman, led a procession of demonstrators carrying firearms, heavy metal chains, and rocks. Predictably, the marchers' first hostile cries against the government attracted the security forces, who arrested al-Rahman and forty-nine of his followers.

The struggle continued in January 1990, when the Egyptian interior minister, Zaki Badr, was removed from office. To test the new minister's mettle, the Jama'a published a list of demands, including the release of their imprisoned comrades and the immediate prosecution of Zaki Badr, and announced plans to disrupt a speech that Sadat's successor, President Hosni Mubarak, was scheduled to deliver. Three days before the speech, state security forces shot and killed a Jama'a commander and wounded six others when Jama'a demonstrators in Asyut demolished jewelry stores as they marched to al-Khashabah Mosque.

These skirmishes, and hundreds of similar incidents over the past twenty years, were the work of Islam's militant underground, which originated in the Jam'iyyat al-Takfir wa'l-Hijra (Society of Excommunication and Emigration) of the 1970s. The various takfir groups (the word refers to the practice of identifying nonbelievers) emerged from the radical wing of the Muslim Brotherhood, the Islamic fundamentalist movement founded in 1928 by schoolteacher Hasan

al-Banna.[2] Following the teachings of Sayyid Qutb, a radical Muslim Brotherhood ideologue imprisoned by Nasser and executed in 1965, the takfir groups
believed that Egyptian society had regressed to a state of *jahiliyya*, or pre-Islamic
ignorance, as a result of the accommodation of the ulama and government
officials to the imperialist policies and worldview of the West. Few of the ulama
can be trusted in this Westernized environment, the radicals warned, for it was
under the supposed guardianship of these scholars of religion—who in medieval
times had been the reliable pillars of Islamic orthodoxy—that the current troubles
began.

During the century of Western dominance that began with British rule in
1882, Egyptian society was introduced to alcohol in abundance, nightclubs,
televised serials of violence and sex, rock and roll music, and the decadent,
non-Muslim values carried by these Western imports. Today radicals argue that
the decline of Egypt and the entire Arab world, coupled with the failure of secular
ideologies like Marxism (adopted by, among others, the Palestine Liberation
Organization) and Arab nationalism (a political ideology popularized by Nasser),
make the present historical era a time of extreme crisis calling for extreme
measures. Egypt must be returned to its authentic identity in Islam, they insist,
and that will happen only when the agents of jahiliyya, including the rulers, are
overthrown.

Several tactical approaches to revolutionary Islam fall under the general
category of takfir. Shukri Mustafa, the leader of a radical group called the Society
of Muslims, teaches that anyone who rejects the principles of his group therefore
rejects Islam and is a pagan, subject to the seizure of property and even death.
According to 'Abd al-Rahman of the Jama'a, however, the blame lies with the
rulers of society, who have disregarded Islamic law. Mustafa and al-Rahman agree
that Egyptian society has abandoned the essential Islamic principle of the
sovereignty of God. The movements they lead employ the principle of resistance
to whatever is seen as contrary to Islam in Egyptian society. The commandment
found in the Holy Qur'an, the word of Allah recited to the Prophet Muhammad,
summarizes their program: "Fight against them until there is no *fitna*
[polytheism], and the religion is entirely God's" (8:39).

Considering themselves to be the only true Muslims, the takfir groups and their successor organizations of the 1980s debated whether it was necessary to flee the "re-paganized" society altogether and form militant sects in the deserts and small villages outside the major population centers, there to prepare for the future armed conflict with the nonbelievers. Others arrogated to themselves the authority to act as rulers of Egyptian society on the pretext that the existing ruling order was not committed to Islam. Today radical fundamentalists provoke the Egyptian authorities in the conviction that the government's pattern of response demonstrates its un-Islamic character. Under the terms of an unwritten social contract between the current Mubarak government and the Islamic groups, social and religious activity is permissible, as is a limited degree of political organization and participation (although explicitly religious parties are banned and must organize under the banner of a secular party). However, the Jama'a believe that because the Qur'an describes the caliph as the representative or viceregent of God on earth, the caliphate is the ideal form of government for Islam; thus the movement rejects any other political system, including the liberal democratic "experiment" in Egypt. Lawmakers who put human or secular law first are tyrants, by this way of thinking, because people are free and equal only when they serve Allah alone. Based on positive civil laws, the Egyptian Parliament cannot promulgate Islamic religious law in toto. Thus the radical Jama'a condemned the participation of the Muslim Brotherhood in the 1984 and 1987 parliamentary elections as a "great sin and offense." "The Parliament is worthy only of burning," the radicals proclaimed.[3]

The radicals were recruited, beginning in the 1970s, from among a generation of educated Egyptians, many of them trained as engineers in secular academies, who could not find jobs in the underdeveloped economic system. Their activity, centered in the cities of Upper Egypt and in certain poor neighborhoods in Cairo, was designed to sway the opinions of the marginalized and oppressed, of which there are an increasing number in Egypt's overcrowded cities. Nonetheless, the radicals' solutions and basic ideology proved to be too extreme to win the support of the masses, who choose not to risk imprisonment as long as their basic, modest material needs are met and order is maintained.

*With massive over-crowding, widespread unemployment, and a population that is 70 percent illiterate and largely mired in poverty, Egypt offers the right ingredients for alternative political/social movements such as Islamic fundamentalism to gain a large following.*

Many of Egypt's radical elements would bring about the systematic implementation of Islamic law by force.

Unlike the radicals, who are a minority even among fundamentalists, the current generation of the Muslim Brotherhood eschews violence and attempts to participate openly in mainstream Egyptian society. Taking advantage of Mubarak's modest liberalization program, the Brotherhood enjoys a wider audience for its seemingly more moderate program of Islamization. Working under the aegis of the Labor party in the early 1990s, the Brotherhood has sought to transform Egyptian society from within, by pursuing a gradualist program of social legislation and education.

Despite these ideological and tactical rifts between the Muslim Brotherhood and the radicals, the groups share basic goals and, at times, resources.[4] All those who are described as fundamentalist, fringe radicals and mainstream politicians alike, believe that the ruling order should systematically apply Islamic law (*Shari'a*) and advance a program of moral reconstruction guided by the Qur'anic principle "Command what is right and forbid what is wrong."

"Forbidding what is wrong" encompasses a number of teachings that non-Muslims, and many nonfundamentalist Muslims, find scandalous in the contemporary world. Perhaps the most important example is role of women in

*Many Muslim women dress and live in the traditional manner, but with economic conditions forcing more women to work outside the home some observers question whether the next generation will turn more "Western." Here, two veiled women walk with a young girl who is dressed in blue jeans and a "Sesame Street" sweatshirt.*

society. Fundamentalist Islam is associated with a return to the veiling of women and to strict observance of Shari'a ordinances establishing men as the exclusive owners of property (in which category wives are sometimes included) and as the sole holders of rights in interpersonal relations. In fundamentalist-influenced Muslim societies, schools, transportation, offices, and other public institutions are segregated by gender. (In Cairo, for example, one car per train of the metro is reserved for the exclusive use of women.) The consistent emphasis on a restriction of women to traditional domestic roles—though it has been modified somewhat in Iran, Egypt, and elsewhere by the economic necessity of women entering the work force—is so pervasive that sociologist Martin Riesebrodt has characterized Islamic fundamentalism as essentially a patriarchal protest movement against selected aspects of secularized modernity such as the Western women's liberation movement.[5]

Egyptian preacher Shaykh Mitwali Sharawi articulates the fundamentalist sensibility on this question:

> When God speaks of the adulterer and the adulteress, he is specific. Who
> is he referring to when he speaks of the adulteress? The woman, but in

order to indict both the woman and the man equally, God chose to refer
to both in such a distinct manner as to avoid confusion. She is the one
causing provocation. Thus God told men not to be tempted by women;
and he told women not to uncover themselves. So, then who is the
source of provocation? The woman is!

Because the woman is the source of provocation and "[a] man is less likely to
incite temptation among women," adds a teacher at the Mahmoud Mosque,
"Islam does not stipulate detailed criteria of dress for men as it does for women."[6]

Supporters of the feminist movement in the West no doubt find it
surprising, then, that young women are extensively involved today in the Islamic
movements in activist positions described by anthropologist Andrea Rugh as
"different from the supportive roles they played as sisters and wives of the earlier
Muslim Brotherhood."[7] One female activist argues that in the Islamic view,
women are fully equal to men, but not in the "Western sense of equality,"
whereby divinely ordained differences between the sexes are denied. The author
of a master's thesis on the participation of women in the original Islamic
community at the time of the Prophet, this woman sees herself as a defender of
an "authentic" role for women in Islam that includes taking leadership without
disrupting the patriarchal order instituted by God.[8]

The message of "the Islamic current" is propagated in the network of
hospitals, clinics, schools, and orphanages established throughout Egypt (and the
entire Arab world) by branches of the Muslim Brotherhood and other fundamentalist groups. There are various levels of this Islamic current, however, and
presently there is a struggle within the larger movement in Egypt to define the
best and most effective means of realizing the common goal of implementing
Islamic law. Adil Hussein, the editor of *al-Sha'b* (*The People,* an organ of the
Islamic movement in general and the Muslim Brotherhood in particular) and a
highly visible leader of the Muslim Brotherhood, favors the political route. A
former socialist, Hussein has heard the criticism that he is jumping on the Islamic
bandwagon just at a time when it seems to be gaining momentum and articulating
a distinctive and persuasive political message. He responds simply by arguing that

*Egyptian newspaper editor Adil Hussein, an Islamic fundamentalist who nonetheless distances himself from Muslim radicals who seek restoration of extreme punishments dictated by the Shari'a.* (Courtesy Steve York and Associates Film and Television Production)

Islam is the best hope for Egyptians seeking a viable and culturally authentic political identity—as long as one understands Islam properly.

"You will find Islamists who say things which in our opinion are extremely backward and rigid," Hussein complains. "They are the ones who call for the return of the society of Medina, which perished fourteen hundred years ago, certain aspects of which cannot survive today. So we disagree with them on a host of issues." Hussein thereby distances himself from the radicals, who would (among other measures) restore the *huddud* penalties of the Shari'a, which mandate the stoning of adulterers, the mutilation of thieves, and the death penalty for apostates. "However," Hussein continues, "it is also true, I think, that if democracy in Egypt were widened so that debate could be open to all, then such a debate would attract many of those young people who have adopted violent and extremist positions."

Hussein puts forward the rational, compromising face of Islamic fundamentalism by dismissing "positions that are foolish in their enmity toward everything Western . . . foolish in their understanding of contemporary society, their exaggerated wariness of anything new." "None of this will go away," he maintains, "unless there exists an atmosphere of democracy which allows for freedom and debate."

The question that policymakers, educators, and everyone interested in the future of Egypt—and, indeed, of the Middle East—are debating in the early 1990s is whether Adil Hussein and others like him in Algeria, Tunisia, Jordan, and elsewhere are to be believed when they say that Islamic fundamentalism can be a force for democratic change.

# Islam and Islamic Fundamentalism

We have begun this chapter with a discussion of Egypt because it offers an important example of an almost universal struggle today in the Muslim world to define Islam's role in political and cultural life. Islam is not confined to the Middle East, of course; indeed, more Muslims live in Indonesia than in any other country. Islamic fundamentalist-like movements also exist outside the Middle East, in South Asia (the Jamaat-i-Islami, for example, which was born in Pakistan) and Southeast Asia (where *dakwah,* or missionary-style, movements are popular). In the 1990s, as we shall see, political Islam is also on the rise in Africa and, possibly, in Central Asia.

In assessing the prospects for the worldwide democratization of Muslim societies, some Western observers do not differentiate between Islam and Islamic fundamentalism. Rather, they tend to equate the two (although they would never think of identifying Christianity with its fundamentalist wing). According to American University political scientist Amos Perlmutter, for example, there are no viable distinctions to be made among Islamic movements around the world. "Islamic fundamentalism of the Sunni or Shia variety in Iran, Iraq, Egypt, Jordan, the West Bank and Gaza, the Maghreb and also Algeria," he contends, "is not merely resistant to democracy but wholly contemptuous of and hostile to the entire democratic political culture. . . . [It] is an aggressive revolutionary movement as militant and violent as the Bolshevik, Fascist, and Nazi movements of the past." Perlmutter asserts that the world's 800 million Muslims should be viewed as one monolithic force. "The issue is not democracy but the true nature of Islam," he writes. "Is Islam, fundamentalist or otherwise, compatible with

*The Islamic revival has swept Egyptian society, reinforcing and extending the traditional patterns of Arab life. This storefront mosque in Cairo overflows for Friday prayer, stalling midday traffic.*

liberal, human-rights oriented Western-style representative democracy? The answer is an emphatic 'no.'"[9]

Islam is seen as fundamentalist in nature for three interrelated reasons. First, the argument runs, scriptural inerrancy is already built into the Islamic tradition. In fact, because all Muslims believe that the Qur'an is the actual word of God dictated to and recited by the Prophet Muhammad, no one within the believing community has suggested that it be read any way but literally. Thus the question of inerrancy never has arisen in the case of the Qur'an as it did in the case of the Christian Bible, which is understood by the majority of Christians to be the work of a number of inspired writers who had different perspectives on various questions. Second, say those who see the current wave of fundamentalism as the true face of Islam, the very word *Islam* means "submission" and the ultimate goal of the believer is to submit all realms of life to Allah's will. Because the divine will is literally and nonmetaphorically identified with the Qur'an, the Sunna (examples of the Prophet), and their codification in Islamic law, all Muslims, the argument continues, have an infallible blueprint for ordering the community. The fundamentalists, by this reasoning, are simply doing their duty as Muslims when they seek to implement the Islamic law fully and comprehensively. Finally, those who equate Islam and fundamentalism point to the fact that Muslim societies, with the lone exception of Turkey, have not succeeded in enforcing the separation of religion and state. In Islam this kind of compartmentalization is unthinkable (unless a committed secularist like Kemal Atatürk in Turkey comes to power), for no aspect of life is to be excused from strict obedience to the will of the Creator.

Therefore fundamentalism is also sometimes called "political Islam" because it seeks to bring about an Islamic state. In the words of Javid Iqbal, a justice of Pakistan's supreme Islamic court, in theory an Islamic state is "Allah's state, or the Kingdom of God on earth, and the Muslims constitute Allah's party (*hizbullah*)." This makes it different from a secular state in a number of practical ways, he says.

> A state which is managed and administered in accordance with Islamic law is technically called *dar al-salam* (country of peace). If a *dar al-salam* or an Islamic state is politically or economically subjugated by a non-Muslim power, it will be transformed into *dar al-harb* (country of war), and the Muslims shall be left with only two alternatives: either to conduct a jihad in order to regain their independent status or to migrate (*hijra*) to some Muslim country.

> In an Islamic state the people are not vested with ultimate sovereignty, nor does absolute authority rest with the head of the state or with parliament. Ultimate sovereignty and absolute authority vest in God, and the only principle operative in an Islamic state is the supremacy of Islamic law.

> A modern secular state must have three features: it must be fully sovereign; it must be national; and it must have well-defined territories. When these three features exist, a state can legitimately claim to be a

sovereign state. However, an Islamic state, although sovereign from this accepted standpoint, is not fully sovereign because according to the faith of Islam, ultimate sovereignty vests only in God. Strictly speaking, it is also not a national state, because the Muslim community (*umma*) is a community of faith and consists of peoples who may belong to different tribes, races, or nationalities, and may speak different languages and be different colors, but who share a common spiritual aspiration, i.e., their faith is Islam. Consequently, an Islamic state is a multinational state. An Islamic state is not a territorial state in the strict sense of the term, because it aims and aspires to become an universal state. Nevertheless it is not a utopia or imaginary state. It has to be initially founded as a territorial state, although the territories are expected to expand.[10]

In accounting for the rise of Islamic fundamentalisms, many scholars point to the favorable circumstance of the Arab Muslim strength and unity experienced during the oil crisis and embargo of the 1970s, and to the decline of other alternatives to Islam as an expression of Muslim solidarity. In addition to these and other external circumstances, however, the internal arguments mentioned above must be taken into account by any serious student of comparative fundamentalisms, because of their salience and appeal to many Muslims around the world who identify Islam with a simple, basic approach to life and who rely on the teachings of religious scholars or informed laymen in order to understand the basic requirements of Islam as a way of submission. The scope and number of Islamic movements reflects something of the ease with which the fundamentalist version of Islam is popularized, especially when external circumstances are favorable.

Fundamentalism is, however, a *version* of Islam, a particular construction of Islam under certain circumstances, rather than the essence of Islam. Like Judaism, Islam is indeed a religion of law and the law's systematic application is its goal. But, as with Judaism, the interpretation of law in Islam, and the discussion about how, when, and where it ought to be applied, has led historically to a number of different expressions of Islam as an authentic, orthodox way of submission to the will of God.

People who equate Islam with one way seen as fundamentalist overlook the variety within its historical tradition, beginning with the basic division between Sunni Islam, adhered to by roughly nine out of ten Muslims, and Shi'ite Islam, the minority expression of Islam which is identified in most Western minds with fundamentalism as a result of the Iranian revolution and the regime of Ayatollah Khomeini. In examining the construction of fundamentalism from the vast historical resources of Sunni Islam, we hope to demonstrate that Islamic fundamentalism—like fundamentalisms in other traditions—is one among many possible modern constructions of the tradition. By *construction* we mean a particular presentation of the tradition, a presentation that selects and weighs certain historical precedents and teachings more heavily than others. Reference to the Shi'ite tradition, which follows our discussion of Sunni Islam, will serve to demonstrate that an uncontested, single, monolithic fundamentalism does not even exist; rather, there are many fundamentalisms within Islam.

# Forging Fundamentalism from the Historical Sources of Sunni Islam

Like its counterparts in Judaism and Christianity, Islamic fundamentalism is essentially a modern phenomenon. It emerged as a self-conscious movement of resistance to the agents of secular modernity, primarily the European colonialists (and their indigenous disciples), who built or took control of the major social and political institutions of the Middle East in the nineteenth century and especially after the defeat of the Ottoman Empire in World War I.

Although fundamentalism is a modern phenomenon, Islamic fundamentalists are influenced by the writings of premodern reformers such as Ahmad Ibn Hanbal (d. 855) and Ahmad Ibn Taymiyya (d. 1328). These learned jurists opposed the incorporation of non-Muslim practices into Islamic life and stressed the comprehensive and universal nature of the message of God as presented in the Qur'an. As the following discussion demonstrates, fundamentalists also draw on other historical examples and figures in constructing an antisecularist and antimodernist presentation of Islam.

## *The Shari'a*

Today's fundamentalists in the Sunni Arab world are responding to and at times challenging a well-organized religious institution that was developed in the Ottoman Empire, which lasted for more than six centuries (1301–1920). This religious institution, headed by a dignitary known as the Shaykh al-Islam, who was situated atop a hierarchy of religious scholars, controlled all higher education and the administration of justice in the empire. It was also responsible for the formulation of laws based on the Shari'a. The Shari'a is drawn from the relatively small number of legal edicts in the Qur'an (although some, like the rules of inheritance, are quite detailed) and from other laws based on the Sunna (the words or example of the Prophet) as recorded in the Hadith (traditions).

As we have noted, the implementation of the Shari'a, which incorporates and subsumes the central ethical and theological principles of the religion, is the shared goal of all Islamic fundamentalists. It is not true, however, that all fundamentalists, much less all Muslims, agree with one another regarding the interpretation of the Shari'a. The same could be said, of course, of Christians in relation to the New Testament, and of Jews in relation to the Torah.

The early religious scholars of Islam debated the principles of Islamic law, and although there was general consensus regarding the practical duties of ordinary people, four different Sunni schools of interpretation eventually emerged. None of these schools produced or drew upon any one authoritative legal text. Instead, the unfolding and elaboration of the Shari'a proceeded by means of a continuing series of religious rulings (*fatwa*) pronounced by *muftis* (religious scholars with advanced expertise in Islamic jurisprudence).

Thus the body of Islamic law was hardly inflexible: the judge of any Shari'a court could and routinely did modify its prescriptions slightly to meet local conditions. He could do this by retrieving and emphasizing one or more appropriate texts over others in the vast written corpus. The important point, to which we shall return, is that the Shariʻa—and thus Islam itself—presents the paradox of an immutable reality that in its evolving interpretation is so highly adaptable as to be elastic. On the one hand, Islamic law is a fixed set of divinely revealed laws and principles binding on all Muslims at all times. On the other hand, as a code that is intended to preserve Islam in varying historical circumstances, it is flexible and changing in practice.

The scope and application of Islamic law is thus a matter of interpretation, and this is why the question of who is doing the interpreting, and under what conditions, is and has been of grave importance to Muslims. Between the two forms of Islam, Sunnism and Shiʻism, there are important differences on this central question. After the eighth century a pattern developed in Sunni Islam whereby the religious institution was allowed to adjudicate personal, civil, and criminal law, but was not allowed to interfere in the external policies of the political institution (the caliphs, or Muslim rulers, lost effective political power in 945) or even in the form of government adopted by the political power. (As we shall see, the Shiʻites in Iran and elsewhere took a different attitude toward religious and political authority.)

Within the Sunni religious institution, each of the four schools of jurisprudence developed its own rites and practices through a process known as *ijtihad,* by which qualified muftis were allowed to use independent judgment in interpreting the primary sources of Islam. In the first half of the tenth century, the period of independent reasoning and flexible interpretation of the law ended when a consensus developed to close the gates of ijtihad, presumably to forestall further adaptations and splintering.[11]

## *The Wahhabi Model in Arabia*

Sunni fundamentalists in the twentieth century reject much of the medieval commentary that followed the closing of the gates of ijtihad. They turn instead to historical episodes which embody their view of Islam. One such example is the founding of Wahhabism.

In the eighteenth century, Ottoman rule extended across North Africa and throughout most of the Balkan peninsula. As the empire became fragmented and mismanaged during the latter part of the century, Islamic movements of renewal began in Cairo, the smaller cities of Yemen, and the holy sanctuary cities of Mecca and Medina in the Arabian peninsula. One such movement was established on the Arabian peninsula by Muhammad Ibn 'Abd al-Wahhab (1703–87), a Sunni Muslim who followed the strict medieval Hanbalite school of legal interpretation. Long before Sayyid Qutb made the same judgment regarding twentieth-century Egypt, the founder of Wahhabism designated Arabia as a jahiliyya society and denounced popular religious practices such as the veneration of saints' tombs as unwarranted innovations (*bid'a*). Settling in the town of al-Dar'iyyah (near present-day Riyadh), he converted the ruler, Prince Muhammad Ibn Sa'ud, to this view. Their alliance created the foundations for a new state, based on the Qur'anic principle of *tawhid*, the transcendent unity of God. The Saudi kingdom "enforced" the transcendence of God by institutionalizing a political system that was designed to promote and protect a personal and social lifestyle in strict accord with the prescriptions of the Qur'an.[12]

The Wahhabi state was based on the close cooperation of a learned teacher (*shaykh*) and an able commander (*emir*). In this system, charismatic religious leadership was not as essential as it would be elsewhere—to Shi'ite Muslims, for example, living in Iran under a different political system and with a different theological heritage—but the militant character of this reform movement, coupled with the puritanical zeal of its founder, established Wahhabism as an important model for Islamic fundamentalists in the nineteenth and twentieth centuries.

## *The Impact of Colonialism and Westernization*

The Industrial Revolution had a profound social and economic impact on the Arab world in the nineteenth century. Dramatic improvements in transportation opened new markets and stimulated an infusion of Western capital, the introduction of the rudiments of a Western-style financial system, and most important, an

influx of European immigrants who worked in agriculture, banking, and government administration. As export agriculture expanded, the traditional merchant
class declined.

Because Arab societies had not developed economic or political institutions
capable of regulating the pace and direction of Western influence, the rapid
distortion of traditional economic patterns quickly led to dependence on the West
and eventually to the assertion of direct Western colonial control of the Islamic
world. The French came to control Algeria in 1830, Tunisia in 1881, Morocco
in 1911, and Syria and Lebanon after World War I. The British occupied Egypt
in 1882, conquered the Sudan by 1898, and took control of the territories which
became modern Iraq and Jordan. They also controlled Palestine through international mandate following World War I. Even the small states in the Persian
Gulf, South Arabia, and Libya were under some form of European control by
that time.

After this colonization there were substantial differences in the character
of modern developments in different Muslim regions, depending upon the
character of the ulama, the state of Islamic education immediately prior to
colonization, and the colonial policy of the particular colonizing power.[13] But
the social dislocation which ensued was in most cases traumatic and widespread.
By the late nineteenth century, for example, the sequestering of large tracts of
land for corporate agricultural purposes created a landless peasant class in some
areas. Traditional urban elites were also displaced, as in the case of the ulama,
who gradually relinquished their hegemony over legal and educational matters
to a new class of Western-influenced bureaucrats.

Resistance to foreign rule in the nineteenth century took the form of *jihad*
(holy struggle) revivalist movements which anticipated Islamic fundamentalism
in certain aspects. In the Sudan, for example, Muhammad Ahmad (1848–1885)
proclaimed himself to be the Mahdi, a figure in Islamic eschatology whom God
sends at the turn of each century to return Muslims to the straight path.
Empowered by this aura, Ahmad was able to successfully lead a movement to
expel the Ottoman Egyptian forces from the Sudan in 1885 and establish an
Islamic state. "The Sudanese Mahdi rejected the corrupt practices of the Turko-

Egyptian rulers and fought the British, but he did not reject modern military technology," historian John Voll writes. "Although he is frequently described as an opponent of foreign rule and an enemy of Western intrusions into the Islamic world, he also opposed certain local religious customs, engaged in ijtihad, and in other ways recalled the example of Ibn 'Abd al-Wahhab."[14]

In the nineteenth century the success of Sunni fundamentalist-like movements was isolated, however, as the majority of the educated Arabic-speaking people were absorbed in the process of appropriating Western political and technological forms.

Egypt was one of the first countries in the Arabic-speaking world, or in the larger Islamic world, to undertake a major program of Westernizing reforms. Muhammad 'Ali (d. 1849), an Albanian Turk installed by the Ottomans as governor of Egypt after the withdrawal of the French, began a program of rapid modernization and Europeanization of the Egyptian military, government, and economy. He and his successors in the nineteenth century established educational institutions designed to transform the life and thought in Egypt from a traditional Islamic pattern inculcated by the Qur'anic schools to a modern secular and nationalistic worldview taught by schools specializing in the sciences and Western languages. 'Ali and his followers brought the ulama and the leaders of popular Islamic organizations under more direct government control. Subsequently, the leadership of Egyptian political and social life passed to the Westernizers.

Educated young Muslims in the cities were scandalized by these developments and by the intellectual and moral crises created by the rapid introduction of Western ideas and technology into a society that had been medieval in outlook for centuries. Accordingly, many influential Muslim intellectuals wanted to adapt Muslim practices and beliefs to the exigencies of a modern industrialized economy without betraying their Islamic heritage. They came to be known as modernists.

Islamic modernism seemed at first to offer a way between the "atheism" of the undisciplined Westernizers and the calcified traditionalism of al-Azhar, the major Islamic educational institution in Egypt. Jamal al-Din al-Afghani (1838–97) and Muhammad 'Abduh (1849–1905) proposed a major reform of Islamic teaching and practice that would incorporate science and other forms of secular knowledge. Shaykh 'Ali 'Abd al-Raziq called for the abolition of the caliphate, denying that it had a textual basis in the Qur'an or the Sunna. The caliphate was not the legitimate Islamic form of government, he argued, for God had given Muslims the freedom to choose their political systems. 'Abduh advanced this argument. In the Qur'anic institution of *shura* (consultation) he found evidence for the modernists' conclusion that Islam is democratic in nature.

The modernists recommended a return to the example of the pious ancestors (*salaf*), especially the companions of the Prophet. Like the Wahhabis of Saudi Arabia, and like future Egyptian fundamentalists, the modernists practiced ijtihad, rejected the "superstitions" of popular religion, and appropriated the concept of tawhid. But they did not repudiate Western ways in principle and although they did return to the traditional sources, they did not seek a program of Islamization, the construction of a purified society on a pristine Islamic model. In the rhetoric and approach of Islamic modernism, however, lay the seeds of Islamic fundamentalism. These were nurtured by one of 'Abduh's students, Rashid Rida (1865–1935), whose al-Manar school rejected the rationalist tendencies in the thinking of other modernists.

The efforts of Islamic modernists were eclipsed, however, by events which moved Egypt, and the Sunni Arab world in general, closer to a secular model of government. During World War I, the British declared Egypt to be a protectorate, but would not allow a delegation (*wafd*) of Egyptians to act independently at the Peace Conference. A series of nationalist demonstrations in 1919 against British hegemony led to the formation of the Wafd political party. In 1922 Great Britain declared Egypt to be an independent monarchy under the rule of King Fuad, a descendant of Muhammad 'Ali. The British maintained their military control over the country, and the Wafd became a mass nationalist political party. In this context the Egyptian elite (and many Islamic modernists), opposing British domination but preferring to retain the parliamentary model of government, embraced nationalism as a secular movement.

Although the Egyptian masses did not abandon Islam, Rashid Rida's intellectual project of recovery of Islamic sources lacked an organizational base and was increasingly marginal to the main political movements of the day. Islam suffered another setback of sorts in the 1920s, when Turkey, under the leadership of its first president, Kemal Atatürk, provided a viable model for secularization by separating religion from the state, abolishing the caliphate, and bringing education, law, and literature in line with Western standards. Atatürk's program had the effect of disestablishing Islam. Even as this process unfolded in Turkey, the Westernizing trend intensified in Egypt. Many Egyptian women refused to wear the veil, entered the work force, became politically active, protested against polygamy (a practice legitimated by Islamic personal law), and demanded the elimination of the Shari'a courts. Egyptian men adopted European lifestyles and ways of thinking. Religious education at al-Azhar suffered as young men pursued training elsewhere and embraced the principle of intellectual freedom.

## *The Muslim Brotherhood*

The first movement in Egypt that may be called fundamentalist arose in response to these interlocking threats of Westernization and the erosion of Islam. Hasan al-Banna (1906–1949), a teacher at an elementary school in Ismailiyya, mocked the traditionalist ulama even as he berated them for abandoning the defense of Islam to enjoy the procurements offered by the state system. If Islam were to go under, he warned, al-Azhar and its privileged functionaries would lose their endowments as well. In 1928 al-Banna founded the Muslim Brotherhood, an organization that reflected his own unique intellectual and moral development.

The influences on al-Banna's personal development were diverse, and like many fundamentalist leaders after him, he synthesized these various influences into an innovative approach to religion and to social issues. His father, a watchmaker, was also a scholar steeped in the rigorous Hanbalite school of Islamic law. But Hasan al-Banna was formally educated in the state system rather than in Islamic schools attended by religious scholars. Thus he absorbed the strengths, and noted the weaknesses, of the Western-influenced approach to the world. Another major influence on al-Banna came from a brotherhood of Sufis

*Fundamentalist groups like the Muslim Brotherhood in Egypt are often motivated by what they see as the encroachment of Western values into Muslim culture. These young men defiantly dance to American rock music in front of the Mohammed Ali mosque, Egypt's largest.*

(Islamic mystics) which he briefly joined. Their intense piety and religious fervor attracted al-Banna, but his Hanbalite austerity and literalism moved him to repudiate the cultic and pagan elements that had crept into Sufism.

In organizing the Muslim Brotherhood, al-Banna drew upon each of these influences. He grafted Sufi devotional practices (such as the daily recitation of the Qur'an) and membership requirements (like the taking of an oath) onto a program of political activism based in a network of social welfare services. The Brotherhood worked through mosques and recruited from among the ulama, but was not confined to, or defined by, either of these traditional institutions. As with subsequent Sunni fundamentalist movements, the Brotherhood's inner core was composed not of ulama (who were identified with the state and thus with the problem) but of ordinary Muslims who studied the sources of Islam on their own and attempted to put them directly into practice. Al-Banna described the movement as "a Salafiyya message, a Sunni way, a Sufi truth, a political organiza-tion, an athletic group, a cultural-educational union, an economic company, and a social idea."

Al-Banna, like fundamentalists elsewhere, sought to return all things, the state as well as the society, to the control of God. Thus he repudiated the separation of religious and political power as inimical to the principles of pristine Islam. Accordingly, the movement he founded sought to inspire Muslims to live a life of intense observance of the basic principles of Islam as a means of combatting "the wave of atheism and lewdness [that] engulfed Egypt" as part of what he felt was a Western crusade, "more dangerous than the political and military campaigns by far," to corrupt Islam from within. The Europeans had established schools and scientific and cultural institutes, al-Banna observed, "in the very heart of the Islamic domain, which cast doubt and heresy into the souls of its sons and taught them how to demean themselves, disparage their religion and their fatherland, divest themselves of their traditions and beliefs, and to regard as sacred anything Western."[15] Under the aegis of the Muslim Brotherhood, activists formed Islamic countersocieties, published Islamic newspapers, and preached and taught Islamic ethics and social relations to offset the influence of the Europeans.

The movement spread rapidly and by 1935 it had established schools for girls as well as boys, trade schools, and home-based textile industries in over fifty villages and towns in the Nile delta area and in Cairo. Underscoring the principle that Islam is a comprehensive way of life, the Brotherhood built a network of social service institutions that provided direct assistance to displaced rural migrants newly arrived in urban areas. "Such concrete, practical assistance was not available from either the more traditional associations like the Sufi Brother-hoods or the government agencies. The Muslim Brotherhood was perceived as making the effort to meet widespread human needs and grew rapidly in the 1930s."[16]

The formal organization of the Brotherhood rapidly evolved from a small core of people in Ismailiyya and Cairo to a guidance council elected by a consultative assembly, whose members were drawn from regional branches of the expanding movement. Rank and file members worked daily in "battalions" or "families" at the local level. During World War II, as the group was radicalized and became involved in acts of violence, a secret apparatus was created to defend the movement against the police.

## *The Radicalization of the Brotherhood*

By the middle of the twentieth century a generation of Westernized Arab elites in Egypt, Syria, Algeria, and elsewhere had come to enjoy wealth and influence in their respective societies. As Arab countries gained independence from the colonizing powers, they did not thereby automatically discard the powerful colonial institutions and, more importantly, the patterns of education, government, and business established by the Europeans. To the contrary, most Muslim rulers willingly involved their countries in the world financial system—as debtors—and their subjects sought to enjoy the standards of material living commonplace in the West.

The newly independent nations were nonetheless faced with profound questions of identity. Now that the Western tide was receding, they asked: Who are we Egyptians? Whom, or what, do we as Syrians wish to emulate? Should we, as Jordanians, return to the patterns of the Ottoman era? Should a new world be created by drawing upon the best of the West and the East?

The Muslim Brotherhood proposed an Islamic solution to the problem of identity. Al-Banna taught that identity should be rooted not in the nation but in Islam, thereby advocating pan-Islamism in the face of Egyptian nationalism and inspiring the spread of the Muslim Brotherhood into the Sudan, Syria, and the Maghreb. The Brotherhood called for the restoration of the caliphate as a symbol of Islamic unity and dedicated itself to work for a society governed by Islamic law applied systematically and comprehensively to all areas of life.

After World War II the movement reached a peak of influence, with half a million people actively involved and another half-million supporters and sympathizers. The government countered by promoting a new wave of Islamic modernism, personified by the poet and literary critic Taha Husayn (1889–1973), who held that "independent Egypt must become a part of Europe, for that is the only way to become a part of the modern world." In response the Brotherhood attempted to recruit from among the Western-influenced class, thereby shifting the realm of political Islam from the shaykhs to the lawyers, doctors, engineers, pharmacists, and army and police officers. "The Muslim Brotherhood was thus the first Islamic association to appear in modern Egypt with the goal of seizing power," notes Egyptian historian Abdel Azim Ramadan.[17] The Brotherhood established itself on the international front as well, supporting the Palestinian cause against Israel, participating in the 1948 war between Israel and the Arab League, and violently opposing the 1949 armistice agreement.

In 1948, sensing the growing influence and radicalization of the Brotherhood, Egyptian Prime Minister Nuqrashi Pasha struck a preemptive blow by attempting to dissolve the organization and detaining its most important leaders. This initiative led to his assassination by Brotherhood radicals; in retaliation, Hasan al-Banna himself was murdered. His successor as Supreme Guide of the Brotherhood, Hasan al-Hudaybi, supported the military officers of the July Revolution, only to break with them when they came to power in 1952 and dissolved the Brotherhood shortly thereafter. The conflict reached a climax when the Brotherhood attempted, unsuccessfully, to assassinate Egypt's new president, Gamal Abdul Nasser, who ordered a thorough suppression of the Brotherhood and imprisoned hundreds of its leaders.

One of those imprisoned leaders, the former modernist literary critic Sayyid Qutb, had been converted to radical Islam after a disheartening two-year visit to the United States (1948–50). Qutb derived many ideas from the seminal Pakistani fundamentalist thinker Maulana Abul Ala Maududi (1903–79). Maududi's influence on Qutb and other Sunni Muslim fundamentalists was indeed enormous. Founder of the Jamaat-i-Islami, an Islamic fundamentalist organization in Pakistan with branches throughout South Asia, Maududi was a systematic thinker and a prolific writer, a dynamic orator, a seasoned politician, an astute and indefatigable organization builder, and a charismatic leader who almost single-handedly shaped modern Muslim discourse on the social, economic, and political teachings of Islam. "Maududi gave a new language—a political language—to Islamic discourse," political scientist Mumtaz Ahmad writes. "Terms first used by Maududi, such as 'the Islamic system of life,' 'Islamic ideology,' 'Islamic politics,' 'the Islamic constitution,' 'the economic system of Islam,' and 'the political system of Islam,' became common parlance for Muslim writers and political activists everywhere."[18] Familiar with the issues of modern social science disciplines, Maududi plumbed the Qur'an and Hadith in order to construct a system entailing Islamic law and political theory, Islamic economic and social relations, and Islamic philosophy and culture. He then presented this Islamic system as an ideological alternative to both Western liberalism and Soviet Marxism. Translated into all the major languages of the world, Maududi's books were and are widely read in most Muslim countries.

Qutb studied Maududi's concept of *iqamat-i-deen* (the establishment of religion)—the total subordination of the institutions of civil society and the state to the authority of the Shari'a. In the process of formulating his ideas on Islamic ideology, Maududi was greatly impressed by the then-emerging methods and organizational strategies, if not the ideologies, of communism and fascism. "His frequent references in his writings to the ideological purity, organizational discipline, and ascetic character of the communist and fascist movements seem quite consistent with the way he later proceeded to organize his own party," Ahmad writes. "Maududi came to the conclusion that the best way to transform a society was to create a small, informed, dedicated, and highly disciplined group which would work to assume social and political leadership." In August 1941, Maududi founded the Jamaat-i-Islami to give institutional shape to his ideas on the reconstruction of Muslim society based on Islamic principles and to prepare and train a cadre of Islamic workers who could act as a vanguard of an Islamic revolutionary movement.

Qutb adopted the notion of *saleh jamaat* (a righteous group), or a "holy minority," that would one day capture political power and construct the Islamic system in its entirety. He began his own program by establishing the need for such a radical approach. Qutb turned Western philosophy and culture against itself: drawing on the writings of cultural critics like Arnold Toynbee and Alexis

Carrel, he found ample documentation for his charge that Western culture offered only unbridled individualism and moral depravity. In his view Westernized Egyptian society was "the most dangerous jahiliyya which has ever menaced our faith," as he argued in the popular *Signposts on the Road* (1964). "For everything around is jahiliyya: perceptions and beliefs, manners and morals, culture, art, and literature, laws and regulations, including a good part of what we consider Islamic culture." Such a diagnosis of West-induced ills was not new, but the medicine Qutb prescribed was. To throw off the yoke of jahiliyya, nothing less than a jihad, an Islamic holy war, must be mounted.

The notion of a revolution against the state was anathema to mainstream Sunnism, which had long ago tied its fortunes to the ruling order. Qutb's profound influence on his own and later generations of radical fundamentalists stemmed from the fact that he succeeded in articulating the theological foundations for such a revolt in terms acceptable in mainstream Sunni thought. In addition to plumbing the Islamic sources for passages congenial to his views, Qutb accomplished this interpretive feat by making a selective retrieval of the writings of the great medieval theologian Ibn Taymiyya, whose orthodoxy and moral authority (and austerity) were beyond question. Ibn Taymiyya was not quite an obvious choice; although he had harshly and consistently criticized the thirteenth-century Mamluk empire for its laxity and corruption, he never called for its overthrow. Therefore, Qutb turned to Ibn Taymiyya's lesser known polemics against the Mongols, "barbarians" who had overrun Syria, but who had converted to Sunnism. Ibn Taymiyya offered the radical opinion that reciting the profession of faith was insufficient to establish membership in the *umma* (universal Islamic community): the Mongols were "deviants," not only because they continued to violate the sexual and behavioral codes of Islamic law, but because, in Ibn Taymiyya's judgment, a Sunni ruler becomes illegitimate if he does not apply a substantial part of the Shari'a in his realm.[19]

Reasoning from this principle and by analogy, Qutb concluded that the devout Muslim had no duty to obey the illegitimate rulers of twentieth-century Egypt, where "the Shari'a is not the sole source of all legislation." This, Qutb said, was the major divergence between the regime he proposed and the Egyptian regime.[20] For these opinions he paid with his life in 1965, but his influence spread after his death. During the presidency of Anwar Sadat in the 1970s, Qutb's disciples came from the growing pool of disaffected young Egyptians whose path of upward mobility had been blocked by corruption, mismanagement, and malaise in the Egyptian economy.

## The Islamic Current in Egypt in the 1990s

Today the Mubarak government's policy toward "the Islamic current" is carefully calibrated in an attempt to prevent the radical fundamentalists from gaining influence with the traditional centers of Sunni Islam, which in turn are believed to influence public opinion. The Mubarak policy has been largely successful to this point, although because of the extremes with which it is dealing the government has sometimes appeared slightly schizophrenic in its relation to Islam. On 26 December 1991, for example, a government court, apparently motivated by the political desire to uphold the regime's image as defender of the faith, sentenced the novelist Alla Hamed, his publisher, and a book distributor to eight years in prison. Just as the Ayatollah Khomeini had done in the case of Salman Rushdie, the Egyptian court declared Hamed's 1988 novel, *A Distance in a Man's Mind*, to be blasphemous; the protagonist's suggestion that Islam is not "for all times and places," the court ruled, "threatened national unity and social peace." Encouraged by the government move, representatives of al-Azhar, the home of the Islamic establishment, impounded a number of "forbidden" books on display at the Cairo International Book Fair, including a treatise on Islam and women's rights and a series of works on the relationship between Islam and politics by Egypt's senior security court judge. Apparently, al-Azhar's putative partner in defending the faith, President Mubarak, found this move to be a bit *too* inspired, for he subsequently intervened to lift the ban on the books. Moderation rather than zeal in upholding Islam remains his policy.[21]

*Approximately one-third of Egypt's mosque preachers are paid by*
*the government, which regularly previews their Friday sermons.*
*As in most Muslim societies, the prayers and sermons are broadcast*
*to the entire neighborhood over speakers mounted on every mosque's*
*minarets, like these on Amr Ibn el Aas, Cairo's oldest mosque.*

By permitting a mild version of "the Islamic current" to hold sway over public perceptions, the Arab secular elites in power in Egypt are taking a calculated risk that may boomerang. They may be encouraging a long-term cultural shift away from secular principles toward a political fundamentalism that seeks to inform every aspect of Egyptian life. Currently Egypt lives with many varieties of Islamic fundamentalism within its borders, and over the course of the forty years since Nasser came to power in 1952, the secularized military state has gradually perfected the fine art of constraining and containing Islamic militancy. This it has done, in the Mubarak years, through a sophisticated (if, as we observed, occasionally schizophrenic) policy combining partial appeasement, co-optation, ruthless repression, constant surveillance and infiltration of radical cells, and a crushing monopoly over the media.

The Muslim Brotherhood today publishes a weekly newspaper, supports the Labor party, and has representatives in the Egyptian Parliament. Since it adopted Islam as an ideology for political and national renewal during the parliamentary elections of 1987, the Labor party has explained its policies according to an Islamic framework and has been at least partially successful in mobilizing public opinion behind these policies. The party has emphasized the role Islam should play in promoting regional cooperation and conflict resolution. Islam as a cultural system, and individual Islamic countries, have sufficient normative and material capabilities to influence the world and shape its destiny. So says Adil Hussein, one of the leading articulators of the Labor party's positions.

Meanwhile, the radical Islamic movement endures, with monthly incidents of firebombs hurled through the windows of liquor stores and bars, unveiled women harassed by young ruffians, and gun battles with one or more of the dozens of clandestine radical splinter groups that reject the moderation of the Muslim Brotherhood. Young Islamic radicals have taken over student organizations at most universities, and constantly denounce what they perceive as the rampant corruption and inefficiency of the ruling party—corruption which is to be expected, they insist, of a ruling elite which long ago abandoned Islam.

Indeed, the two recent seismic shifts in the political terrain of the Arab world—the display of Arab disunity during the 1990–91 Gulf crisis and the dismantling of the Soviet patron state—have placed "the Arab problem" in bold relief for the secularized elites who have ruled the Arab nations for decades through the apparatuses of a modern security state. With Marxist socialism in ruins, with the myth of Arab nationalism exposed as hollow after the defeat of Nasser in the 1967 war with Israel, and with the hopes for genuine pan-Arabism recently broken with the eclipse of the Ba'th party as a unifying force beyond the borders of Syria or Iraq, secular Arab rulers, whose power is based exclusively on military might, find themselves bereft of authenticating ideologies to bolster their sagging regimes.

For these reasons the tentative moves toward liberalization and democratization in the late 1980s seemed to some observers to be little more than a last-ditch effort to retain effective control of civil society. Under pressure from the West and from internal opponents, the ruling elites in Egypt, Jordan, and Algeria (and, haltingly, even Kuwait, which reportedly ended government censorship of newspapers in the wake of the Gulf war) embarked cautiously on a road of reform that proved perilous whenever the adaptable fundamentalists were allowed, however briefly, to play and win at the democratic game, as they did in Algeria from 1988 until 1992, when the secular government cracked down on the Islamic Salvation Front and cancelled the elections that would likely have brought the fundamentalist party to power.

# The Contemporary Proliferation of Islamic Fundamentalist Movements

As we have seen, there are many different manifestations of the fundamentalist program to implement the Shari'a as the comprehensive basis for state and society. The possibilities range, in the case of Egypt alone, from the revolutionary violence of the radical cells to the mainstream politics of the new Muslim Brotherhood. These various programs share both a critical attitude toward the values of Western-style modernization and a basic approach to the foundational sources of Islam. Fundamentalists see these sources as providing a blueprint for contemporary society, the specifications of which may be drawn from the political situation in any given country, as well as the repertoire of instrumental possibilities offered by modern science and technology rightly applied.

This range of fundamentalist strategies is on display in the 1990s as fundamentalist movements prosper in an expansive geographic arc stretching from Western Africa across the Maghreb into the Middle East, and extending toward the republics of Central Asia and across the Indian subcontinent into Southeast Asia. Compelling evidence of the vitality of political Islam is found not only in this impressive swath of the Earth, but also in Europe, where non-Muslim societies are increasingly "threatened," or so many of their leading politicians feel, by the influx of Muslim immigrants, many of whom gather in enclaves seemingly ripe for the growth of Islamic countercultural movements.

These movements frighten many Western observers. Their very tenacity and ferocity in the face of overwhelming odds is daunting to the Westerner who prefers his or her religion mild and nonthreatening. And, at this moment in history, Islamic fundamentalisms seem to be gaining. But the individual movements do not by any means constitute one unified movement; indeed, there is a fierce competition between two fundamentalist patrons for the allegiance of the various regional movements.

# Fundamentalisms in Iran and Saudi Arabia: Two Models for Export

While the Egyptian Muslim Brotherhood spawned Islamic fundamentalist movements in the Sudan, Syria, Palestine, Jordan, and elsewhere, today these erstwhile satellites are increasingly independent if not entirely autonomous, and they are almost all in need of an ideological and organizational sponsor. In the 1990s the two main rivals for hegemony over the world of political Islam are the Islamic Republic of Iran, established after the Shi'ite-led revolution of 1978–79, and the Kingdom of Saudi Arabia, the oldest fundamentalist regime, dating back to the eighteenth-century alliance between the Wahhabis and Prince Ibn Sa'ud.

One might expect that the Iranian Shi'ites would be much more successful in influencing other Shi'ite groups such as the hostage-taking *Hizbullah* (Party of God) in Lebanon (which it has funded and supplied with arms and personnel), while the Saudis would hold sway over fellow Sunnis. To an extent this has been true. But in the 1990s there have been some surprising alliances, such as the one between Iran and the Sudan, based on shared commitments to a revolutionary style of Islamic activism that does not sit well with the conservative fundamentalist Sunni establishment of Saudi Arabia. The Sudan has been able to tap both sources: Iran has sent military advisors, 2,000 Revolutionary Guards, and President Hashemi Rafsanjani (for a diplomatic visit), while radical groups collect money in Saudi Arabia for jihad against the Christian-dominated Sudanese south.[22]

Iran's revolutionary model proceeds directly from the unique historical experiences of Shi'ite Muslims and the theological concepts developed from them. One of these is the notion that Shi'ites are destined to be the oppressed of the earth until the justice that was originally denied them is restored with the return of a messiah figure known as the Hidden Imam (the twelfth imam, or religious leader who went into hiding in 930).

The most powerful symbol of the Shi'ite religious experience of injustice was the murder of the third imam of the Shi'ites, Husayn 'Ali, the grandson of the Prophet. In 680 he journeyed to Kerbala in southern Iraq to protest the ascension of the Umayyad ruler to the caliphate. There Husayn and his family and friends were killed by Umayyad troops. His martyrdom is annually commemorated at Ashura rituals of mourning throughout the Shi'ite world—rituals which the Ayatollah Khomeini and his followers used as platforms for the dissemination of their revolutionary message in the 1970s.

For the greater part of Shi'ite history, the memory of Kerbala was expressed through a tradition of political quietism among the Shi'ite minority. In planning his return to Iran after exile by the Shah, however, Ayatollah Khomeini selected carefully from among the plethora of doctrines, practices, and interpretations available in the Shi'ite tradition. Following the twentieth-century philosopher Ali Shari'ati, Khomeini reinterpreted and developed the long-neglected Shi'ite doctrine of the "guardianship of the jurist" so as to support absolutist, theocratic rule in Iran. Thus, as Abdulaziz Sachedina comments, the Shi'ite fundamentalists' "retrieval of relevant teachings that would enable them to build an Islamic system adaptable to modern circumstances is selective. . . . [T]heir fundamentalism can be designated as an activist type of reaction involving creative interpretation of religious ideas and symbols to render them applicable to contemporary Muslim history."[23]

In ruling postrevolutionary Islam, Khomeini was intent upon bringing the society into conformity with what he perceived to be the full scope of the Shari'a, including the imposition of its penalties for adultery, theft, and other criminal acts. The death sentence that Khomeini pronounced against Salman Rushdie, the Pakistani expatriate, British citizen, and former Muslim, was scandalous to Western sensibilities, but it clearly reflected the world as seen through the eyes of a Muslim *marja'-i-taqlid*, a "source of imitation," who believed himself to be the Supreme Jurist, obligated to govern the Islamic Republic in the absence of the Hidden Imam. By Khomeini's reckoning Rushdie, the author of *The Satanic Verses,* a novel which included an offensive portrayal of the Prophet, was guilty of apostasy. Such Western notions as the independent sovereignty of Great Britain and the rights of its citizens, including former Muslims, were simply not recognized. Khomeini acted on faith—a faith shared by millions of Muslims who have perpetuated the calumny on Rushdie long after the Ayatollah's passing from the scene. This shared faith remains a legitimating principle for putatively Islamic regimes, as well as for the post-Khomeini Islamic Republic of Iran.

Khomeini was also intent on exporting his brand of fundamentalism to the rest of the Islamic world, which he felt had too long been under the sway of Saudi Arabia, the other major patron of Islamic political movements. As we have seen, Wahhabi fundamentalism did not develop, as did later fundamentalisms, in opposition to Western modernization. The alliance between the political and religious leaders that made Saudi Arabia viable as an Islamic state allowed the religious elite to enjoy a relatively stable existence there. This state of affairs was a good thing in a land so rich with oil, governed by Islamic law, and home to the holy cities of Medina and Mecca, the latter being the most sacred site in Islam and the destination of hundreds of thousands of Muslim pilgrims making the *hajj* annually. In short, the Saudi kings and shaykhs desired to preserve the status quo in their land while propagating the spread of Islamic fundamentalism elsewhere.

That policy became complicated, however, after the revolution in Iran legitimated and popularized an anti-Western animus that came to be identified with Islam itself. Although the Saudi monarchy referred to itself as "custodian of the Holy Places," many Muslims believed that a cozy relationship with the United States rendered that claim hypocritical. Muammar Qaddafi of Libya accused the Saudis of defiling the holy places by allowing their American-made military aircraft to fly in the air space above Mecca and Medina, and called for the internationalization of the holy cities. Ayatollah Khomeini, in his last will and testament, mocked the efforts of the Saudis in distributing copies of the Qur'an throughout the world and called Wahhabism an "aggressive sect that leads unsuspecting people to be controlled by the superpowers, whose aim is to destroy true Islam."[24]

The Iranians also used the occasion of the pilgrimage, or hajj, to advance their notions of Islamic revolution. This inspired agitation in Riyadh, and the stage was set for the often violent confrontations of the past decade. Small Iranian demonstrations occurred in the pilgrimage of 1980, but in 1981 and 1982 there were serious clashes between Iranian pilgrims and the Saudi security forces. In 1986, Iranian pilgrims who were thought to be importing arms were arrested and prevented from undertaking the hajj. The 1987 pilgrimage, however, proved the most violent, with 402 pilgrims killed and Saudi Arabia and Iran blaming each other for the deaths.

Although Iran formally boycotted the hajj after 1987, there were explosions during the 1989 pilgrimage, and in 1990 the Saudi reputation suffered further damage when over fourteen hundred pilgrims were crushed to death in a tunnel. The Lebanese movement Hizbullah spoke of "a new massacre," and Iran referred darkly to a "criminal conspiracy" and called for the Saudis to be stripped of their custodianship of the holy places.[25] In the Gulf crisis of 1990–1991 even the lifelong secularist Saddam Hussein, newly clad in the robes of Islam, was able to argue that the land containing the holy cities of Mecca and Medina had, like Palestine, fallen prey to occupation. He spoke of the need to liberate Mecca, "hostage of the Americans," from troops of the Western-led coalition.

Perhaps the most serious outcome of the Gulf crisis for the Saudis, however, was that it inspired the emergence of radical, anti-Western fundamentalist groups within Saudi Arabia itself. During the war the Saudis were careful to secure a fatwa from Shaykh Bin Baz which sanctioned the presence of "diverse nationalities among the Muslims and others for the resistance of aggression and the defense of the country." The council of senior religious officials also specifically endorsed King Falud's decision to allow foreign troops into the country and said that the Shari'a required both that the Muslim ruler be prepared to defend Muslim land and that he "seek the help of whoever has the power that enables them to perform the task." Another fatwa in January 1991 sanctioned the use of force against the Iraqis and declared the battle against Saddam a jihad. Non-Muslim soldiers had an important role to play in defeating "the enemy of God." Some religious scholars felt that the presence of Western troops violated the moral integrity of the holy peninsula and that the foreigners harbored their own nefarious goals. In May 1991 a large number of ulama gave a detailed memorandum to the King outlining a comprehensive program of reform and calling for the creation of a *majlis al-shura,* or consultative assembly, whose members would be chosen according to competence, and not according to rank or sex, for

"Islamization" of the judiciary, military, economy, and media, and for abstention from all "non-Islamic pacts and treaties."[26]

In February 1992 the King acceded to this request, reportedly as one way of heading off the growing influence of the radical underground. As a result of this debacle, however, the Saudis set themselves squarely against revolutionary Islam and discontinued or reduced funding to many radical groups throughout the Muslim world.

## *Rising Movements*

Despite the tumult introduced into the world of Islamic fundamentalism by the Gulf crisis, Sunni and Shiʻite movements alike are on the rise in the Islamic world. In Afghanistan, for example, the four Sunni fundamentalist parties and several smaller Shiʻite groups "won" the thirteen-year war waged first against the occupying army of the Soviet Union and then against Soviet-backed President Najibullah, who resigned on 18 April 1992. This victory, coming as it did after Pakistan suspended aid to the rebels and at a time when many observers had been predicting that the revolutionary movement might collapse, was a testimony to the endurance and zeal of men and women who fight for what they see as an absolute cause. Afghan tribalism and its factional tendencies were momentarily transcended in a joint military operation conducted for the sake of Islam. Indeed, the Afghan War is the first war since World War II in which Soviet troops were defeated. It is the first liberation war won by a movement which proclaims Islam, not nationhood or socialism, as its goal.

Although the Mujahidin, or Muslim fighters, seek a state governed by Shariʻa, they do not fit the mold of Islamic movements elsewhere and thus demonstrate something of the diverse possibilities when radical Islam becomes politicized. The resistance movement was based on an unlikely alliance of the young, educated, urban laymen and the traditional segment of Afghan society, mobilized by the traditionalist ulama under the banner of an Islamic jihad. The Islamic resistance in Afghanistan was thus an amalgam of forces; in the words of Olivier Roy, "it was at the same time a war of liberation, a traditional jihad, and

*Among the enemies targeted by radical Islamists are the Jews in Israel. At the fundamentalist Philistine mosque in Gaza, this preacher inveighs against Western and Jewish culture: "One day the rock and the tree will rise up and announce 'There is a Jew under me; kill him.'"*

a modern revolutionary movement to establish an Islamic State."[27] By August 1992 this unlikely alliance had fully collapsed as Afghanistan was once again plunged into civil war, this time between rival Islamic factions.

The fortunes of the Palestinian fundamentalist group Hamas also seemed to be rising in 1992, in the aftermath of Iraq's defeat in the Gulf war of 1990–91 and the collapse of the Soviet Union—both powers had supported Hamas's secular rival, the Palestine Liberation Organization. Hamas violently opposes negotiations with Israel and is committed to the liberation of Palestine through the escalation of the intifada.

The Muslim Brotherhood preceded Hamas as the Islamic movement in the territories of the West Bank and Gaza occupied by Israel after the 1967 Six Day War, but the Brotherhood did not confront the Israeli army and focused its energies instead on establishing a large social welfare network in the Gaza Strip. There Shaykh Ahmad Yasin emerged as a charismatic and influential leader; his Islamic Assembly infiltrated the mosques and the Islamic University. But on the West Bank, in spite of the spread of religious associations, the Brotherhood failed to establish a network or to identify a viable leader.

Only with the appearance of groups described by the generic term Islamic Jihad in 1983, groups that made struggle against Israel their central religious duty, did Islam become integral to the politics of the occupied territories. In the process, the Muslim Brotherhood itself, from whom the members of Jihad were recruited, was radically transformed—or, one might say, returned to its militant roots. Islamic Jihad was inspired by the writings of Sayyid Qutb and by the example of the Shi'ite revolution in Iran. In 1986 and 1987, through a series of anti-Israeli guerrilla operations, Islamic Jihad played an important role in inciting the intifada, which quickly became organized through local and regional committees of Hamas. While Jihad declined, Hamas has operated within the occupied territories from the early days of the uprising. In February 1988 the Muslim Brotherhood formally adopted Hamas as its militant arm and made the liberation of Palestine in its entirety—"from the [Jordan] river to the sea"—its new priority.[28]

During the Gulf crisis the leadership of Hamas was caught between public opinion favorable to Saddam Hussein on the one hand, and its financial dependence on the Gulf states on the other. Through a cautious policy it managed not to alienate either "constituency" and emerged from the Gulf crisis in a position of greater strength relative to the PLO.

In neighboring Jordan, to take a third example of Islamic fundamentalism "on the rise," the Muslim Brotherhood, established there in 1934, now forms the largest single block in Parliament. The Brotherhood achieved this prominence with the reluctant support of King Hussein, who announced in April 1989 that the first elections in twenty-two years would be held the following November.

The King was responding to a general economic crisis precipitated by decades of economic mismanagement. Popular outrage at the level of court corruption led to the outbreak of five days of serious disturbances. The riots seemed to call for drastic measures, and the King decided to initiate a process of democratization in Jordan. "Islam is the Solution" proclaimed the campaign banners of the Brotherhood, which took thirty-four out of the eighty seats in Parliament in the November election. (Twenty-two of those seats were won by the Muslim Brotherhood and the remaining twelve by Islamic independents.)

The Gulf crisis precipitated by Iraq's invasion of Kuwait afforded the new Muslim parliamentarians an occasion to flex their political muscles. On 18 January 1991 Parliament issued a statement declaring:

> We salute Iraq's refusal to go along with American demands and ask it to play its historic role in resisting the great Satan who is threatening every Arab country and belief. . . . God will decree victory for the Iraqi people and humiliation for all enemies of God and humanity. Tell those infidels they will be overcome and cast into the furnace of hell.[29]

The long-standing antipathy of various Islamic movements toward the West was exacerbated now by the deployment of Western forces in the arena of conflict. The rhetoric of Muslims in Jordan's Parliament approximated that of radical leaders in the streets, including Shaykh Abu Zant, who was quoted as declaring:

> This battle is not between Iraq and America but between Islam and the Crusaders. . . . It is not between Saddam and Bush but between the infidel leaders and the Prophet of Islam. . . . Why is Iraq the focus? Because the Zionists and American enemies don't wish to see the Arabs or Muslims possess any power that can stand against Israel. . . . The Saudis have lost their credentials as Muslims by allowing foreign forces to come to our Holy Land, which only God can protect! They have brought the Americans, and what the Americans have brought to the Holy Land is V.D. and AIDS.[30]

Popular resentment increased against the American role in the war after U.S. air attacks on Jordanian truck convoys traveling Iraqi roads. In another example of the delicate political balancing act for which he is famous, King Hussein awarded the Brotherhood with five cabinet seats in January 1991. The Muslim Brotherhood and Islamic bloc members of Parliament urged the King to side openly with Iraq in the war. Relations with the United States reached an all-time low, and the King's speeches became more pro-Iraqi in tone and earned a strong rebuke from President Bush. The American aid program to Jordan came under review in Washington.

While ultimately dependent on the King as the fulcrum of the political system, Islamic activists were a formidable political force in their own right. They enjoyed control of Jordanian mosques, schools, and social welfare centers, from which they were able both to respond to the currents of popular disquiet and to shape it. Furthermore, the Muslim Brotherhood's control of the ministries of education, religious affairs, health, and social development from January to June 1991 provided it with an ideal opportunity to enhance its domestic profile and consolidate its power over grass-roots supporters.

Like many other Islamic activists currently on the rise, however, the Muslim Brothers in Jordan proved themselves to be superb protestors but absurd rulers. They refined the art of social and political criticism and deferred to no other group or movement in their ability to organize mass demonstrations, but they have not been able to articulate a coherent domestic program—much less a viable international policy. In Jordan, their desire to control the social order sparked a heated debate in Jordan's secular community after a series of Brotherhood rulings affecting the segregation of the sexes in the workplace, banning fathers from watching daughters in school sports, and ordering prayers (in which America is attacked) in state schools. "The basic issue underlying [these] episodes is the nature of democratic life in Jordan and the relationship between the majority and the minority," writes Beverley Milton-Edwards. "Many secular-minded Jordanians, particularly in the middle classes, have felt imposed upon by the Islamists, and the debate over the rules of the game that is behind such tension remains basically unresolved as Jordan travels down the road of democratization."[31]

Having encouraged popular dissatisfaction without contributing to a solution of Jordan's manifest economic and political difficulties, the Brotherhood seemed to squander the momentum it gained during the Gulf crisis. King Hussein removed members from the cabinet, for example, after they alienated a majority of the Jordanian public and when they opposed his decision to participate in peace talks with Israel.

Nonetheless the Islamic activists are increasing their political presence and power in all sectors of society. In June 1991, for example, they won control over the executive board of yet another of Jordan's professional associations. And although the National Charter approved by King Hussein in 1991 mandates a multiparty system, provides for greater rights for women, and enhances the freedom of the press, it also declares that the Shari'a will be the source of all law in the country. This may be a sufficient opening for greater Islamic political activism in the future.

## *New Horizons*

In other parts of the Middle East, political Islam is or has been under tight supervision or control. However, the collapse of the Soviet Union, the defeat of Saddam Hussein, and the initiation of peace talks in the Middle East have contributed to a changing world order in which political forces are realigning and tribal forces that would reshape national boundaries are enjoying new opportunities for influence. In this situation the possibility exists that the 1990s will witness the rise of newly vital movements: in Libya, where unstructured Islamic groups, who clash frequently with state security forces, are the greatest internal threat to Qaddafi's regime; in Syria, where the Muslim Brotherhood has residual support despite having been outlawed and ruthlessly repressed; and in North Africa, where the secular governments of Algeria, Tunisia, and Morocco have struggled to contain burgeoning Islamic groups.

In Iraq, organized clandestine Shi'ite movements of opposition to the regime have existed since the Islamic Da'wa (Call) party was established in

*A veiled woman walks along a street in Algeria under graffiti reading "Soon the Islamic state!"* (Agence France-Presse)

October 1957 in Najaf by Ayatollah Muhammad Baqir al-Sadr (born in 1933 and executed by the Ba'thist authorities in April 1980). To date, this is one of the two most important political organizations among the fundamentalist Shi'ite opposition groups, the other being the Supreme Assembly for the Islamic Revolution in Iraq (SAIRI), which came into being in November 1982 in Tehran and is heavily dependent on financial and other Iranian government support. Since the mid-1980s SAIRI has been recruiting Iraqi exiles and Iraqi prisoners of war to its regular army unit; its sources claimed during the Gulf war that they could easily mobilize fifty or even a hundred thousand fighters outside and inside of Iraq when the time came to strike at Saddam and his henchmen.

While the exact sizes of the various movements are difficult to gauge, their aims are clear. In essence, they all believe that Iraq should become an Islamic republic, similar (though not necessarily identical) to Iran, and they make it clear that they will not tolerate the continuation of traditional Sunni supremacy in Iraq. Even though they accept Western science and technology, all the Shi'ite fundamentalist movements are committed to combating Western (or "imperialist" and sometimes "Christian" or "Crusader") cultural, economic, and other influences in the region.[32] Faced with various scenarios in 1991, as it became clear that the Iraqi military machine was defeated by the allied forces and that Saddam

Hussein could be toppled, many state department strategists in Washington seemed to prefer envisioning a crippled Saddam Hussein in power to a Shi'ite regime presumably funded and supported by Iran. The latter remains a possibility in the eventual absence of Saddam.

Perhaps the most important contest for Muslim allegiances being waged today, however, is taking place between Iran, Saudi Arabia, and Turkey over the resource- and technology-rich republics of Central Asia—lands which some observers are already referring to collectively as "Islamistan." Independent Azerbaijan, Uzbekistan, Kirgizstan and Tajikistan are experiencing an Islamic revival in the absence of Soviet religious repression, but the fundamentalist Islamic Renaissance Party has failed to this point to mount an organized mass movement in any of the republics. The fortunes of fundamentalist Islam as a worldwide political movement that is capable of directing material as well as spiritual development may rise or fall with its success in rallying Muslims in these regions.

In May 1992, Hassan al-Turabi, head of the fundamentalist National Islamic Front in the Sudan, appeared for a series of closed meetings in Washington, D.C., to proclaim, among other things, that fundamentalist Islam is indeed a worldwide political movement on the rise. "The Islamic awakening began as a spiritual, an individual event, but it has become increasingly political," he said. "We have not yet translated everything into new forms and programs. But the blueprint is emerging."[33] To those who criticize the Islamic fundamentalist leadership as politically ineffectual, Dr. Turabi responded by acknowledging that the various programs of Islamization in the Middle East and North Africa are "in the first stages of a process that will unfold for a long time to come." Is it a surprise that we must learn how to govern effectively, he asked rhetorically, after being kept from real power during the colonial period?[34]

For his Washington appearances Dr. Turabi wore a pinstriped business suit in place of his customary garb, the traditional flowing white robe and half-foot-high turban. He described himself as a unique type of Muslim activist poised to lead the Islamic movement into a new era. Indeed, Dr. Turabi, a walking synthesis of traditional Islamic learning and Western, post-Enlightenment sophistication, is an exemplar of the late-twentieth-century Muslim fundamentalist charismatic

*A Muslim district in Paris. France is now home to an estimated four million Muslims. The spread of Islam into Western Europe has given rise in some quarters to a new wave of xenophobia and, among the Muslim immigrants, to an "enclave mentality." A radical reassertion of Islamic identity is one way of protecting the family from persecution, disintegration, or assimilation to a foreign or secular culture.*

leader. An elegant Sudanese legal scholar and philosopher with advanced degrees from the University of London and the Sorbonne, he languished in prison for a number of years in the Sudan, which afforded him the opportunity, he says, to read more in the Qur'an and the schools of Islamic law than any jurist alive. This experience gave him a vantage point from which to lead a return to Islam "as a comprehensive way of life," and to inspire the movement to "renew religion as a broad base from which to integrate society." The "Islamic Awakening," he said, will ultimately transcend the ethnic, tribal, and national lines that currently divide and weaken Muslims (in Africa and elsewhere); the West will simply have to learn to live with this new and growing power bloc.

Dr. Turabi is widely regarded as the de facto power in the Sudan, where a militant Islamic government nominally led by General Omar Hassan al-Bashir seized control in a 1989 coup. Since then, according to Amnesty International and other human rights groups, the government has tortured political dissidents and engaged in other systematic violations of human rights.[35] Despite these

charges, which he dismisses as the result of occasional excesses that are un-
avoidable in revolutionary movements, al-Turabi presents himself as an exponent
of a moderate Islamic fundamentalism, in which the application of Islamic law
will be conducted with respect for individual dignity and property, and with
respect for the rights of women and minorities. Islamic fundamentalism serves to
unite Muslims in a powerful bloc that overcomes the weaknesses in the current
electoral process in the Sudan, where, he claims, political parties have been little
more than ethnic and tribal groupings, ultimately ineffective in leading the nation
down the path of development and modernization.

When pressed on the details of the Islamic blueprint for societies, however,
Dr. Turabi speaks from the tradition of Hasan al-Banna and Sayyid Qutb, arguing
that the "establishment religious scholars" of Islam have become corrupted;
accordingly, he says, the role of religious adjudication must be subordinated to
the popular will. Dr. Turabi warned, however, that Western notions of democracy
cannot be taken as the model for self-rule in Islamic nations, which are ultimately
governed by Qur'anic principles of consensus. Al-Turabi's critics, who are
growingly apprehensive about the trend toward Islamic governments, charge that
the same may be said of the Islamic fundamentalist understanding of human rights
in the context of the Shari'a.

# Conclusion

Muslim fundamentalists of various stripes do seek to establish the Shari'a as the
explicit, comprehensive, and exclusive legal basis for society—a goal not shared
by the vast majority of Muslims. The renewed commitment to this long-standing
fundamentalist goal, strengthened immeasurably by the current proliferation of
Islamic movements in the Middle East and in South, Central, and Southeast Asia,
comes at a time when other ideological systems are perceived as bankrupt and
none but Islam is accepted as a total and integrative way of life. Thus the rise and
salience of Islamic fundamentalism may be considered as part of a worldwide
quest for authenticity and for a stable communal and personal identity in an age

of "high modernity." In the concluding chapter we will discuss the processes of high modernity, processes which threaten to erode self-defining differences between peoples and which have led to "new tribalisms" in many parts of the world.

It may be said at this juncture, however, that the general commitment to the implementation of Islamic law across the board does not lead all Muslim fundamentalists down the same path. Like any complex legal code developed over time, the Shari'a admits of many interpretations and diverse applications, each of which is unavoidably selective. Even Muslims who would be considered progressives by any Western standard have styled themselves as fundamentalists dedicated to the proper interpretation and application of the Shari'a.

University of Khartoum professor Akmed An Na'im, a leader of an Islamic reform movement in the Sudan called the Republican Brothers, argues, for example, that a fundamentalist retrieval of Islamic law may be reconcilable with Western notions of human rights in civil society. Imprisoned without charge in 1984 by Sudanese President Numiery, a self-proclaimed fundamentalist, An Na'im protested that Numiery's brand of Islamic fundamentalism, shared by other Islamic radicals in the Middle East, was a mistaken attempt to impose the Shari'a as an antidote to Western neocolonialism and cultural domination. He argued that the elements of Shari'a invoked by Numiery (and Khomeini)—the prescriptions revealed to Muhammad in Medina dealing with penal law, civil liberties, and the treatment of minorities and women—promoted a "historically dated Islamic self-identity that needs to be reformed." Islamic economic and social justice and the exercise of legitimate political power depend upon the retrieval of the teachings of the Prophet in Mecca, which provide, in An Na'im's judgment, "the moral and ethical foundation" of the tradition. "The Medina message is not the fundamental, universal, eternal message of Islam. That founding message is from Mecca," he writes. "This counter-abrogation [of the Medina code] will result in the total conciliation between Islamic law and the modern development of human rights and civil liberties."[36]

Rare is the disputant in such a conflict who does not claim to be upholding "the fundamentals." Rather, the battle is often over what they are, where they are to be found, how and by whom they are to be interpreted. In demanding the retrieval of the Mecca prophecy, An Na'im concludes, "we [Republican Brothers] are the *super-fundamentalists*."

The possibility of a "progressive" fundamentalism in power does not ensure, of course, the existence of one. If the fundamentalists do eventually come to power in Algeria, for example, they may or may not behave in accord with the best interests of either the West or the Algerian people. But there is more than one way to implement Islamic law. The situation may allow, or necessitate, the kind of shrewd compromise with secular governments and economies that has characterized the "conservative fundamentalist" monarchy in Saudi Arabia. Or the situation in Algeria may eventually approximate that of Egypt, in which lip service, public ceremony, co-opted senior ulama, and occasional deferential rulings of government (that is, secular) courts serve as a panacea in lieu of the actual implementation of the Islamic law. Whatever route the Islamic activists take in North Africa, or Central Asia, or in the dakwah movements of Southeast Asia, one can be sure that they will proclaim themselves to be the genuine defenders of the fundamentals of Islam in the twentieth century.

*CHAPTER FIVE*

# THE SPIRIT OF FUNDAMENTALISM

The study of modern religious fundamentalisms reveals a great deal about the world in which we live. In what follows we lift up and examine themes implied in the previous chapters as a way of reflecting upon the lessons that fundamentalisms offer to people who would better understand religion in the modern world, and to people who are more generally concerned with the effects of modernity on society and culture.

From our survey of fundamentalisms in Christianity, Judaism, and Islam, it is clear that each fundamentalist group or movement is in many ways like *any* social movement driven to seek political power. Thus fundamentalist movements attract their fair share of scurrilous types, people who are simply vengeful and exploitative. They also attract people who are merely insincere, being motivated more by a quest for power, prestige, or wealth than by a commitment to the values espoused by the movement. In these cases religion is seldom more than the latest and perhaps most convenient vehicle for self-aggrandizement or for class revolt. In the latter case, we have noted that fundamentalist movements swelled in numbers under conditions of severe economic and social depression or oppression. Egypt, for example, experienced a pattern in the 1970s and 1980s that was followed throughout much of the Sunni Arab world. Both the Muslim Brotherhood and its radical splinter groups became especially appealing to young men who were stuck in bureaucratic backwaters. Many of these recruits to the

Brotherhood were well-trained engineers who had been educated in a Western-ized, secularized school system and were promised a life of advancement and socioeconomic progress, only to see these hopes dashed in a postindustrial and underdeveloped society. Islam became the solution.[1]

It is equally clear, however, that many fundamentalists—including many of those motivated by economic needs and frustrations—are educated and sophisticated people who are genuinely concerned about the moral, social, political, and economic failures of their respective societies and who believe that the answer lies in a return to religious values and lifestyles. This news may disappoint or frustrate social scientists who long ago wrote religion off as a solution or antidote to social ills, but it is fascinating and even hopeful to those of us nonfundamentalists who agree that society loses something essential to its humanity when it attempts to trivialize or constrain the religious impulse—the impulse to acknowledge the sacred as the deepest source of human identity. Where, then, do fundamentalists succeed in defending religion's "rightful place" in society? And, from the perspective of nonfundamentalists who take religion seriously, where, how, and why do fundamentalists fail?

## The Impact of Fundamentalisms

First it must be said that fundamentalists possess accurate antennae. They picked up long before others did the cultural signals which occasioned their counterat-tacks, like those in defense of the family or of women who are victims of pornography. To Americans troubled by the growth of a morally impoverished (and armed) youth subculture of a permanent underclass in the United States, for example, the analysis of the "New Morality" by Christian fundamentalist Bob Jones, Jr., may not sound as hysterical today as it did in 1968, when he warned of "the debilitating philosophy of permissiveness" that would make people "take sin for granted" and cause us eventually to look upon hedonism, pornography, excessive materialism, and blind ambition not as the means of corruption but "as a way of life that we must accept."[2]

*American fundamentalists profess bafflement that such a permissive society would bar them from praying in public schools.* (By permission of Doug Marlette and Creators Syndicate)

Fundamentalists' antennae also pick up signals of corruption and approaching doom in Israel, where the shrewd polemics of Gush Emunim rabbis appeal to Jews who worry that Judaism is being or has been replaced by secular Zionism as the "glue" that cements ethnic and personal identity. In Sunni Egypt and Shi'ite Iran, fundamentalists were among the first to criticize the eclectic process of state building that occurred after independence, when Western models of development were transplanted and adopted uncritically, rather than gradually adapted to people with different historical traditions, experiences, and values. People who are concerned about the future course of developing societies could do worse than to study the cultural criticism found in the sermons and tracts of fundamentalist leaders.

Of course fundamentalists are not only observers and critics of society's choices; they are also activists who propose alternative choices grounded in their religious worldviews. Much of the renewed attention, favorable and unfavorable, given to religion in the United States in the 1970s and 1980s was in large part inspired by fundamentalists' attempts to move into the mainstream of public debate. Gush Emunim–style fundamentalism occurred in the context of a general return to Judaism by segments of the Israeli population in the euphoria following the 1967 Six Day War. The Kookists who would later form Gush Emunim played upon, advanced, and some would say, exploited the renewed sense of national-ethnic-religious pride following the stunning victory of Israel over its Arab adversaries.

While American Christianity made a comeback of sorts after its temporary eclipse in the 1960s, and while Israeli rabbis struggled to preserve Judaism as a religious as well as an ethnic identification, Islam never really fell from its status as the cultural force that bequeaths legitimacy on governments in the Middle East, North Africa, parts of South Asia, and Indonesia and Malaysia. Islamic symbols and rhetoric have been appropriated by all parties in the ongoing debate about the pace and direction of modernization and cultural development.

Thus the leaders of the Islamic Salvation Front are not the first Algerians to define the independent Algerian state in Islamic terms. After engineering a coup d'état in 1965, Houari Boumediene, educated at Cairo's al-Azhar University, placed great emphasis on the connection between Islam and Arabization, and the national charter of 1976 depicted Islam as the force behind Algeria's social revolution. In Syria, Iraq, and Egypt secular leaders of the 1950s and beyond legitimated Arab socialism by rooting it in an indigenous Arab Islamic heritage and thus distinguishing it from American capitalism and Soviet communism alike. But the Arab socialists did not attempt to restore an Islamic polity, and Islam was not the central principle but only a component in the national ideology. Allegiance to Islam was seen as a requirement in winning mass support, but the fundamentalists opposing these regimes pointed repeatedly to the fact that the allegiance was nominal; it was, in John Esposito's words, "a controlled use of religion to legitimate government's policies."[3]

Having helped to restore or maintain religion's place in society, do fundamentalists gain widespread acceptance of their programs? The intensity of their protest and the absolutism of their religious language seem to have contradictory effects. On the one hand, secularists and other nonfundamentalists in Egypt, Israel, and the United States do not accept the entire package of metaphysics, religion, and sociocultural criticism presented by fundamentalists; nonfundamentalists also tend to reject the tactics and the condemnations of the more radical fundamentalists. On the other hand, fundamentalists have reminded otherwise apathetic people that great issues demand response. Ironically, anti-pluralist fundamentalists have thereby contributed to the expression of pluralism: their protests have spawned counterprotests by moderate or liberal believers and nonbelievers alike, initiating a wide-ranging and searching debate in the very societies they seek to transform.

In April 1992, for example, Buffalo, New York, was the scene of a mass countermovement organized in response to Operation Rescue, which discovered that it was not the only protest group inspired by an oppositional mentality. The evangelical and fundamentalist Christians, including Roman Catholics, were confronted by abortion rights activists and by the state, which arrested 597 anti-abortion protestors during the two-week "Spring of Life" Operation. (Only 18 abortion rights advocates were jailed.) "We have been extremely effective," said Katherine Spillar of the Feminist Majority Foundation, a group that orchestrated defense plans for the five clinics under siege by Operation Rescue. "They have not accomplished anything."[4] In Israel, a similar dynamic has emerged in response to Jewish fundamentalism. Organizations like Peace Now have grown in numbers and influence in proportion to the perceived strength of the settler movement.

We alluded to the special status of Islam in the cultural and political life of the societies for which it is the majority faith, and it may be appropriate here to see Islam as an exception to the general pattern by which fundamentalists find their niche in pluralist societies. Because North African, Middle Eastern, and many Asian societies derive a sense of shared history, identity, and solidarity from their common Islamic heritage and from the notion of membership in a transnational worldwide *umma*, political Islam has not been a minority movement detached from the cultural mainstream. Instead, as we have seen in the case of Egypt, Islamic fundamentalism draws strength from a more generalized, multilayered revival of religious observance which is evident in increased mosque attendance, the proliferation of religious literature, religious programming in the media, the birth of new Islamic associations and student groups, and the success of dakwah movements such as the ones in Malaysia and Indonesia, which seek to deepen the Islamic identity of the Muslim population. Given these vast social sources of potential support for an "Islamic solution" to endemic social problems, it is little wonder that Islamists have amassed a considerable following for their programs of social reconstruction based on the Shari'a.

However, as we have seen, fundamentalist movements vary significantly within each religious tradition, and so does the nature of fundamentalist activism: not all fundamentalists express their disdain for secular society by breaking the law or by engaging in civil disobedience—especially in the United States, where other avenues of influence are open to dissenters. The Reverend Donald E. Wildmon leads an organization, the American Family Association, that plays by the rules of the game. Using market values and the courts to his advantage, Wildmon has organized Christian boycotts of advertisers who support "morally objectionable" television programs. In 1992 he filed a law suit against the producers of a documentary film on censorship and prevented the broadcast of the film in the United States. And in some notable instances fundamentalist critiques of American society have been acknowledged by opponents on the left. People for the American Way, an organization that often lines up against fundamentalists in the public debate, supports fundamentalist opposition to public school textbooks which overlook religious themes in American and world history and society.

As we mentioned, it is difficult to remain a radical or hard-line fundamentalist in a pluralist and open democratic society—precisely because there is usually someone listening to you, agreeing at least in part with your protest, and willing to compromise on some points in order to join forces for the sake of increased political influence. That is one reason why some erstwhile Christian fundamentalists now prefer the label "neo-evangelical"; it better describes the approach of activist Christians who must keep their fundamentals to themselves a bit more than they did before they entered into political coalitions with feminists against pornography, with moderate Roman Catholics against abortion, with blacks against the drug culture.

Indeed, the attempt to characterize fundamentalisms across cultures leads to generalizations that must be examined in each case for exceptions and for modification. In our first chapter, for example, we noted that fundamentalists view crisis situations as an opportunity to awaken their undecided or ambivalent countrymen or coreligionists to the mortal threat to community and identity posed by liberal religion and/or by secular governments. And in the individual chapters on Christianity, Judaism, and Islam, we described particular cultural crises that served as catalysts for fundamentalist beginnings or growth (for example, the Israeli setback in the Yom Kippur War as a stimulus to Gush Emunim; the moral and cultural crises of the 1960s in America as a stimulus to Christian fundamentalist activism). We must add that fundamentalists do not simply *react* to crises; the many successful movements such as the Muslim Brotherhood and the Jamaat-i-Islami, and institutions such as Bob Jones University and the Mercaz Harav Yeshiva, do not depend on crises to sustain them in the long run. Fundamentalists are well-organized in preparation for such crises and they understand basic human needs and meet them well. We pointed, for example, to the network of social service institutions—hospitals, day-care centers, schools, and colleges—that fundamentalists establish when they fear they will not get a fair break from the surrounding world. Sociologist Robert Wuthnow comments perceptively:

> The success of fundamentalism is also due to the groups' ability to amass vast resources. Were they simply reacting to crises, they could not have lasting influence. But they are careful stewards of resources. They build colleges and seminaries when times are good. They train grass-roots leaders. By distinguishing themselves from outsiders, they make sure that their followers spend time together, thinking about the right ideas and inculcating faith among the young. Indeed modernity is very much their friend in this respect because it encourages them to think rationally, to plan ahead, to study, to engage in gainful employment, to strategize politically, and to model their own organizations on the business or government agencies in which they work.[5]

Critics have described the fundamentalist method of community building as "totalistic" or "totalitarian," and as involving strict processes of indoctrination; but images of theocratic dictatorships, cultic obedience, and the exploitation of vulnerable youth are appropriate only in a small number of cases of fundamentalist-like politicized religion. To say, on the other hand, that fundamentalists "envision a mode of life, emanating from religious principles, that embraces law, polity, society, economy, and culture" is simply to include fundamentalisms among those human societies that have tried to integrate all spheres of human life. Capitalist societies have done no less in trying to inform law, politics, and the economy with theories about prices, profits, and human motivations. "Modernity perhaps encourages most of us to lead compartmentalized lives in which our religious beliefs do not affect our work, our view of money, or our attitude toward the environment," Wuthnow writes. "To seek ways of informing those spheres more effectively with our religious convictions is certainly not to become totalitarian fundamentalists."[6]

# Fundamentalisms and the Construction of Tradition in Late Modernity

Throughout this book we have stressed that the spirit of fundamentalism is constructive rather than destructive. Stereotypes about religious fundamentalism remain strong enough, however, that this argument will surprise many readers who continue to think of fundamentalists as aberrant, threatening, regressive, or barbarian—to take only a few of the words used to describe them by their enemies. Our argument is part of a revisionist approach to the topic, which scholars, including many of those working on the Fundamentalism Project, have found more illuminating than hackneyed diatribes against "narrow-minded true believers."

To argue that fundamentalisms are constructive in spirit is not to deny that their programs begin with polemical attacks, some of them very fierce and unyielding, against religious or political systems, modes of belief and practice, liberal approaches to sacred texts, or irreligious lifestyles. Fundamentalisms are *reactive;* they begin in an "anti-" mode—as antimodernist, or antisecularist, or antifeminist, or anticommunist—but they are not mere protest movements. Fundamentalists are innovative world-builders who act as well as react, who see a world that fails to meet their standards and who then organize and marshal resources in order to create an alternative world for their followers to inhabit and vivify. In creating and sustaining an alternative world—whether it be the world of the Christian academy, or the world of the West Bank settlement, or of a Muslim Brotherhood chapter—fundamentalists are *interactive*. As modern people they are engaged in contemporary processes of community building, electioneering, political organizing, and education, and they live amidst other modern people who do not share their tenacious commitment to religious "fundamentals." Fundamentalists worry about the growing secularity of their host societies and wish to restore God, or in the case of Hindu, Sikh, and Buddhist fundamentalisms, a comparable conception of the divine, to a central place in the everyday consciousness of all people in society.

In this sense fundamentalists are missionaries who, like all good missionaries, speak in the language of the people to whom the message is being addressed. They are enormously creative in formulating and modifying their ideas according to the needs and aspirations of common people; as devotees of sacred texts and traditions, they know how to sustain a rich, common language that animates personal experience and forges bonds with other believers. Indeed, the discursive and communal richness of fundamentalism is, as Robert Wuthnow observes, "a form of 'cultural capital,' giving people status within their religious communities much in the same way that wealth or education might give them prestige in the secular world."[7]

As missionaries and world builders, however, fundamentalists are inevitably caught up in the implicit as well as explicit values of our age, which the British social philosopher Anthony Giddens has described as "late modernity" or "high modernity." By this Giddens means to indicate a time of increasingly rapid acceleration of the processes unleashed by the high-tech revolution of this century, processes that have led late modern institutions to "differ from all perceived forms of social order in respect of their dynamism, the degree to which they undercut traditional habits and customs, and their global impact."[8] The consequences of the mass communications technologies of late modernity alone suggests something of the extent of the transformation of self-consciousness and self-understanding that occurs when viewers and listeners around the world are exposed instantaneously to events, alternate cultures, and a seemingly endless variety of choices of lifestyle and belief.

Furthermore, the media communicate these options in discrete bits and pieces, often seemingly self-contained, which now exist independently of their former historical (temporal-spatial) context. In late modernity, Giddens says, one finds an increased level of self-awareness and an appreciation by people, especially community leaders and modern professional elites, of the ways in which identities can be "constructed" by a selective appropriation of elements—teachings, behaviors, patterns of organization—of complex and once-coherent social systems. Among these social systems that are now selectively retrieved are the rich, detailed, and previously well-integrated religious systems known as traditions. Giddens speaks of "disembedded" bits of tradition, relocated across time and space, recontextualized by the communications media and modern transportation, which allow easy crosscultural interaction, and recombined with other disembedded bits to form the raw material for new configurations of "modernity" and "tradition." Late modernity is thus parasitic, feeding off many different historical bodies; and these processes of late modernity are consciously or unconsciously internalized by people living in the cultures of late modernity—including fundamentalists.

Fundamentalists are constructive in this most modern of ways: they, too, draw upon selective "bits" of religious tradition and of modernity. Fundamentalists fuse passages of sacred texts with modern political ideologies; they adopt bureacratic organizational structures and resource management techniques from the secularists who oppress them; they harness the latest technological innovations to fulfill ancient religious requirements. Fundamentalists idealize sacred lands, "freezing" them at one time and place and lifting them out of their complex and changing historical contexts to serve as emblems of communal identity and as the raison d'être of political movements.

In this fundamentalists are not to be singled out. As Giddens and other theorists have noted, almost every modern social movement follows this process of selection and identity construction, but fundamentalists construct their identities while claiming the special privilege of absolute authority: the revealed word of God escapes the erosion incumbent upon these processes. We may be using modern instruments and methods, the fundamentalists argue, but we are immune to the consequences of modernity because we are protected by a source of truth that is by definition outside of, over and above, the temporal-spatial order and the vicissitudes of history. Giddens points to the great appeal of any system that would present itself as trustworthy and authoritative in the context of late modernity:

> Modernity is a post-traditional order, but not one in which the sureties of tradition have been replaced by the certitude of rational knowledge. Doubt, a pervasive feature of modern critical reason, permeates into everyday life as well as philosophical consciousness, and forms a general existential dimension of the contemporary social word. Modernity institutionalizes the principle of radical doubt and insists that all knowledge takes the form of hypotheses: claims which may very well be true, but which are in principle open to revision and may have at some point to be abandoned. Systems of accumulated expertise, which form important disembedding influences, represent multiple sources of authority, frequently internally contested and divergent in their implications. In the settings of what I call high or late modernity—our present-day world—the self, like the broader institutional context in which it exists, has to be reflexively made. Yet this task has to be accomplished amid a puzzling diversity of options and possibilities.[9]

Into this field stride fundamentalist leaders cloaked in the authority of sacred scriptures or hallowed traditions—scriptures and traditions which are, however, being interpreted according to the exigencies of the age. Sayyid Qutb needed an Islamic rationale for jihad against jahiliyya society, and from the lesser known writings of Ibn Taymiyya and selected quotations from the Qur'an and Sunna, he constructed a compelling one (compelling to devout Sunni Arabs disgruntled by the efforts of their religious scholars to protect Islamic values from Western encroachments). It was not the only construction of Islam—or of mid-twentieth-century Egyptian society—but it inspired trust in a significant segment of the population.

"In circumstances of uncertainty and multiple choice, the notions of trust and risk have particular application," Giddens writes, and it must be said that existential trust is what fundamentalists build in their followers. They fend off the confusions of a world of "disembedding mechanisms and abstract systems" by providing a sense of "ontological security." To move from the language of the secular philosopher to the more comfortable vernacular of the Christian fundamentalist, we quote Bob Jones III: "The quality of faith found here [at Bob Jones University] is enduring, based on the forever-settled Word of God. The quality of the people is radiant—they shine as lights in a dark world. The quality of the atmosphere is pure—the benefit of the Lord's abiding presence."[10] Jones, no less than Rabbi Levinger of the Gush Emunim, understands that a system of thought and behavior guaranteed by ancient wisdom and divine blessing establishes the kind of trust that, in Giddens' formulation,

> provides an inoculation which screens out potential threats and dangers that even the most mundane activities of day-to-day life contain. Trust in this sense is basic to a protective cocoon which stands guard over the self in its dealings with everyday reality. It brackets out potential threats . . . which were the individual to seriously contemplate them, would produce a paralysis of the will and feelings of engulfment. Trust is a medium of interaction with the abstract systems which both empty day to day life of its traditional content and set up globalizing influences. Trust generates that leap into faith which practical engagement demands.[11]

The apocalyptic imagination of fundamentalisms ironically serves to establish and reinforce this sense of trust. In the sacred scriptures or traditions we have the key to unlock the secrets of God's plan, the fundamentalist proclaims. This interpretive key is also a superb means of building trust by setting clear boundaries around the fundamentalist world in order to protect it from erosion and from being overwhelmed by the forces of darkness.

# Conclusion: Holy Lands and the Fundamentalist Imagination

Disputes about the rightful ownership and proper meaning of sacred land play an important role in regional conflicts around the world. In the fall of 1990 in Ayodhya, India, for example, rioting Hindu "fundamentalists" clashed with local Muslims. Activists of the VHP (World Hindu Society) were seeking control of a small plot of land in the eastern Gangetic plain which is the site of a mosque established by the first Mogul emperor of India in 1528. This same hill is known to pious Hindus as the ancient birthplace of King Ram, the human incarnation of Lord Vishnu and the prime exemplar of orthodox Hindu virtues. Working with and through factions of the Bharatiya Janata Party (BJP), the VHP activists filed legal claims and petitioned Parliament for their "right" to build a temple to the god Rama on the site. With the failure of the legal means, zealots within the VHP inspired the Ayodhya riots, which led to increased political polarization in India and eventually figured in the fall of the Prime Minister V. P. Singh.

In East Jerusalem, twenty-one Palestinians were killed on 8 October 1990, when Israeli security forces stormed the hill which Jews call Temple Mount and Muslims call Haram al-Sharif. As in Ayodhya, a relatively small plot of land serves as an identity-defining sacred space for the pious believers of two different religious traditions. The only structure left standing from the ancient Jewish temple destroyed by the Romans in 70 C.E., is the retaining wall that supported the hill upon which the temple stood. Haredi Jews, among many others, flock to this Western Wall (also called the Wailing Wall) beneath Temple Mount to mourn the centuries-long interruption of temple worship. Meanwhile, standing literally above the Jews keening at the supporting wall below, Palestinian Muslims pray within two holy mosques erected where the temple once stood. These Palestinian Muslims recall not the temple worship of the Golden Age of Solomon, but the Prophet Muhammad's mystical "night journey" to *al-aksa* ("the farthest place"). From a large stone or slab of rock upon which Abraham ventured to sacrifice his son, the Prophet ascended into the seventh heaven on his steed, whose hoofprint

*Built in 691 C.E., the Dome of the Rock is an Islamic shrine in Jerusalem. Often referred to as the third holy place, after Mecca and Medina, the Dome stands over the rock on the Temple Mount from which the Prophet ascended to heaven, on horseback, in the Night Journey. The place may also have been the site of the Holy of Holies in the Temple of Solomon.*

is still discernible to believers in the stone. This stone has been preserved for centuries under the Dome of the Rock, the other mosque on Haram al-Sharif, a magnificent gold-domed shrine that has become a landmark on Jerusalem's skyline.

Messianic Jews believe that the Temple must be rebuilt on this site before the Messiah comes to Israel. The riots and deaths on 8 October 1990 occurred after Palestinians atop the mount hurled stones on Jewish worshippers below after rumors had spread among the Palestinians that a small group of radical Jews were planning to ascend the mount to lay the cornerstone of the (third) Jewish Temple.

*Sacred space in cramped quarters. When two religions revere and seek to control sacred sites literally on top of each other, tension is inevitable. Here, Jewish haredim pray at the Western Wall, a retaining wall of the Second Jewish Temple (built by Herod in 20 B.C.E. and destroyed by the Romans in 70 C.E.). In October 1990 rumors spread in Jerusalem's Arab quarter that Jews planned to storm the mount, and Palestinians atop the wall began throwing stones at the Jewish worshipers below. When Israeli security forces retaliated, twenty-one died in the ensuing violence.*

The tragic incident galvanized the Palestinian resistance movement, breathing new life into the intifada and especially into its Islamic vanguard, the fundamentalist movement Hamas. The October 8 confrontation unleashed what Hamas has termed "the war of the knives"—a new round of knifings and reprisals in the occupied territories and in Israel proper.

We have already noted the similar situation in Saudi Arabia, when in the weeks following the Iraqi invasion of Kuwait, coalition forces led by the non-Muslim troops of the United States established bases of operations hundreds of miles east of the site of the Islamic holy cities Mecca and Medina. To Muslim fundamentalists and "situational fundamentalists" like Saddam Hussein, King Fahd no longer warranted the cherished title "Guardian of the Holy Lands" because he permitted American "infidels" to occupy the desert kingdom.

These and other recent incidents of religiously inspired violence, which unfold like mini-Armageddons over the ownership and significance of sacred space, give powerful testimony not only to the perdurance and revival of centuries-old intra-religious conflicts within the context of a supposedly progressive and secularizing world order, they also carry important implications for the secular governments and state security forces that have time and again been drawn inexorably into these clashes. These skirmishes over sacred space are a vivid microcosm of the far-reaching and complex battles over the definitions of national, regional, and communal identity that we have discussed in this book. The postcolonial twentieth century is an era in which new "nations" are struggling to establish a new-old civil and political order, to appropriate Western technologies and instrumentalities to feed, clothe, nurture, and house their indigenous masses, and to preserve human dignity and respect the integrity of the cultural traditions and ways of life of their peoples.

In negotiating their way through late modernity, fundamentalists in Third World nations are attempting to repeal the secular reordering of the world which occurred during and after the two world wars of this century, that is, within a generation extending roughly from 1919 (the defeat and fragmentation of the Ottoman Empire in World War I) to 1948 (the establishment of the "secular" states of India in 1947 and Israel in 1948). Fundamentalist-inspired conflicts over space described and held as sacred represent a rejection of the postcolonial nation-state as conceived of and imposed by the victorious colonizing Western powers. When fundamentalists reimagine that world, however, they inevitably draw upon the concepts and assumptions of their opponents.

According to the World Hindu Society, for example, India is a Hindu *nation* and full rights within it are to be ascribed only to those whose "Hinduness" is evident; by this system, Muslims, Sikhs, and other religious minorities must become "Hinduized"—a vague formula that suggests at the very least a conformity to Hindu standards for the purification of outsiders. India is decidedly not to be defined by the secularist and pluralist model of the West, which embraces an egalitarian approach to humanity and fails to discriminate on the basis of right belief. To the Hindu fundamentalists humanity is defined by right belief—rather, by right praxis, or conduct—and the rights accruing to that humanity flow from right practice. Radical Sikhs in the Punjab call their homeland a sacred "land of purity" (Khalistan) and demand that the Indian government make good on the promises of the secular constitution that protects the free expression of religions. In order to practice their faith, the *gursikh* (pure Sikhs) maintain, they must be separate, uncontaminated by Hindus, Muslims, Jains, and other non-Sikhs; they must, therefore, secede from India and establish a separate Sikh state.[12] And, as we have seen, religious Zionists in Israel believe that the secular Zionists who founded the state and who continue to govern it are their unwitting allies in a divine plan to redeem "the Whole Land of Israel." They believe the boundaries of the current state will be gradually expanded to cover the biblical Promised Land—a goal which carries with it immense geopolitical obstacles and ultimately implies the forced expulsion of Palestinian Arabs from the occupied territories.

These skirmishes over sacred space are not the vestigial impulses of dying breeds of religious zealots. They are, instead, episodes in a competition for hegemony, for the power to name and claim land, to define or delimit individual rights, to privilege certain classes or elites over others, to shape the law, political economy, and international relations of a given state. This competition is conducted, under the banner of religion, not only by pious believers but also by secular elites and counter-elites who respect or fear or seek to exploit popular religious fervor. In this game of appropriating religion for political ends, Saddam Hussein may compete with the Ayatollah Khomeini, although the former is perceived by many as a crassly opportunistic charlatan and the other as "the genuine article," that is, as a true believer. In late modernity the manipulation of the religious tradition no less than of the religiopolitical situation can come at the hands of clerics and laymen and nonbelievers alike.

Nonetheless, in naming and appropriating sacred space, especially sacred lands, for geopolitical ends, fundamentalists and ersatz fundamentalists alike are drawing upon one of the most powerfully evocative realities of common human experience—the anchoring of personal and communal identity in a particular place and time. We identify ourselves with a place of origin, a homeland, a place where we were brought to life physically or spiritually, or where we grew to maturity. If the nonfundamentalist coreligionist, or even the secularist, who does not literally accept the doctrines and practices of the faith, is ever to be mobilized in a common sociopolitical cause with the fundamentalist, it will likely be over *this* fundamental—over land, title, name, identity—all wrapped into one in a place of significance. The secular Zionist whose Torah is a cultural icon rather than a literal guide to daily living, but whose family perished in the Holocaust, may cherish "the Promised Land" as fiercely as the Gush Emunim member who interprets the phrase in strict eschatological terms and engages in Torah study.

To call a place sacred is not to marginalize it or veil it from the gaze of outsiders; it is, instead, to elevate and enhance the significance and centrality of the place. To name it sacred is to render it a repository of hopes, needs, identities, and meanings, and to establish it as the symbolic center of human striving and thus the focal point for social, political, and religious self-interpretation; for whoever controls the meaning of the sacred center controls the identity of the people and the nation, and thus controls destiny. For the secularized person, then, sacred space is still strangely evocative and powerful as a symbol of the identity and very existence of a people. To venerate the shrine or tomb or battlefield may be no more, and no less, than to proclaim with one's very being the conviction that the deeds and existence of this people carry a significance beyond the mundane; these places are invested with what Peter Berger has called "signals of transcendence."[13]

We have seen that fundamentalists today in various religious traditions, sensing and studiously reflecting upon the evocative and defining power of the sacred, attempt to harness this power for what, upon close scrutiny, turns out to be an almost bewildering variety of political, social, and religious ends. United only by a common conviction that the sacred is under sustained attack by the forces of secularization, fundamentalists seek to reconsecrate the world.

History is vast and within it different peoples have occupied the same regions during different periods. Today those same surviving peoples, with their particular pasts, empowered in the late twentieth century by small arms technologies, mass communications, imported revolutionary ideologies, and accessible versions of their own militant religious histories, are more capable than ever of disrupting a postcolonial "order" that has been revealed in our lifetimes as paper-thin.

The fundamentalist imagination is contained, however, when limits are set by civil society to the process of retrieving a past and constructing a future. The United States is notable in the twentieth century for a relative absence of religious violence in general, and especially for the absence of religious violence intended to undermine the Constitution and governing foundational principles of the Republic. Among the many polyglot and deeply pluralistic modern nations, the United States has been relatively successful in providing different immigrant groups hailing from hundreds of regions and particular historical backgrounds with essentially one national story and identity. The national myth has its founding hero (George Washington), its sacred binding scriptures (the Constitution, the Declaration of Independence, and the Bill of Rights), its saints and martyrs (Lincoln, Kennedy, and King), its high holy feast days (Fourth of July, Veterans Day, Memorial Day), and its most brilliant feature, a certain American pioneer lack of closure, an open-endedness that allows new heroes to fit into the mix—a black civil rights leader, for example, or an Irish Catholic president.

This is precisely because the American founding ideal is revolutionary: that all are equal simply by being human; that competing interests, even if based on ethnic, racial, or religious identities, must compete within this foundational political-philosophical framework. James Madison predicted that no one sect or cult or party would win out in America because all parties, sects, and cults could organize, speak freely, worship openly, and promote political candidates—as long as they recognized the civil law and the rights upon which this creative, ordered pluralism was based. In other words, the key to America's success has been its ability to endorse competition as lawful, indeed as the very fibre of political and economic life, and to provide assurances, through a federal system and a semi-welfare state, that within that competition the losers retain full civil and political rights and participation—they are not, in theory at least, to be vanquished, exiled, executed, sold into slavery, or otherwise deprived of full rights. Those who lose the competition will not kill one another, will not revolt, but will be administered to by a federal government that benevolently restrains the play of the free market and attempts, successfully and unsuccessfully, to weaken monopolistic political and economic powers.

A great deal of the credit for America's success as a democratic experiment has to be attributed to an accident of history that the Middle East and much of South Asia has not enjoyed (and of course to the good fortune of Americans that their nation's founders were wise enough to recognize what is distinctive about the American experiment and to build upon it). Most Americans were newcomers to this land and none had (or were able to persuade others of) a historic religious claim to it. No American immigrant could lay claim to this tree, mountain, rock, valley—and when one did identify a sacred space, there was a vast expanse of territory waiting for others. The occasions for ethnic clashes were also muted through need for joint collaboration. Americans succeeded as a pilgrim people here through connivance, winking, looking the other way when we didn't like someone's faith or traditions because he gave us good business. Is it too much to suggest that we still do this? Jewish merchants were among the wealthiest and smartest in the New Amsterdam colony that we came to know as the state of New York; the Dutch colonists did not like the Jews, suspected them of all kinds of kabbalistic oddities and thought them miserly—in short held all the prejudices against them which Jews have historically borne—but they needed them. And so they creatively connived.

In this pluralistic, democratic context "pure" separatist, boundary-setting fundamentalism has a difficult time surviving; to survive at all, even in qualified form, fundamentalists must collaborate with "outsiders." In our system a hard-core fundamentalist minority cannot bring the government down; to gain influence it must form coalitions, make compromises, soften its separatist stance.

This is the hope that many secularists and religious liberals hold for societies like Israel and Egypt as well: that radical fundamentalist or other extremist imaginings will be contained by the rules of a social contract that allows for a vigorous competition between different models of society. Because of their own internal diversity, fundamentalists may be forced to compete among themselves, as well as with nonfundamentalists, in order to play a significant role in charting the direction of nation and society.

# THINKING ABOUT FUNDAMENTALISM

*The Glory and the Power,* like any book, may fall into many kinds of hands. Some readers may be people who fear or sneer at hard-line religious movements and at individual believers who are uncompromising in their convictions, militant in their expression, and full of designs for changing the public order. Other readers will have explored these pages in order to understand the movements that are playing such a large part in determining the world's destiny and which are not insignificant on the North American scene.

Throughout the writing of the book, the authors have kept both of these kinds of readers in mind, but we have not neglected a third—fundamentalists themselves, or people who, if they do not describe themselves as fundamentalists, match the outlines described in this book and are at least "fundamentalist-like." Every sixth American describes himself or herself to the poll taker as "conservative Protestant" or as belonging to a denomination classified as such. (A glance at the "Churches and Synagogues" section of the telephone *Yellow Pages* will show that almost no church bodies have the word *fundamentalist* in their name.) Not all of these religious conservatives are fundamentalists; many are moderate evangelicals or pentecostals or members of the non-fundamentalist wings of the Southern Baptist Convention, the Lutheran Church/Missouri Synod, the Christian Reformed Church, and the like. However, one can safely estimate that at least every eighteenth American citizen (and as many as one in twelve) is a Protestant fundamentalist.

We hope fundamentalists have not read this work as a long essay posing "us" versus "them." It would not be an unfamiliar experience for them to be overlooked, belittled, or the subjects of scoffing; from time to time one notices that public voices which cannot speak disparagingly about Catholics, African-Americans, Hispanics, Jews, or other minorities, can get away with inhumane characterizations and caricatures of fundamentalists. The authors recognize that this century has seen Marxists, secularists, rationalists, scientists, feminists, and liberals who certainly bear a family resemblance to some religious fundamentalists when it comes to intolerance.

In *The Glory and the Power*, we have made a determined effort to be fair-minded, to try to understand the new movements. Some observers see a danger in taking fundamentalisms so seriously. Will not such efforts, some ask, contribute to the growth of movements they see as malignant and threatening, by giving them credibility and finding in them some measures of plausibility? This book has tried to position itself between all the schools; our goal has not been to champion the fundamentalist cause but to understand why it persists in our modern day.

We have not found fossilized, vestigial, and static movements. Fundamentalists are innovative, often on the rise, and usually dynamic. They and those who oppose them may want to make some assessments about the prospects for fundamentalisms in the future. These vary, of course, from culture to culture, and accident, surprise, and contingency mark every turn in history, so it is impossible to predict or even to project with much confidence. It is difficult to find any nonfundamentalist lay person or professional—sociologist, psychologist, anthropologist, poll taker, historian, or theologian—who thirty years ago foresaw the rise of new and neofundamentalist movements in North America and around the world. If they—we—all missed the signs, what assurance do we have that anyone can guess better about the future?

Still, there are some useful things to be said about present trends. For example, one can note the different prospects for fundamentalisms in free republics and pluralistic societies where the separation of church and state has been established and where religious and secular parties contend on equal terms, versus the prospects in societies which have never had such separation, whether in the thinking of the people or the law of the land. In the former, fundamentalists can at best hope to gain power in the public order by engaging in dialogue and debate. Being in the minority while seeking votes, they have to build coalitions and make alliances. Some of these tend to compromise the purity of movements and the fundamentalists turn "evangelical" or "moderate" and "mainstream"—if they do not retreat again into pure isolation and lose their significance. It has been said that there is more modernism in most fundamentalists in such cultures than there is fundamentalism in most moderns, a fact which gives the latter an advantage just as it throws more fear into the custodians of fundamentalist groups and traditions.

So it is that one can picture in North America large numbers of people who are fundamentalist but who find the term no longer useful, or find some features of the fundamentalist way of life to be not only bad public relations but not fairly descriptive; they begin to "blend into the woodwork" of conservative Protestantism. In reaction, others may become even more firm about being fundamentalist and quite militant about using the term in self-description. If the past is any guide, a past which has consistently seen hard-liners turn softer-liners and people "at the margins" moving toward the mainstream and center, there will again be new movements at the edges which will revitalize fundamentalism and make new moves in and against the mainstream culture.

Tactics of fundamentalists change. Around 1980, feeling newly invigorated, fundamentalists in the United States made alliances with secular ultraconservatives to form a New Christian Right. Linking with the presidential campaigns and administrations of the popular Ronald Reagan, who courted them, they aspired to gain access and influence in the White House, the Supreme Court and lower courts, the Congress and state legislatures, and in centers of mass communications, entertainment, and commerce. They worked through several celebrity point-men, often television evangelists who were recognized in the whole culture. They made some alliances, enjoyed some gains, and then seemed to reach their limits with that strategy.

Consciously or unconsciously (probably more the latter, no conspiracy theory being operative here), they changed strategy. A dozen years later one pictures fundamentalisms as informed by any number of lesser known and non-celebrity individuals who inspire loyalties and quicken the energies of millions of citizens on many fronts in countless communities. There are not fewer fundamentalists than there were during the prime years of the New Christian Right. If they are not as frequently in the national headlines, they are constantly in action on the local level. Most frequently they take aim at the Constitution and the anti-abortion cause in its interpretation. Now and then they put real energies into a constitutional amendment permitting prayer in public schools. Often they attack federal agencies such as the National Endowment for the Arts and the National Endowment for the Humanities.

More frequently, however, their actions are regional or local. They block abortion clinics in Wichita or Buffalo and make national news. They change the policies of a local hospital and make local news. A censorship case in Cincinnati does not seem to have much to do with life in Portland, Oregon, or Portland, Maine. An endeavor to have "creation research" taught against or alongside evolution in California schools seems to have little to do with textbook choice in Delaware. A fight over the figure of Jesus in the creche on a courthouse lawn in Kansas seems remote from the lawns of Connecticut. Yet these many movements have much in common and taken together they do keep changing the fabric of American society.

Around the world there is a different picture. While outside the Protestant party of Northern Ireland and some immigrant populations on the Continent, true religious fundamentalisms as of this writing still make only rare appearances in northern and western Europe (one can picture a kind of belt marked "Few Fundamentalists" running from Europe across Canada and the northern United States and running to Japan), everywhere else fundamentalisms seem to be attracting the loyalties of more and more people. That is certainly the case in Latin America among Protestants and some Catholics. It is true of the Zion Christian Church, with its explosive growth in South Africa and among Muslims in nations like Nigeria. In the entire historically Islamic world—from North Africa through the Middle East and now incorporating the Asian republics of the old Soviet Union and extending down through the subcontinent of Asia and the island worlds of the southern Pacific—fundamentalisms keep growing, taking aim on polity and policy.

Now, after the end of the two-superpower situation of the Cold War, the worldwide trend is toward tribalism of a sort, in which peoples oppose and fight other peoples along cultural-linguistic-ethnic-religious lines, and in which the last element, the religious, is an ever more important factor. What about the future of such movements? So long as there is poverty people will need empowerment and will often call upon their God to provide it. So long as there are threats to their identities, people will claim their God as agent of the formation of their groups and as one who would bless them uniquely and charge them to act particularly. But we should neither overestimate nor underestimate these movements. Among American policymakers, underestimators were taken off guard by events in American politics of the 1980s, by the Iranian Revolution of 1979, and by foreign policy developments everywhere around the world. Underestimators who opposed fundamentalisms lost ground to them and could make no sense of the ground their opponents kept winning.

Overestimators, on the other hand, may make their own contribution to domestic and international unrest and imbalances. Fundamentalisms often reach limits. The Ayatollah Khomeini was not able to export his Shi'ite revolution. Neither Shi'ite nor Sunni Muslims have effected a Muslim-wide front of united fundamentalisms. The government of Egypt as of now is blocking the progress of the Muslim Brotherhood. Publics here and there grow weary of fundamentalists' legal impositions on them, and moderate them or even react against them. The whole human future is not necessarily one of peoples against peoples, of tribalism fired by religion. The global network of mass communications, the impulse to develop international markets, the experience of people who travel and find reasons for empathy with other kinds of people—these add up to counterforces against fundamentalisms, so fundamentalisms should not be overestimated.

In short, a complete balance sheet cannot be drawn. Poverty and deprivation, so prevalent throughout the modern world, often fuel reactive movements. We must seek to comprehend the resentments of people scorned by others and the aspirations of those who seek to find or uphold their group identity while insisting on the integrity of their religious faith and their right to try to convert others to it. Fundamentalisms have to be reckoned with as will-to-power movements, just as they are quiet motivators of people in day-to-day existence in personal life. Fundamentalists, one hopes, will come to see why most will fail to convert, share their identity, or coalesce with them in power moves. Convictions are deep, passions are strong, and words of moderation will often sound like the advice of betrayers or subverters.

That having been said, we may hope that humans as individuals and in groups will find better ways than they have in the immediate past to interact while guarding their own integrity. In one formula, "the highly committed people are not civil and the highly civil people are not committed." The sounds of explosives and denunciations have been louder than argument and more frequently heard than conversation. But conversation permits people to be themselves while hearing others and remaining open to certain measures of change in the give and take which sustains human life. To make a contribution to that conversation is the goal of *The Glory and the Power*.

# NOTES

## Introduction

1. In order to minimize the use of scholarly apparatus we do not include a note after every direct quote from the transcripts of *The Glory and the Power* documentary film series, produced by the William Benton Broadcast Project in conjunction with WETA TV and FM, and the BBC; the films were aired on PBS stations nationally in June and July of 1992. In our introduction, the Randall Terry quotes are taken from *Fighting Back*, a film by Bill Jersey; the Daniela Weiss quotes are found in *This Is Our Land*, a film by Jane Treays; the Adil Hussein quotes are from *Remaking the World*, a film by Steve York.

2. As former White House Counsel Charles Colson, now a born-again Christian, puts it: "According to a recent article in the *New York Times*, I am a totalitarian theocrat. The authors implied that I am anxious and confused about my faith, given to apocalyptic visions, possibly a sadist, and basically opposed to fiction, psychology, journalism, and assertive women. In other words, according to the authors' definition, a fundamentalist." Colson found this mischaracterization to be "symptomatic of the growing tendency to substitute symbols and slogans for reason and argument in public discourse." Colson opposes the distortions of the term *fundamentalism*, especially by other Christians. "I recently heard a pastor warn his flock against falling away from the faith and getting involved in 'sex, drugs, and fundamentalist sects.' In much of the church's intramural battling, Christians have used the word against one another." See Chuck Colson, "The Scarlet F," *Jubilee*, April 1991, p. 7.

## Chapter 1: The Fundamentals of Fundamentalism

1. Gerhard Ebeling, *The Nature of Faith* (Philadelphia: Muhlenberg, 1961, p. 174).

2. The sociologist Max Weber first employed the notion of "elective affinities" (*Wahlverwandtschaften*) to describe the relationship between ideas and interests. Max Weber, *Gesammelte Aufsätze zur Religionssoziologie* (Tübingen: Mohr, 1947), p. 83. Also see Richard Herbert Howe, "Max Weber's Elective Affinities: Sociology within the

Bounds of Pure Reason," *American Journal of Sociology* 84 (September 1979): 366–85.

3. On South Asian fundamentalisms, see the following essays in Martin E. Marty and R. Scott Appleby, eds., *Fundamentalisms Observed* (Chicago: University of Chicago Press, 1991): Daniel Gold, "Organized Hinduisms: From Vedic Truth to Hindu Nation," pp. 531–93; T. N. Madan, "The Double-Edged Sword: Fundamentalism and the Sikh Religious Tradition," pp. 594–627; and Donald Swearer, "Fundamentalistic Movements in Theravada Buddhism," pp. 628–90.

4. See the discussion of Pius IX in Josef L. Altholz, *The Churches in the Nineteenth Century* (Indianapolis: Bobbs-Merrill, 1967), pp. 73–90.

5. Quoted in Ian Lustick, *For the Land and the Lord* (New York: Council on Foreign Relations, 1988).

6. See also Gabriel Almond and Emmanuel Sivan, "Fundamentalism: Genus and Species," a paper published at the November 1991 conference of the Fundamentalism Project, Chicago.

7. See Jurgen Habermas, *The Theory of Communicative Practice,* vol. 2 of *Lifeworld and System: A Critique of Function and System,* trans. Thomas McCarthy (Boston: Beacon Press, 1987).

8. Martin Buber, *I and Thou,* trans. Walter Kaufmann (New York, 1970). Tillich's discussion of technical reason is summarized in *The Protestant Era,* trans. James Luther Adams (Chicago: University of Chicago Press, 1948), pp. 55–65, and can be found throughout his three-volume *Systematic Theology* (Chicago: University of Chicago Press).

9. The definition is taken from Martin E. Marty and R. Scott Appleby, "An Interim Report on a Hypothetical Family," in Marty and Appleby, *Fundamentalisms Observed,* p. 835.

# Chapter 2: Fighting Back:
# Protestant Fundamentalism in the United States

1. Randall Terry, speaking in the Bill Jersey film *Fighting Back.* Otherwise unattributed quotes from Terry, Bob Jones, Jr., Beneth Jones, and Bob Jones III in this chapter are also from the transcript of this film documentary.

2. Frances Fitzgerald, "Reflections: Jim and Tammy," *New Yorker,* 23 April 1990, pp. 67, 69.

3. Pat Robertson, *The New World Order* (Dallas: Word Publishing, 1991), p. 6.

4. See Martin E. Marty, *Righteous Empire: The Protestant Experience in America* (New York: Harper and Row, 1970; pb edition, Harper torchbooks), pp. 93, 139, 180, 204, 216.

5. See the discussion of premillennialism in George Marsden, *Fundamentalism and American Culture: The Shaping of Twentieth Century Evangelicalism, 1870–1925* (New York: Oxford University Press, 1980).

6. For a discussion of fundamentalism and creationism, see George Marsden, "The Evangelical Love Affair with Enlightenment Science" and "Why Creation Science?" in his recent collection of essays, *Understanding Fundamentalism and Evangelicalism* (Grand Rapids, Mich.: Wm. B. Eerdmans, 1991), pp. 122–81.

7. For a full discussion of this issue, see Mark A. Noll, *Between Faith and Criticism: Evangelicals, Scholarship, and the Bible in America* (San Francisco: Harper and Row, 1986).

8. See Marsden, *Fundamentalism and American Culture*, pp. 14–16, 110–16.

9. See the discussion of organization in Nancy T. Ammerman, "North American Protestant Fundamentalism," in Marty and Appleby, eds., *Fundamentalisms Observed*, pp. 22–38.

10. On the establishment and growth of Bible colleges, see Quentin Schultze, "The Two Faces of Fundamentalism Higher Education," in Martin E. Marty and R. Scott Appleby, eds. *Fundamentalisms and Society: Reclaiming the Sciences, the Family, and Education* (Chicago: University of Chicago Press, forthcoming, 1993).

11. Jerry Falwell, *Listen, America!* (New York: Doubleday, 1980), pp. 15–16.

12. Ibid., p. 19.

13. Ammerman, "North American Protestant Fundamentalism," p. 41.

14. Ibid., p. 44.

15. Falwell, "Prologue," *Listen, America!*.

16. Ibid.

17. Smith is cited in Susan D. Rose, *Keeping Them Out of the Hands of Satan: Evangelical Schooling in America* (New York: Routledge, 1988), pp. 35–36.

18. Ibid., pp. 37–38.

19. Quoted in Nancy T. Ammerman, *Bible Believers: Fundamentalists in the Modern World* (New Brunswick, N.J.: Rutgers University Press, 1987), p. 76. On Christian academies, see also: Alan Peshkin, *God's Choice: The Total World of a Fundamentalist Christian School* (Chicago: University of Chicago Press, 1986); and R. Scott Appleby, "Keeping Them Out of the Hands of the State: Two Critiques of Christian Schools," *American Journal of Education* 98, no. 1 (November 1989): 62–81.

20. See James Moore, "The Creationist Cosmos of Protestant Fundamentalism," in Marty and Appleby, eds., *Fundamentalisms and Society.*

21. For a full account of the Arkansas case, see Langdon Gilkey, *Creationism on Trial: Evolution and God at Little Rock* (San Francisco: Harper and Row, 1985).

22. Moore, "The Creationist Cosmos."

23. Rebecca Klatch, *Women of the New Right* (Philadelphia: Temple University Press, 1987), p. 3.

24. Virginia Bessey, ibid., p. 25.

25. Quoted ibid., pp. 50–51.

26. Ammerman, "North American Protestant Fundamentalism," pp. 47–49.

27. A description of the game, and of the inspiration provided by Willow Creek Church, is found in "First Baptist Reminder," a weekly publication of the First Baptist Church of Dallas.

28. Quotes from John Peloza, Jim Corbett, and Dennis MacDonald in this section are taken from the transcript of *Fighting Back.*

# Chapter 3: Gush Emunim: A Fundamentalism of the Land

1. Gideon Aran, "Jewish Zionist Fundamentalism: The Bloc of the Faithful in Israel (Gush Emunim)," in Marty and Appleby, *Fundamentalisms Observed,* p. 265.

2. Ehud Sprinzak, *The Ascendance of Israel's Radical Right* (New York: Oxford University Press, 1991).

3. Moshe Halbertal, "When Gush Comes to Shove," *New Republic,* 23 March 1992, p. 33.

4. Rabbi Avraham Kook, quoted in Aviezer Ravitzky, "Religious and Political Messianism in Israel," in Emmanuel Sivan and Menachem Friedman, eds., *Religious Radicalism and Politics in the Middle East* (Albany: State University of New York, 1990), pp. 20–21.

5. Ravitzky, ibid.

6. Aran, "Jewish Zionist Fundamentalism," pp. 270–71.

7. Rabbi Zvi Yehuda Kook, quoted in Aviezer Ravitzky, "Religious and Political Messianism in Israel," p. 18.

8. Unless otherwise noted, quotes from Rabbis Eliezer Waldman and Moshe Hirsch in this chapter are taken from the transcript of *This Is Our Land,* a film by Jane Treays.

9. Samuel C. Heilman, *Defenders of the Faith: Inside Ultra-Orthodox Jewry* (New York: Schocken Books, 1992) provides a careful description of haredim culture.

10. Rabbi Hirsch, quoted in Clyde Haberman, "A Palestinian Who is a Jew Fights Israel," *New York Times,* 1 May 1992, p. A4.

11. Aran, "Jewish Zionist Fundamentalism," p. 272.

12. The war was inconclusive in military terms, but the Arab states had taken Israel by surprise initially and regained some of the territory on the Sinai peninsula lost in the 1967 war. For discussions of the various perceptions, see Fred J. Khoury, *The Arab-Israeli Dilemma,* 3rd ed. (Syracuse: Syracuse University Press, 1985), pp. 370–86; and Albert Hourani, *A History of the Arab Peoples* (Cambridge, Mass.: Harvard University Press, 1991) pp. 416–19. One might have expected that an aggressive, triumphalist movement like Gush Emunim would have gotten off the ground organizationally, as well as emotionally, on the wave of an Israeli military victory rather than after what was perceived by many as a humiliating defeat.

13. Halbertal, "When Gush Comes to Shove," p. 34.

14. Ibid.

15. See Sprinzak, *The Ascendance of Israel's Radical Right,* p. 153.

16. Ibid., p. 160.

17. Daniela Weiss, quoted in Peter Ford, "The Vision of the 'Land of Israel' Falters in Wake of Likud's Loss," *Christian Science Monitor,* 10 July 1992, p. 1.

18. For a thorough discussion of this concept, see Sprinzak, *The Ascendance of Israel's Radical Right,* pp. 124–27.

19. Gideon Aran, "Jewish Zionist Fundamentalism," p. 275.

20. Quotes from Michael Lighter, Esther Karish, Emona Elon, Daniela Weiss, and Avraham Burg are from the transcripts of *This Is Our Land.*

21. Sprinzak, *The Ascendance of Israel's Radical Right,* p. 157.

22. Michael Fishbane, *Judaism* (San Francisco: Harper and Row, 1987), p. 122.

23. Myron J. Aronoff, "The Institutionalization and Cooptation of a Charismatic, Messianic, Religious-Political Revitalization Movement," in David Newman, ed., *The Impact of Gush Emunim* (London: Croon-Helm, 1985), pp. 185–86.

24. Peter Berger, *The Heretical Imperative* (Garden City, New York: Anchor Press, 1979).

25. See Fishbane, *Judaism,* p. 124.

26. Halbertal, "When Gush Comes to Shove," p. 36.

27. On this point, see Samuel C. Heilman and Menachem Friedman, "Religious Fundamentalism and Religious Jews: The Case of the Haredim," in Marty and Appleby, *Fundamentalisms Observed*, pp. 250–54.

28. See Haym Soloveitchik, "The Role of Texts in the *Haredi* World," in Martin E. Marty and R. Scott Appleby, eds., *Accounting for Fundamentalisms: The Dynamic Character of Movements* (Chicago: University of Chicago Press, forthcoming, 1993).

# Chapter 4: Remaking the World of Islam

1. The account of violence by Muslim groups is narrated in Abdel Azim Ramadan, "Fundamentalist Influence in Egypt: The Strategies of the Muslim Brotherhood and the Takfir Groups," in Martin E. Marty and R. Scott Appleby, eds., *Fundamentalisms and the State: Remaking Polities, Economies, and Militance* (Chicago: University of Chicago Press, forthcoming, 1993).

2. For a history of the Muslim Brotherhood, see Richard P. Mitchell, *The Society of the Muslim Brothers* (London: Oxford University Press, 1969).

3. Quoted in Ramadan, "Fundamentalist Influence in Egypt."

4. For example, in an interview published 30 January 1990 in the newspaper *al-Sha'b*, an organ of the Islamic movement in general and the Muslim Brotherhood in particular, 'Abd al-Rahman commented upon the meaning of the violent skirmishes: "There will be no room here for a discussion or mutual understanding with the new minister [of the interior] unless or until he and his men return to the Truth."

5. Martin Riesebrodt, *Fundamentalismus als patriarchalische Protestbewegung* (Fundamentalism as a Patriarchal Protest Movement) (Tübingen: J. C. B. Mohr, 1990).

6. Quotes are taken from *Remaking the World*, a film by Steve York.

7. Andrea Rugh, "Reshaping Personal Relations in Egypt," in Marty and Appleby, eds., *Fundamentalisms and Society.*

8. This woman is featured in *Remaking the World.*

9. Amos Perlmutter, "Wishful Thinking about Islamic Fundamentalism," *Washington Post,* 22 January 1992.

10. Javid Iqbal, "Democracy and the Modern Islamic State," in John L. Esposito, ed., *Voices of Resurgent Islam* (New York: Oxford University Press, 1983), pp. 252, 254.

11. See the discussion of Shari'a in W. Montgomery Watt, *Islamic Fundamentalism and Modernity* (Routledge: London, 1988), pp. 25–29. The four Sunnite rites are the Hanafite, the Malikite, the Shafi'ite, and the Hanbalite, which take their names from their nominal founders: Abu-Haniffa (d. 767); Malik ibn-Anas (d. 795); ash-Shafi'i (d. 820); Ahmad ibn-Hanbal (d. 855).

12. See John Voll, "Fundamentalism in the Sunni Arab World: Egypt and the Sudan," in Marty and Appleby, eds., *Fundamentalisms Observed*, p. 350–52.

13. See Fazlur Rahman, *Islam and Modernity: Transformation of an Intellectual Tradition* (Chicago: University of Chicago Press, 1982), p. 43.

14. Voll, "Fundamentalism in the Sunni Arab World," p. 353.

15. Hasan al-Banna, quoted ibid., p. 356.

16. Voll, ibid.

17. Ramadan, "Fundamentalist Influence in Egypt."

18. Mumtaz Ahmad, "Islamic Fundamentalism in South Asia: The Jamaat-i-Islami and the Tablighi Jamaat," in Marty and Appleby, eds., *Fundamentalisms Observed*, p. 464.

19. Emmanuel Sivan, *Radical Islam: Medieval Theology and Modern Politics* (New Haven: Yale University Press, 1985), p. 99.

20. Ibid., p. 93.

21. See R. Scott Appleby, "The Arab Problem and the Islamic Solution," *Christian Century,* 19 February 1992, pp. 190–91.

22. "Islam Resumes its March," *Economist* 323, no. 7753 (4 April 1992), p. 47.

23. Abdulaziz Sachedina, "Activist Shi'ism in Iran, Iraq, and Lebanon," in Marty and Appleby, eds., *Fundamentalisms Observed*, p. 406.

24. See James Piscatori, "Religion and Realpolitik: Islamic Responses to the Gulf War," in James Piscatori, ed., *Islamic Fundamentalisms and the Gulf Crisis* (Chicago; American Academy of Arts and Sciences, 1991), pp. 7–8.

25. Ibid.

26. Ibid., pp. 8–10.

27. Olivier Roy, "Afghanistan: An Islamic War of Resistance," in Marty and Appleby, *Fundamentalisms and the State.*

28. Jean-François Legrain, "A Defining Moment: Palestinian Islamic Fundamentalism," in Piscatori, ed., *Islamic Fundamentalisms and the Gulf Crisis,* pp. 70–87. Also see Zeev Schiff and Ehud Yaari, *Intifada: The Palestinian Uprising—Israel's Third Front* (New York: Simon and Schuster, 1990).

29. Quoted in "Pro-Iraq passions build in Jordan," *Middle East Mirror,* 21 January 1991.

30. Quoted by Milton Viorst, "A Reporter at Large: The House of Hashem," in *New Yorker,* 7 January 1991, p. 32.

31. Beverley Milton-Edwards, "A Temporary Alliance with the Crown," in James Piscatori, ed., *Islamic Fundamentalisms and the Gulf Crisis,* p. 105.

32. For an elaboration of this analysis, see Amatzia Baram, "From Radicalism to Radical Pragmatism: The Shi'ite Fundamentalist Opposition Movements of Iraq," in Piscatori, ed., *Islamic Fundamentalisms and the Gulf Crisis*, pp. 28–51.

33. Judith Miller, "A Muslim Cleric Hones the Fusing of Religion and Politics," *New York Times*, 17 May 1992.

34. One of the authors of the present volume, Scott Appleby, attended one of the al-Turabi sessions and took the notes that form the basis of this summary.

35. Miller, ibid.

36. Abdullahi Ahmed An Na'im, "The Reformation of Islam," *New Perspectives Quarterly* (Fall 1987): 51.

# Chapter 5: The Spirit of Fundamentalism

1.  See Amira El-Azhary Sonbol, "Egypt," in Shireen T. Hunter, ed., *The Politics of Islamic Revivalism: Diversity and Unity* (Bloomington: Indiana University Press, 1988), pp. 23–29.

2.  Bob Jones III, "Bad Medicine: A Discussion of the New Morality," pamphlet (Greenville, South Carolina: Bob Jones University Press, 1968).

3.  John L. Esposito, "Islam and Muslim Politics," in Esposito, *Voices of Resurgent Islam*, p. 9.

4.  "Rescue Ends Peacefully," *Chicago Tribune*, May 8, 1992.

5.  Robert Wuthnow, "Fundamentalism in the World," *Christian Century*, 29 April 1992, p. 457.

6.  Ibid.

7.  Ibid., p. 456.

8.  Anthony Giddens, *Modernity and Self-Identity: Self and Society in the Late Modern Age* (Stanford, Calif.: Stanford University Press, 1991), p. 1.

9.  Ibid., pp. 2–3.

10. Bob Jones III, "A Word from the President," in "Open the Doors: Bob Jones University," pamphlet (Greenville, South Carolina: 1992).

11. Anthony Giddens, *Modernity and Self-Identity*, p. 3.

12. See Madan, "The Double-Edged Sword," pp. 594–627.

13. Peter Berger, *A Rumor of Angels* (New York: Anchor Books, 1990).

# RECOMMENDED READINGS

Ajami, Fouad. *The Arab Predicament*. Cambridge: Cambridge University Press, 1981.

———. *The Vanished Imam: Musa al-Sadr and the Shi'a of Lebanon*. Ithaca: Cornell University Press, 1986.

Ammerman, Nancy T. *Bible Believers: Fundamentalists in the Modern World*. New Brunswick, N.J.: Rutgers University Press, 1987.

———. *Baptist Battles: Social Change and Religious Conflict in the Southern Baptist Convention*. New Brunswick, N.J.: Rutgers University Press, 1990.

Andersen, Walter K., and Shridhar D. Damle. *The Brotherhood in Saffron: The Rashtriya Swayamsevak Sangh and Hindu Revivalism*. Westview Special Studies on South and Southeast Asia. Boulder, Colo.: Westview Press, 1987.

Antoun, Richard T., and Mary Elaine Hegland, eds. *Religious Resurgence: Contemporary Cases in Islam, Christianity, and Judaism*. Syracuse, N.Y.: Syracuse University Press, 1987.

Arjomand, Said Amir. *The Shadow of God and the Hidden Imam*. Chicago: University of Chicago Press, 1984.

Averrill, Lloyd J. *Religious Right, Religious Wrong: A Critique of the Fundamentalist Phenomenon*. New York: Pilgrim Press, 1989.

Aviad, Janet. *Return to Judaism: Religious Renewal in Israel*. Chicago: University of Chicago Press, 1983.

Azari, Farah. *Women of Iran: The Conflict with Fundamentalist Islam*. London: Ithaca Press, 1983.

Bakash, Shaul. *The Reign of the Ayatollahs*. New York: Basic Books, 1986.

Barkun, Michael. *Disaster and the Millennium*. New Haven: Yale University Press, 1974.

Barr, James. *Fundamentalism*. Philadelphia: Westminster Press, 1978.

Beale, David O. *In Pursuit of Purity: American Fundamentalism Since 1850*. Greenville, S.C.: Unusual Publications, 1986.

Boone, Kathleen C. *The Bible Tells Them So.* Albany, N.Y.: State University of New York Press, 1989.

Bruce, Steve. *The Rise and Fall of the New Christian Right.* Oxford: Oxford University Press, 1988.

———. *Pray TV: Televangelism in America.* London: Routledge, 1990.

Caplan, Lionel, ed. *Studies in Religious Fundamentalism.* Albany: State University of New York Press, 1987.

Esposito, John L., ed. *Voices of Resurgent Islam.* New York: Oxford University Press, 1983.

Falwell, Jerry. *Listen America!* New York: Doubleday, 1980.

———. *The Fundamentalist Phenomenon.* Garden City, N.Y.: Doubleday-Galilee, 1981.

Giddens, Anthony. *The Consequences of Modernity.* Stanford: Stanford University Press, 1990.

Gilkey, L. *Creationism on Trial: Evolution and God at Little Rock.* San Francisco: Harper and Row, 1985.

Ginsburg, Faye D. *Contested Lives: The Abortion Debate in an American Community.* Berkeley: University of California Press, 1989.

Greenawalt, Kent. *Religious Convictions and Political Choice.* New York: Oxford University Press, 1988.

Haeri, Shahla. *Law of Desire: Temporary Marriage in Shiʻi Iran.* Syracuse: Syracuse University Press, 1989.

Heilman, Samuel. *Defenders of the Faith: Inside Ultra-Orthodox Jewry.* New York: Schocken Books, 1992.

Hunter, James Davidson. *Evangelicalism, The Coming Generation.* Chicago: University of Chicago Press, 1987.

Hunter, Shireen T., ed. *The Politics of Islamic Revival: Diversity and Unity.* Bloomington, Ind.: Indiana University Press, 1988.

Kahane, Rabbi Meir. *Uncomfortable Questions for Comfortable Jews.* Secaucus, N.J.: Lyle Stuart, 1987.

Kelley, Dean M. *Why Conservative Churches Are Growing.* New Haven: Yale University Press, 1988.

Kelly, George A. *The Battle for the American Church.* Garden City, N.Y.: Image Books, 1981.

Kincheloe, Joe. *Understanding the New Right and Its Impact on Education.* Bloomington, Ind.: Phi Delta Kappa Educational Foundation, 1983.

Klatch, Rebecca. *Women of the New Right.* Philadelphia: Temple University Press, 1987.

Kepel, Gilles. *Muslim Extremism in Egypt: The Prophet and the Pharoah.* Translated by Jon Rothschild. Berkeley: University of California Press, 1985.

Kramer, Martin, ed. *Shi'ism, Resistance and Revolution.* Boulder, Colo.: Westview Press, 1987.

LaHaye, Tim. *Battle for the Mind.* Old Tappan, N.J.: Revell, 1980.

Larson, Edward J. *Trial and Error: The American Controversy over Creation and Evolution.* Revised edition. New York: Oxford University Press, 1989.

Lawrence, Bruce B. *Defenders of God: The Fundamentalist Revolt against the Modern Age.* San Francisco: Harper and Row, 1989.

Lefebvre, Marcel. *I Accuse the Council.* Dickinson, Texas: Angelus Press, 1982.

———. *An Open Letter to Confused Catholics.* England: Fowler Wright Books Ltd., 1986.

Lernoux, Penny. "The Fundamentalist Surge in Latin America." *Christian Century* 20 (January 1988).

Lewis, Bernard. *The Political Language of Islam.* Chicago: University of Chicago Press, 1988.

Liebman, Charles S., ed. *Religious and Secular: Conflict and Accommodation Between Jews in Israel.* Jerusalem: Keter, 1990.

Liebman, Charles S., and Eliezer Don-Yehiya. *Civil Religion in Israel: Traditional Religion and Political Culture in the Jewish State.* Berkeley: University of California Press, 1983.

Liebman, Robert C., and Robert Wuthnow, eds. *The New Christian Right: Mobilization and Legitimation.* Hawthorne, N.Y.: Aldine, 1983.

Lindsey, Hal. *The Late, Great Planet Earth.* Grand Rapids, Mich.: Zondorvan Publishing House, 1977.

———. *The Road to Holocaust.* New York: Bantam Books, 1989.

Marsden, George M. *Fundamentalism and American Culture.* Oxford: Oxford University Press, 1980.

———. *Understanding Fundamentalism and Evangelicalism.* Grand Rapids, Mich.: William B. Eerdmans, 1991.

Martin, David. *Tongues of Fire: The Explosion of Protestantism in Latin America.* Oxford: Basil Blackwell, 1990.

Marty, Martin E. and R. Scott Appleby, eds. *Fundamentalisms Observed.* Chicago: University of Chicago Press, 1991.

Maududi, Abul Ala. *The Islamic Law and Constitution.* Lahore: Islamic Publications, 1980.

Mernissi, Fatima. *Beyond the Veil: Male-Female Dynamics in a Modern Muslim Society.* New York: John Weily and Sons, 1975.

Mitchell, Richard P. *The Society of the Muslim Brothers.* London: Oxford University Press, 1969.

Mortimer, Edward. *Faith and Power: The Politics of Islam.* New York: Vintage Books, 1982.

Mottahedeh, Roy. *The Mantle of the Prophet: Religion and Politics in Iran.* New York: Pantheon Books, 1985.

Munson, Henry Jr., *Islam and Revolution in the Middle East.* New Haven: Yale University Press, 1988.

Mutahhari, Ayatullah Murtaza. *Fundamentals of Islamic Thought.* Berkeley: Mizan Press, 1985.

Nandy, Ashis. *The Intimate Enemy: Loss and Recovery of Self under Colonialism.* Delhi: Oxford University Press, 1983.

Nasr, Seyyed Hossein. *Islamic Life and Thought.* Albany: State University of New York Press, 1981.

Neuhaus, Richard John. *The Naked Public Square: Religion and Democracy in America.* Grand Rapids, Mich.: William B. Eerdmans, 1984.

Neusner, Jacob. *Messiah in Context.* Philadelphia: Fortress Press, 1984.

Noll, Mark A. *One Nation Under God? Christian Faith and Political Action in America.* San Francisco: Harper and Row Publishers, 1988.

Peshkin, Alan. *God's Choice: The Total World of a Fundamentalist Christian School.* Chicago: University of Chicago Press, 1986.

Pipes, Daniel. *The Rushdie Affair: The Novel, the Ayatollah, and the West.* New York: Birch Lane Press, 1990.

Piscatori, James P. *Islam in the World of Nation-States.* Cambridge: Cambridge University Press, 1986.

Piscatori, James P., ed. *Islamic Fundamentalisms and the Gulf Crisis.* Chicago: American Academy of Arts and Sciences, 1991.

Provenzo, Eugene, Jr. *Religious Fundamentalism and American Education: The Battle for the Public Schools.* Albany: State University of New York Press, 1990.

Rahman, Fazlur. *Islam and Modernity.* Chicago: University of Chicago Press, 1982.

Robertson, Pat. *America's Dates With Destiny.* Nashville, Tenn.: Nelson, 1986.

Rose, Susan. *Keeping Them Out of the Hands of Satan: Evangelical Schooling in America.* New York: Routledge, 1988.

Roy, Olivier. *Islam and Resistance in Afghanistan.* New York: Cambridge University Press, 1986.

Ruthven, Malise. *A Satanic Affair: Salman Rushdie and the Rage of Islam.* London: Chatto and Windus, 1990.

el-Saadawi, Nawal. *The Hidden Face of Eve: Women in the Arab World.* Boston: Beacon Press, 1982.

Sachedina, Abdulaziz A. *Islamic Messianism: The Idea of Mahdi in Twelver Shi'ism.* Albany: State University of New York, 1981.

Sahliyeh, Emile, ed. *Religious Resurgence and Politics in the Contemporary World.* Albany: State University of New York Press, 1990.

Said, Edward W. *Orientalism.* New York: Vintage Books; 1979.

Silk, Mark. *Spiritual Politics: Religion and Politics Since World War II.* New York: Simon and Schuster, 1988.

Sivan, Emmanuel. *Radical Islam: Medieval Theology and Modern Politics.* New Haven: Yale University Press, 1985.

Sivan, Emmanuel, and Menachem Friedman, eds. *Religious Radicalism and Politics in the Middle East.* New Haven: Yale University Press, 1988.

Springborg, Robert. *Mubarak's Egypt: Fragmentation of the Political Order.* Boulder, Colo.: Westview Press, 1989.

Sprinzak, Ehud. *The Emergence of the Israeli Radical Right.* New York: Oxford University Press, 1990.

———. *The Ascendance of Israel's Radical Right.* New York: Oxford University Press, 1991.

Stoll, David. *Is Latin America Turning Protestant? The Politics of Evangelical Growth.* Berkeley: University of California Press, 1990.

Tambiah, Stanley. *Sri Lanka: Ethnic Fratricide and the Dismantling of Democracy.* Chicago: University of Chicago Press, 1986.

Tibi, Bassam. *The Crisis of Modern Islam: A Preindustrial Culture in the Scientific-Technological Age*. Translated by Judith von Sivers. Salt Lake City: University of Utah Press, 1988.

Voll, John O. *Islam, Continuity, and Change in the Modern World*. Boulder, Colo.: Westview Press, 1982.

Warburg, Gabriel R., and Uri M. Kupferschmidt, eds. *Islam, Nationalism, and Radicalism in Egypt and the Sudan*. New York: Praeger, 1983.

Watt, W. Montgomery. *Islamic Fundamentalism and Modernity*. London: Routledge, 1988.

Weber, Timothy P. *Living in the Shadow of the Second Coming*. Chicago: University of Chicago Press, 1987.

Wright, Robin. *Sacred Rage*. New York: Simon and Schuster, 1986.

Wuthnow, Robert. *The Restructuring of American Religion: Society and Faith since World War II*. Princeton, N.J.: Princeton University Press, 1988.

# INDEX